ENGLISH SYNTAX

ENGLISH SYNTAX

A Book of Programed Lessons

PAUL ROBERTS

An Introduction to Transformational Grammar

Harcourt, Brace & World, Inc.
New York   Chicago   Atlanta   Dallas   Burlingame

© 1964 by Harcourt, Brace & World, Inc.

All rights reserved. No part of this book may be reproduced in any form, by mimeograph or any other means, without permission in writing from the publisher.

Printed in the United States of America

CONTENTS

Acknowledgments vii
1   The Sentence   1
2   The Noun Phrase   9
3   Kinds of Nouns and More Determiners   19
4   Post-Article Structures in the Determiner   29
5   The Verb Phrase   39
6   Types of Verbals   46
7   Verbs of the *have* Class, Adverbials   54
8   The Auxiliary   62
9   The Rest of the Auxiliary   71
10 Practice with the Auxiliary   79
11 Adverbials Again   88
12 Transformation   97
13 *Yes/no* Questions   106
14 The *do* Transformation   114
15 Other Occurrences of the *do* Transformation   122
16 *Wh* Questions   132
17 Possessives   143
18 More Possessives   151
19 VI and VT   160
20 Other Varieties of Vt_3 170
21 Vt_{to} and Vt_{ing} 178
22 The Passive Transformation   186
23 Review of Determiners, **T-there**   195
24 Relative Clauses   205
25 The Verb Phrase as Noun Modifier   215

26	Adverbials of Place as Noun Modifiers	224
27	Adjectives	232
28	Ambiguity in Noun Modification	240
29	Sentences Transformed into NP's	249
30	Subordinate Clauses	259
31	Inner and Outer Structure	268
32	Conjunctions	277
33	Correlatives and Conjunctions that Join Sentences	286
34	Series	294
35	Sentence Connectors	303
36	Sentence Modifiers	312
37	Sentence Modifiers Derived from Relative Clauses	321
38	Dangling Modifiers	330
39	Punctuation of Sentence Modifiers	340
40	Practice with Sentence Modifiers	349
41	Predication	358
42	Some Problems in Modification	367
43	Reference of Pronouns	376
44	Review	385
	Abbreviations Used	395
	Some Syntactic Rules of English	397

Acknowledgments

People working in the field of transformational grammar will be aware that much of the treatment in this textbook had not previously appeared in print and may wonder about its provenience. It will not surprise them to learn that most of the new material is the contribution of Professor Noam Chomsky of the Massachusetts Institute of Technology. It was Professor Chomsky who explained to me, in particular, the main outline of the determiner system, the transitive verb system, and the noun modifier system.

Professor Chomsky cooperated with me closely in the preparation of the text. He read the first two versions, and we discussed them at great length, after which considerable revisions were undertaken. Problems of terminology were solved by agreement between us. Chomsky did not, however, read the final version before it was in print, and he therefore has no specific responsibility for it. I must suppose that there are many details of which he would disapprove and wish done otherwise.

I must express my gratitude to others who have helped me approach an understanding of transformational grammar: to Professor Archibald Hill of the University of Texas, who introduced me to the subject; to Professor Robert Stockwell of the University of California, who took me through the first principles; to Professor Robert B. Lees of the University of Illinois, whose works have been a constant source of illumination. In particular, I want to thank Professor Dwight L. Bolinger of Harvard, who read the penultimate version and, in a long exchange of correspondence, helped me to confront more confidently a number of thorny problems.

I am grateful to the following people for teaching the text and contributing valuable suggestions: Annamaria Bocchino, Primino Limongelli, Charles Parish, Richard M. Payne, Silvana Volpones-Cremonese, Walter Edward Wells.

My fondest indebtedness is to the students of the Overseas School of Rome who participated in the tryouts, the sophomore classes of 1961–63 and the senior class of 1962–63. In the course of the work many of them became my friends. I am of course grateful to their Headmaster, Daniel

J. Pinto, whose gracious and enlightened cooperation made the experiment possible.

No acknowledgment is complete without mention of the author's wife. I am grateful to Marcia Roberts, *ce qui va sans dire*, but not for such usual reasons as encouragement and typing. It was she who taught the text for two years at Overseas School, who confronted with great wit and courage the many school problems that so large a departure entrained, and who patiently taught me how to make the material available to high school students.

P.R.
Rome, 1964

Lesson One
THE SENTENCE

We must begin the study of grammar by stating what is meant by *grammar,* since the term has been used to mean many different things. In this text we shall mean by *grammar* "the description of the sentences of a language." This text is a grammar of English. Therefore its purpose is to give a description of English sentences.

One might think that the next step would be to say what we mean by *sentence*. We could of course give various definitions of sentence. We could say that a sentence is "a group of words expressing a complete thought" or "a group of words that begins with a capital letter and ends with a period." But obviously these definitions do not get us very far. We want answers to such questions as these: "Just what groups of English words express complete thoughts?" "Just what groups of words are written with a capital letter at the beginning and a period at the end?"

It will be seen that this whole text is an answer—or a partial answer—to these questions. Since its purpose is to give a description of English sentences, it is itself, as a whole, a definition of the term *English sentence*. We shall not have completed the definition of *sentence* until we reach the end. Even then, we shall not have said nearly everything that might be said about English sentences. The sentences of any language are extremely complicated, with all sorts of possible variations. We shall be able to deal here only with the principal structures and thus give only a general answer to the question "What is an English sentence?"

This text covers the area of grammar called *syntax*. This is concerned with the relationships of words in sentences, the ways in which they are put together to form sentences. We begin by making a fundamental distinction between two kinds of sentences: *kernel sentences* and *transforms*. Kernel sentences are the basic, elementary sentences of the language, the stuff from which all else is made. Transforms are the "all else" structures drawn from the kernel to produce all the complications of English sentences.

We shall see that all kernel sentences contain two main parts: a *noun phrase* and a *verb phrase*. The noun phrase functions as the subject of the kernel sentence. The verb phrase functions as its predicate. We will describe the parts of noun phrases and verb phrases. Then we will see how transformations can change and expand the kernel in many ways to create the great variety of sentences possible in English.

Here is one word of caution. There does not exist for grammar, as there does for some sciences, any organization which has the authority to regulate the use of terminology. The result is that grammarians differ in their use of terms. Different grammarians use different terms for the same thing or the same term for different things. By and large, the terms used in this text are familiar and standard ones and are applied in familiar and standard ways. However, there is some departure, inevitably, from the usage of other grammarians. You must therefore be careful to let the text define the terms. Some of them you may have heard used differently. Here you must apply them only as they are applied in the text.

1

A *grammar* is a description of the sentences of a language. An English grammar is a description of English ———— .

2

There are two kinds of sentences: *kernel sentences* and *transforms*. Transforms are built from kernel sentences. Kernel sentences are not built from anything. They are basic. A sentence that is not a kernel sentence is a ———— .

3

A sentence that is not a transform is a ———— sentence.

4

All kernel sentences have two main parts: a *noun phrase* and a *verb phrase*. Using abbreviations, we might say that a kernel sentence consists of NP + VP. Here the letters NP stand for the words ———— .

5

When we say that a kernel sentence consists of NP + VP, the letters VP stand for the words ———— .

6

Instead of saying that a kernel sentence consists of a noun phrase plus a verb phrase, we might say **S** consists of **NP** + **VP**. Here the letter **S** stands for the word _____ .

7

To make the formula more economical, we use an arrow to represent the words *consists of*. Thus we can write **S** → **NP** + **VP**. This means that a sentence consists of a noun phrase plus a _____ .

8

We need to become very familiar with this arrow, because we shall use it a great deal. **S** → **NP** + **VP** means that a sentence _____ of a noun phrase plus a verb phrase.

9

S → **NP** + **VP** means a sentence _____ of a _____ plus a _____ .

10

We can use this kind of formula wherever we need it. For example, we could write **X** → **Y** + **Z**. Whatever **X**, **Y**, and **Z** stand for, the formula means that an **X** consists of a **Y** plus a _____ .

11

Sometimes it is better to interpret the arrow not as *consists of* but as a direction to *rewrite as*. We can say that **S** → **NP** + **VP** means that an **S** consists of an **NP** plus a **VP**. Or we can say that it is a direction to rewrite **S** as _____ + _____ .

12

S → **NP** + **VP** means an **S** consists of an **NP** plus a **VP**. Or it means _____ **S** as **NP** + **VP**.

13

X → **Y** + **Z** means an **X** consists of a **Y** plus a **Z**. Or it means rewrite _____ as _____ + _____ .

THE SENTENCE 3

14

The first direction, or rule, of our grammar is "Rewrite sentence as noun phrase plus verb phrase." Write this as a formula. _____

15

This formula means not only that a sentence consists of a noun phrase and a verb phrase but that the noun phrase comes first and the verb phrase second. In the sentence "The boy came in," the noun phrase is *the boy*. What is the verb phrase? _____

16

Items like *noun phrase* and *verb phrase* are what we call *structures*. Structures generally have several possible uses or functions. In S → NP + VP, the noun phrase functions as the *subject* of the sentence. What words are the subject of the sentence "The boy came in"? _____

17

In "The boy came in," *the boy* is a noun phrase functioning as a _____ .

18

In "The pilot landed the plane," what is the noun phrase that functions as the subject? _____

19

What is the verb phrase in "The child looked up"? _____

20

The NP of S → NP + VP functions as the subject of the sentence. The VP functions as the *predicate*. In "The child looked up," *looked up* is a _____ functioning as a predicate.

21

The terms *noun phrase* and *verb phrase* refer to structures. The terms *subject* and *predicate* refer to functions of structures. Subject is a possible function of a _____ .

22
Predicate is one function of a _____ .

23
A sentence consists of a noun phrase plus a verb phrase. These function as the _____ and the _____ of the sentence.

You may notice that we are not defining subject and predicate except as functions of a noun phrase and a verb phrase in the positions indicated. Probably you are familiar with other definitions, such as "The subject is that which names the performer of an action, and the predicate is that which names the action." It is true that there is usually a performer-action relationship between subject and predicate, particularly in kernel sentences. However, in transforms, as we shall see, the relationship may be quite different. There are also various kernel sentences in which no action is involved: "The boy is here," "It seemed odd."

The important thing to perceive is that it is not the meaning that clues us to the form, but the form that clues us to the meaning. That is, we don't identify the subject by discovering who performs the action. We identify the subject on the basis of form, position, and so on, and this tells us who the performer is in sentences in which the subject is a performer.

24
In "The pilot landed the plane," the noun phrase that functions as subject is _____ .

25
In "The pilot landed the plane," the verb phrase that functions as predicate is _____ .

26
The predicate *landed the plane* contains the noun phrase *the plane*. But this is not the **NP** of **S → NP + VP**. Instead, it is part of the _____ that functions as predicate.

27
What is the noun phrase that functions as subject of "David landed the plane"? _____

THE SENTENCE 5

28

Thus we see that the term *noun phrase* can apply to a single word as well as to a group of words. What is the verb phrase that functions as predicate of "The plane arrived"? _____

29

What is the verb phrase of "The pilot was a woman"? _____

30

The sentence "The pilot was a woman" contains two noun phrases: *the pilot, a woman*. Which of these is the NP of S → NP + VP? _____

31

In "The woman was a pilot," which noun phrase is the NP of S → NP + VP? _____

32

What is the noun phrase that functions as subject of the sentence "She's a pilot"? _____

33

The structure of "She's a pilot" shows that the division between the NP and the VP of S → NP + VP can come within a single syllable. What is the noun phrase in the sentence "It's hot"? _____

34

What is the verb phrase in "It's hot"? _____

35

What is the noun phrase that functions as the subject of "Men eat mush"? _____

36

What is the verb phrase of "Violets are blue"? _____

37

In "Violets are blue," the verb phrase functions as a _____ .

38

What noun phrase functions as the subject of "Sarcasm disturbs David"? _____

39

What noun phrase functions as the subject of "Y equals Z"? _____

40

Thus we find many kinds of expressions that are noun phrases and that function as the subjects of kernel sentences: *the pilot, she, it, men, violets, sarcasm, Y*. Some are one word and some two. What is the verb phrase in "The plane arrived"? _____

41

What is the verb phrase in "The plane arrived on time"? _____

42

We said that **S → NP + VP**. Whatever isn't the **NP** must be the **VP**, or part of the **VP**. What is the **VP** of "The pilot landed the plane smoothly"?

43

Notice that we have begun to define sentence. **S → NP + VP** is a specification of what the main parts of a sentence are. It means that any kernel sentence consists of a noun phrase plus a verb phrase. The noun phrase functions as the subject, and the verb phrase as the _____.

44

It is true that some sentences do not have noun phrases, some do not have verb phrases, and some have the noun phrase and the verb phrase in a different order. But all of these are transforms. **S → NP + VP** is not a description of all English sentences but only of _____ sentences in English.

45

In the sentence "The men ate the mush," there are two **NP**'s. Which is the **NP** of the formula **S → NP + VP**? _____

THE SENTENCE 7

46

In "The men ate the mush," *the mush* is an **NP,** but it is not the **NP** of the formula **S → NP + VP.** Instead, it is part of the ____ .

47

In "The men ate the mush," *the men* is an **NP** functioning as a _____ .

48

In "The pigeons drank the milk," *drank the milk* is a **VP** functioning as a _____ .

49

The arrow of the formula **S → NP + VP** can be read "An **S** consists of an **NP** plus a **VP**," or it can be read as a direction to _____ **S** as **NP + VP.**

50

The formula **S → NP + VP** is the beginning of the definition of *sentence*. But obviously the definition cannot be completed until **NP** and **VP** are also defined. We have given several examples of noun phrases and verb phrases, but we have not yet defined these terms. We will begin to define *noun phrase* in the next lesson.

MAIN POINTS OF LESSON ONE

A grammar is the description of the sentences of a language. There are two kinds of sentences: kernel sentences and transforms.

An English kernel sentence consists of a noun phrase followed by a verb phrase. We indicate this with the formula **S → NP + VP.**

The arrow means *consists of* or *rewrite as*. We can read **S → NP + VP** as "Rewrite **S** as **NP + VP.**"

S, NP, and **VP** are terms referring to particular forms or structures. Most structures have several possible uses or functions. The terms *subject* and *predicate* refer to functions. The subject function is one possible use of an **NP**. The predicate function is one possible use of a **VP**.

The terms *noun phrase* and *verb phrase* are used here to include single words as well as groups of words. *The men, David, I* are all noun phrases. *Landed, landed the plane, landed the plane smoothly* are all verb phrases.

8   ENGLISH SYNTAX

Lesson Two
THE NOUN PHRASE

Since we are studying grammar, we are obviously concerned with grammaticality. We want to know what sentences are grammatical and what sentences are ungrammatical. Because we shall be using these terms frequently, it will be well to note in just what sense we are using them.

For the present our concern is not about what is often called "poor English" as against "good English"—for example, "Me and him done it" as against "He and I did it." We shall have something to say about such problems as we go along. However, our more fundamental task is to separate English from non-English—for example, "He and I did it" from "Did it he and I." There is a sense in which "Me and him done it" is an English sentence. Its forms are used commonly and consistently by people whose native language is English, though usually not by educated people. There is therefore some sense in which it is grammatical. There is a certain grammar to which it belongs, though this is not precisely the grammar of the educated.

However, there is no sense in which *"Did it he and I" is grammatical. It is not part of the grammar of anyone, educated or not. It is not English at all. We call it ungrammatical and indicate that we do so by marking it with an asterisk.

You will often be asked in the course of this study whether particular constructions are grammatical or not. These will all be cases of the kind described above: "He and I did it" versus *"Did it he and I," not "He and I did it" versus "Me and him did it." You will have to answer, at first, not from your conscious knowledge of the grammar but from your unconscious knowledge of it—that is, from your general experience with English. The question "Is this grammatical?" means simply "Is this an English construction or is it not?" When we have described the grammar, we can answer such questions explicitly, by checking with the grammar. We can then also say just *why* a sentence is ungrammatical, if it is. Meanwhile we simply rely on our intuition as speakers of English.

We began the description of English sentences with the rule S → NP + VP. A kernel English sentence consists of a noun phrase plus a verb phrase. We now carry the description further by saying more exactly what we mean by noun phrase and verb phrase. In this lesson we shall begin with the noun phrase.

We have already pointed out that we use the term *phrase* here to mean sometimes groups of words and sometimes single words. *The man, a pilot, this mush, those three youngsters, several of those forty apes* are all examples of noun phrases. However, *David, Sally, I, she* are examples of noun phrases too.

We must now go on to sort out and give names to these different kinds of noun phrases.

51

The main structures that occur in noun phrases of kernel sentences are *determiners*, *nouns*, and *pronouns*. The words *David, man, plane, mush, courage* are examples of nouns. In the sentence "The boy went away," which word is a noun? ____

52

In "The boy went away," the subject is a noun _____ .

53

In "David was hungry," *David* is a noun. It is also a noun phrase, and it functions as a _____ .

54

The sentence "Cows often eat grass" contains two nouns. What are they? _____ , _____

55

In "Cows often eat grass," *cows* functions as a subject, but *grass* does not. *Cows* and *grass* are both nouns. They are also both _____ .

56

In "The plane landed smoothly," which word is a noun? _____

57

In "The plane landed smoothly," *plane* is a noun, but it is not a noun phrase. What is the noun phrase in "The plane landed smoothly"?

---

10 ENGLISH SYNTAX

58

*"Plane landed smoothly" is not a grammatical English sentence. (Remember that we use the asterisk to mark structures that are ungrammatical.) In order to make *"Plane landed smoothly" grammatical, we must add such a word as *the* or *a* or *this* or *every*. These words all belong to the structure called *determiner*. They have the characteristic of occurring before nouns in the noun phrase. What are the nouns in "The pilot needed a plane"? _____ , _____

59

What are the determiners in "The pilot needed a plane"? _____ , _____

60

What are the determiners in "An orange was in the dish"? _____ , _____

61

What is the rewrite of **S**?   S → _____ + _____

62

We now rewrite **NP** in this way: **NP → Det + N**. We have seen that some noun phrases—*the man, an orange*—consist of a noun preceded by a determiner. In the rule **NP → Det + N**, the abbreviation **Det** stands for the word _____ .

63

The rule **NP → Det + N** means that a noun phrase consists of a noun preceded by a determiner. What is the determiner in "Some girls were waiting"? _____

64

What are the determiners in "Some men were eating the mush"? _____ , _____

65

Determiners are of several different kinds. The most common kind are words called *articles*. The English articles are *the*, *a(n)*, and *some*, plus one other that we shall come to in a moment. In "The man arrived," the determiner *the* is an _____ .

66

In "A man arrived" and "Some men arrived," *a* and *some* are articles. They are also _____ .

67

The differs obviously from *a* and *some* in its effect on the noun that follows. *The* gives the noun a definite meaning, specifying a particular one or a particular group. *A* and *some* do not do this. We therefore call *the* a *definite article,* and *a* and *some* are *nondefinite articles.* In "They found the money," *the* is a _____ article.

If you have studied grammar previously, you have probably used the term *indefinite article* rather than *nondefinite article.* There is a distinction, however, between something which is indefinite and something which is simply not definite, and the distinction is of some importance in grammar. The nondefinite article does not necessarily give the noun an indefinite meaning. Some constructions with the nondefinite article are quite definite in meaning. The point is that the definiteness in such constructions is not conveyed by the article, whereas *the* does convey the meaning of definiteness. Originally the word *indefinite* in *indefinite article* did have the meaning *nondefinite,* but it has tended to lose it because of the use of the word in other contexts. Perhaps the terms *specifying* and *nonspecifying* would be better than *definite* and *nondefinite.* However, we shall avoid them here because it seems preferable to stay as close to traditional terminology as possible.

68

In "He bought a book," *a* is a _____ article.

69

In "He needed some money," *some* is a _____ article.

70

We rewrote **NP** as **Det** + **N**. We then saw that a determiner may be an article--*the, a(n),* or *some.* In fact, we shall find that every determiner contains the structure *article,* though not always in these forms. We can

12   ENGLISH SYNTAX

now rewrite determiner in this way: **Det** → **Art**. This is a preliminary rewrite rule for **Det**. There is more to be added later. The abbreviation **Art** stands, of course, for *article*. The three articles so far encountered are ____ , ____ , ____ .

71

Articles are either definite (specifying) or nondefinite (nonspecifying). The nondefinite articles so far encountered are ____ and ____ .

72

We can now add the rule **Art** → $\begin{Bmatrix} \text{Def} \\ \text{Nondef} \end{Bmatrix}$ The brackets mean here, and always, that we have a choice. To have a grammatical English kernel sentence, we must have an **NP**. With some exceptions that we will come to later, the **NP** must contain **Det**. **Det** must contain **Art**. **Art** may be either _____ or _____ .

73

In "Some men passed by," *some* is a _____ article.

74

Now consider the sentence "Men passed by." *Men* is a noun and also a noun phrase. It is apparently a noun phrase without a determiner. Yet our rewrite rule for noun phrase is **NP** → ____ + ____ .

75

Since *men* is an **NP**, either the formula is wrong or *men* must be a case of **Det** + **N**. What is the second **NP** of "The men ate mush"? _____

76

Again, either the formula is wrong or *mush* is a case of **Det** + **N**. We shall find two kinds of noun phrases which do not contain determiners, but *men* and *mush* in the sentences given are not among them. It will turn out that we shall have a simpler grammar of English if, for these sentences, we can somehow preserve the rule **NP** → **Det** + **N**—that is, a rule which says that a noun phrase consists of an **N** preceded by a _____ .

77

In "Men passed by," *men* is an **NP**. It is also an **N**. But the **N** is preceded by nothing. We can preserve the rule **NP → Det + N** only by saying that in some cases the **Det** can be *nothing*. Let us say that *men* in "Men passed by" is an **NP**, and that this **NP** consists of the determiner *nothing* plus _____.

78

The symbol for *nothing*, used in this technical way, is **Ø**. From now on, we shall always use **Ø** instead of the expression *nothing*. In "Men passed by," the noun phrase consists of the structures **Det + N**, and **Det** is _____.

79

We have the rules **NP → Det + N** and **Det → Art**. An **NP** must contain a determiner, and a determiner must contain an article. Therefore, in "Men passed by," where *men* is **Ø + N**, **Ø** must be not only a determiner but also an _____.

80

It remains to be decided what kind of article it is, definite or nondefinite. Do you think "Men passed by" is more similar in meaning to (1) "The men passed by" or to (2) "Some men passed by"? _____

81

Do you think "He bought pencils" is more similar in meaning to (1) "He bought the pencils" or to (2) "He bought some pencils"? _____

82

Do you think "Men are mortal" is more similar in meaning to (1) "The man is mortal" or to (2) "A man is mortal"? _____

83

It should be clear that the sentences with **Ø** as the article are much closer in meaning to those with *a* and *some* than to those with *the*. The definite article *the* specifies the following **N** as a particular one, whereas *a*, *some*, and **Ø** do not. **Ø** is therefore considered a nondefinite article.

Det is **Art**, **Art** is either **Def** or **Nondef**, and **Def** is *the*. **Nondef** is _____, _____, or _____.

14   ENGLISH SYNTAX

We might note here that the question is not whether the **NP** is definite or nondefinite but whether the article is. There is some sense in which both "Men are mortal" and "A man is mortal" are definite, since both **NP**'s have the meaning *all men*. But this definiteness is not conveyed by the articles Ø and *a*. Only *the* has the power of specifying or singling out. Ø, *a*, and *some* do not have this power, though they may sometimes be attached to **N**'s which, for one reason or another, have definite meaning.

84

In "Men eat mush," both the determiners are the nondefinite article _____ .

85

What is the subject of "He ate a banana"? _____

86

Since the subject of a kernel sentence is an **NP,** and *he* is the subject of "He ate a banana," *he* is an **NP**. The rewrite rule for **NP** is **NP** → _____ + _____ .

87

If this rule still holds, *he* in "He ate a banana" must be a case of **Det + N**. The **Det** must be the nondefinite article _____ .

88

In "He ate a banana," *a banana* is a noun phrase. It is composed of the nondefinite article *a* and the noun *banana*. In "The boy ate it," the **NP** *the boy* is composed of the _____ article *the* and the _____ *boy*.

89

In "The boy ate it," *the* is a determiner and also a definite article. *Boy* is an **N** and also a noun. *It* is an **NP;** the determiner is the nondefinite article _____ .

90

In "The boy ate it," *it* is a case of **Det + N**. The **N**, however, is not a noun, like *boy, man, banana*. It is instead what is called a *personal pronoun*. In "He ate a banana," the **NP** *he* is also a personal pronoun. The determiner is the nondefinite article _____ .

THE NOUN PHRASE   **15**

91

Thus an **N** may be a noun, like *boy*, *man*, *banana*, or a personal pronoun, like *it* or *he*. We express this in the rewrite rule **N** → {noun / personal pronoun} There are hundreds of thousands of nouns in English, but only seven personal pronouns. They are *I*, *you*, *he*, *she*, *it*, *we*, and *they*. Cover the list immediately, and see how many of them you can remember. ____, ____, ____, ____, ____, ____, ____.

92

She, *he*, *I*, etc., are called _____ pronouns.

93

The term *personal* refers to the grammatical concept of person. In English grammar there are three possible persons: *first person* means the person speaking and is expressed by *I* and *we*; *second person* means the person spoken to and is expressed by *you*; *third person* means any other person or thing and is expressed by *he*, *she*, *it*, *they*, and all nouns. In the English kernel every **S** must contain an **NP**. Every **NP** of the types so far discussed must contain an **N**, and every **N** must be either a _____ or a _____.

94

Beginning with the very general and abstract structure **S**, we have worked down to where at one point we are dealing with actual words. We have such successively more specific levels as these: **S**, **NP**, **N**, personal pronoun, *he*. In "We looked in," *we* is an **NP** and also an **N**. It is also a _____ .

95

In "We looked in," *we* is an **NP** and therefore a case of **Det** + **N**. In "The men went away," the **Det** is the definite article *the*. What is the **Det** in "We looked in"? ____

96

In "We looked in," *we* is a case of **Det** + **N**, where **Det** is the ∅ form of **Nondef**. Note that here the article has to be ∅. *"The we looked in" is ungrammatical. So is * "Some we looked in." We can now state a gen-

16   ENGLISH SYNTAX

eral rule: "When **N** is a personal pronoun, **Art** must be **Nondef,** and **Nondef** must be **Ø**." What is the **Det** in "I objected violently"? ____

97

We shall see that there are structures in which personal pronouns are preceded by other parts of **Det**. But they are never preceded by the definite article *the* or by the *a* and *some* forms of the nondefinite article. Nouns, however, are accompanied, in different constructions, with any of the articles. In "He ate a banana," *a* is an article. What is the article in "Bananas are expensive"? ____

There are some constructions in which words that occur as personal pronouns are used with articles other than **Ø**: "It's a he." However, *he* is not a personal pronoun here but a noun, like *boy*. The use of *a* has converted it into a noun.

Remember that nondefinite articles do not necessarily make the **N** indefinite. They just don't make it definite. Such words as *he* and *I* are in some sense definite, but this definite meaning is inherent in the pronoun itself; it is not conveyed by any article.

98

In "Violets are blue," is the article **Def** or **Nondef**? ____

99

Give the rewrite rule for **N**.   **N** → ____

100

When **N** is a noun (*people, man, mush, banana*), **Art** is sometimes the nondefinite article **Ø** and sometimes not, depending, as we shall see, on what kind of a noun it is. When **N** is a personal pronoun, **Art** must be **Ø**.

MAIN POINTS OF LESSON TWO

NP → **Det** + **N**. That is, an English noun phrase consists of a determiner plus **N**. (There are two kinds of **NP**'s—proper nouns and indefinite pronouns—of which this is not true. These will be added later to the rule for **NP**.)

THE NOUN PHRASE   17

Det → Art. Every determiner contains at least an article. We shall see that it may contain other structures too. This is just a preliminary rewrite of **Det.**

Art → $\begin{Bmatrix} \text{Def} \\ \text{Nondef} \end{Bmatrix}$ **Art** is either the definite article *the* or one of the nondefinite articles *a, some,* or *Ø.*

N → $\begin{Bmatrix} \text{noun} \\ \text{personal pronoun} \end{Bmatrix}$ **N** is either a noun or a personal pronoun. The personal pronouns are the seven words *I, you, he, she, it, we, they.*

When **N** is a personal pronoun, **Art** must be the *Ø* form of the nondefinite article.

Lesson Three

KINDS OF NOUNS AND MORE DETERMINERS

We can measure the complexity of any part of the grammar by simply counting the number of rules it takes to describe that part. By *rule* we mean a direction of the type $X \rightarrow Y + Z$ and certain other types that we shall encounter later. We find that some parts of the grammar are fairly simple—that is, can be described in relatively few rules. English pronouns are fairly simple. We haven't yet said everything there is to say about them. We still have to account for such forms as *me, him, your, yours*. But all of this can be described with a comparatively small number of rules.

English determiners, on the other hand, are quite complex. The rules must account for a large number of seemingly unrelated structures: *a, the, some, Ø, this, that, few, a few, a few of the, many of the, all, all of the, some of the, a certain, at least three of those first six,* and many more. We shall describe some of this complexity, and perhaps we will be able to see more system in it than appears at first, but a much larger grammer than this one would not have the space to describe all of it.

It is sometimes illuminating to look at the grammar from the point of view of a person learning English as a second language. The native speaker uses the determiners so automatically that he never thinks of their complexity. But to a person learning English as a second language, they represent a great many rules that must be learned. Naturally, he may not be presented with the rules in just the form they are given here, but he must in some way or other come to understand the details of the grammar in order to know what is grammatical and what is not. The English articles alone present a large problem to the speaker of Chinese, Russian, or Italian, and, as we shall now see, there is a good deal more to the English determiner than the articles.

101

In Lesson Two we listed as nouns such words as *David, man, plane, mush, courage*. It is clear that the first of these, *David*, the name of a particular individual, is in some way different from the others. It is what we call a *proper noun*. Which is a proper noun: *woman, girl, Sally?* _____

102

Which is a proper noun: *housewife, Mrs. Alva, secretary?* _____

103

Which is a proper noun: *France, country, nation?* _____

104

Which of the following is not grammatical: (1) We liked the country. (2) We liked a country. (3) We liked the Germany? ____

105

It is characteristic of English proper nouns that they are not used with the articles or with other parts of the determiner. We therefore describe proper nouns as a type of noun phrase different from those described as **Det + N**. We will now enlarge our rule for **NP** to read as follows:

$$NP \rightarrow \begin{Bmatrix} \text{proper noun} \\ \text{Det + N} \end{Bmatrix}$$

Det stands for the word _____ .

It may occur to you that it might be simpler to treat proper nouns as we did personal pronouns: to say that *David*, for example, is a case of **Det + N**, with **Det** the ∅ form of **Nondef**. There is some plausibility in such a description. Like personal pronouns, proper nouns have definiteness built into them and cannot be made more definite by a definite article. However, there are some parts of the grammar in which personal pronouns behave like other **N**'s—for example, like *man, banana, car*—and in which proper nouns behave differently. These will be pointed out as we go along.

106

When we get down to the level of words in the grammar, the rewrite rules simply list the particular items that occur. For example, the rule

20   ENGLISH SYNTAX

for **Def** is **Def** → **the**. The rule for **Nondef** is **Nondef** → **a(n), some, Ø**. The rule for personal pronoun is **personal pronoun** → **I, you, he**, _____, _____, _____, _____.

107

For many categories, of course, it is impractical or impossible to list all the items. We simply give examples for these, putting three dots at the end to show that the list is not complete. For example, we can write the rule for proper nouns in this way: **proper noun** → **David, Mrs. Alva, France** . . . The fact that there are more proper nouns in English than just these three is shown by the _____.

There are some proper nouns in English which have the word *the* as a part of them: *the United States, the Sahara, the Queen Mary*, and perhaps also *the devil, the sun, the moon*. Strictly speaking, however, this is not **Def**, the definite article, but part of the proper noun, something that one learns along with the rest of the word. These facts would be indicated in the grammar in the rewrite rule for proper noun: **proper noun** → **David, Mrs. Alva, France, the United States, Satan, the devil**. General statements can be made about the use of *the* with some proper nouns—for example, in *the Queen Mary* as compared with *Queen Mary*. These would be made in that part of the grammar which also deals with such structures as suffixes and prefixes.

108

What is now our rewrite rule for **NP**?   **NP** → _____

_____ + _____

109

So far, an **NP** is either a proper noun or a **Det** + **N**. We said that an **N** is either a noun or a _____.

110

A noun that is not a proper noun is usually called a *common noun*. We can state the rule for **N** a little more clearly in this fashion:

$$N \rightarrow \begin{Bmatrix} \text{common noun} \\ \text{personal pronoun} \end{Bmatrix}$$

A common noun is always preceded by a _____.

KINDS OF NOUNS AND MORE DETERMINERS

111

There are two main types of common nouns. Some common nouns refer to things that can be counted, and some do not. For example, we say *one chair, two chairs, three chairs*. But we do not say **one courage, two courages, three courages*. Nouns which refer to things that can be counted are called *count nouns*. Which of the following is *not* a count noun: *table, boy, mush?*

_____

112

Common nouns which refer to things that cannot be counted are called *noncount nouns*. *Mush, blood, furniture, sarcasm, despair* are examples of noncount nouns. Which of these is a noncount noun: *building, plumber, wheat, apple?* _____

113

So we have the following developments of **N**:

N → { **common noun** / **personal pronoun** }

common noun → { **count** / **noncount** }

Which of the following is a noncount noun: *woman, sadness, brick, dream?*

_____

114

Nouns which are not common nouns are called _____ nouns.

115

Common nouns are either _____ nouns or _____ nouns.

116

Count nouns have two forms: the *singular form* and the *plural form*. The plural form is the form that means *more than one*. Which of the following is a plural form: *tree, angel, courage, women?* _____

117

The singular form of count nouns is the form that means *just one*. Which of the following is a singular form: *mice, cat, streets?* _____

22   ENGLISH SYNTAX

118

Count nouns in the singular cannot have the Ø form of **Nondef.** "The cat meowed" and "A cat meowed" are both grammatical. *"Cat meowed" is not. What kind of article is *the?* _____

119

The article with count nouns in the singular may be either the definite article *the* or the nondefinite article ____ .

120

Of course, the article may also be the nondefinite *an.* We have not listed this as a separate article because it is just an alternate form of *a,* the choice depending on whether the next word begins with a vowel or a consonant. Which of the following sentences is not grammatical: (1) The cats meowed. (2) Some cats meowed. (3) A cats meowed. (4) Cats meowed? ____

121

When **N** is a plural count noun, **Art** cannot be the nondefinite article *a.* *"A cats meowed" is ungrammatical. When **N** is a plural count noun, **Art** can be definite *the* or nondefinite ____ or ____ .

122

Which of the following is a noncount noun: *spoon, meat, pork chop, picture?*

_____

123

Which of these sentences is not grammatical: (1) He ate some meat. (2) He ate the meat. (3) He ate meat. (4) He ate a meat? ____

124

The rule for the use of articles with noncount nouns is exactly the same as with plural count nouns. **Art** cannot be nondefinite *a.* It can be definite ____ or nondefinite ____ or ____ .

Of course, it is easy to think of contexts in which words ordinarily used as noncount nouns occur with nondefinite *a:* "Prime beef is an expensive meat," "He had a courage such as I had never seen." It is probably best to say that words in such usages have become count nouns for the purposes of those contexts. (The alternative would be to say that the sentences are transforms, with $a(n)$ inserted as part of the transformation.) It might be noted that the process is not reversible ordinarily; that is, count nouns are not easily used as noncount nouns. It is rather hard to think of contexts in which *dream, table, banana* are used as singular noun phrases without $a(n)$.

125

Let us review. Give the rewrite of sentence.   S → _____ + _____

126

Give the rewrite of noun phrase.   NP → _____

_____ + _____

127

We have rewritten **N** as a choice between _____ and _____.

128

We have rewritten common noun as a choice between _____ noun and _____ noun.

129

Det must contain at least _____ .

130

The rewrite rule for **Art** gives us a choice between _____ and _____ .

131

If **N** is a personal pronoun, **Nondef** must be _____ .

132

The nondefinite article *a* occurs only when **N** is a singular _____ .

24   ENGLISH SYNTAX

133

Note that *noun* is an incomplete answer for 132. We do not say * "He ate a meat" or * "He bought a furniture." When **N** is a noncount noun or a plural count noun, **Art** can be _____ , _____ , or _____ .

134

Now compare the sentences "The men were here" and "Several of the men were here." In forming the second sentence, we have added to the first the words _____ .

135

We will call *several of* in the sentence "Several of the men were here" a *pre-article,* because it comes before the article *the.* What is the pre-article in "Many of the men were here"? _____

136

What is the pre-article in "Few of the men were here"? _____

137

In "A few of the men were here," the pre-article is *a few of.* What is the pre-article in "A lot of the men were here"? _____

138

What is the pre-article in "Most of the men were here"? _____

139

We see that before the article we may have such forms as *several of, many of, a few of, few of.* We can indicate this possibility by enlarging the rewrite of determiner: **Det → (pre-article) + Art.** This means that the article may be preceded by a _____ .

140

Note the parentheses in the rule **Det → (pre-article) + Art.** We shall always use parentheses to mean that the item may, but need not, occur. Every noun phrase contains **Det,** and every **Det** contains **Art.** It may, but need not, contain _____ .

KINDS OF NOUNS AND MORE DETERMINERS 25

141

We identify pre-articles by giving a list: **pre-article** → **several of, many of, few of, a few of, a lot of, lots of** . . . The dots at the end mean that the list is not complete. There are many more pre-articles. What is the pre-article in "Both of the students were happy"? _____

142

What is the pre-article in "One of the students was unhappy"? _____

143

What is the pre-article in "Three of the students were unhappy"? _____

You may note that in these structures it is the pre-article, rather than the **N**, which determines whether the noun phrase is singular or plural—that is, whether *was* or *were* occurs in the predicate.

144

What is the pre-article in "A hundred and seven of the students were unhappy"? _____

145

The structures *one, two, three, four, five,* etc., are called *cardinal numbers.* They appear in the kernel sentences of English as part of the pre-article, immediately before the word _____ .

146

Det → **(pre-article)** + **Art** and **Art** → $\begin{Bmatrix} \text{Def} \\ \text{Nondef} \end{Bmatrix}$ The pre-articles may occur before **Art**, and **Art** must be either **Def** or **Nondef**. So far we have illustrated the pre-article only before **Def** (*the*). Suppose, however, we choose **Nondef**. Then we might have such a sequence as this: **several of** + **Nondef** + **boys**. Could *some* or *a* appear here as **Nondef**? ____

147

Both **several of some boys* and **several of a boys* are ungrammatical. So is *several of boys. The sequence **several** + **of** + **Nondef** + **boys** represents an actual utterance, but of course it is not itself an actual utterance. We shall encounter this situation often in the grammar. Before this becomes grammatically sayable, the *of* must be omitted, and **Nondef** must be **Ø**. The sequence **several + of + Nondef + boys** becomes **several boys**. The sequence **many + of + Nondef + tables** becomes _____ _____ .

148

This is a fairly general rule for pre-articles: when the pre-article appears before **Nondef**, the *of* is dropped, and **Nondef** becomes **Ø**. The sequence **a few + of + Nondef + chickens** becomes _____ .

149

The sequence **all + of + Nondef + houses** becomes _____ .

150

We can note here one of the reasons for treating the personal pronouns differently from proper nouns—that is, for considering that personal pronouns have a determiner, consisting at least of the nondefinite article **Ø**, whereas proper nouns do not have a determiner. The pre-article may occur in many structures before personal pronouns: *several of us, many of them, a lot of you,* with the form changing from *we* to *us, they* to *them*. However, we do not have pre-articles before proper nouns.

MAIN POINTS OF LESSON THREE

NP → { proper noun / Det + N } We add *proper noun* as a possible kind of **NP** different from the already discussed **Det + N**.

N → { common noun / personal pronoun } An **N** will then be a common noun (as distinguished from a proper noun) or a personal pronoun.

common noun → { count / noncount } We distinguish two main kinds of common nouns: those that refer to things that can be counted (*table, boy, dream, inspection*) and those that do not (*mush, wheat, courage, despair*).

KINDS OF NOUNS AND MORE DETERMINERS

The kind of article that occurs depends on the kind of **N** that follows. Only nondefinite Ø occurs with personal pronouns. Only *a* and *the* occur with singular count nouns. Only *some*, **Ø,** and *the* occur with plural count nouns and with noncount nouns. Proper nouns are considered as having no determiner at all. For those with which the word *the* occurs (*the United States*), *the* is considered part of the noun rather than a determiner.

Det → (pre-article) + **Art.** This adds to the rewrite of determiner the information that a pre-article can occur before the determiner. Pre-articles are expressions like *several of, many of, a few of,* all including the word *of.* When **Art** is **Def,** the pre-article simply occurs before the definite article *the.* When **Art** is **Nondef,** the Ø form of **Nondef** must occur, and the *of* of the pre-article will be dropped.

Lesson Four
POST-ARTICLE STRUCTURES IN THE DETERMINER

Explanations like that in which *several tables* is derived from **several + of + Nondef + tables** are bothersome to many students because they don't seem "real." The grammarian seems to be playing a game in which he makes up fictitious structures from which to derive real ones. This is, however, a superficial view. The grammarian is going about the very real business of describing the relationships that exist among the structures of the language and of doing so in the most economical way he can devise. We want to observe the quality of nondefiniteness running through *some tables, a table, several tables* as distinct from the definiteness of *the tables, the table, several of the tables.* The best way of doing this seems to be through the concept of the nondefinite article ∅ and the rule for dropping *of* when **Nondef** is ∅.

Of course, we cannot suppose that speakers of English consciously go through such processes in forming noun phrases. Obviously, they do not form in their minds the sequence **several + of + Nondef + tables** and then consciously choose ∅ for **Nondef** and consciously drop *of.* We can, however, imagine that something like this structure does exist in our minds and that we work with this structure, somehow or other, in speaking and understanding English. The operation itself is obscure; nobody knows very much about the thought processes involved in the use of the structure of a language. But we can get some notion of the structure itself.

It should be noted also that the English determiner contains a good deal of complexity which this grammar will not describe in detail. For example, the rule "omit *of* before **Nondef**" applies to most pre-articles but not to all. It doesn't apply, for instance, to the pre-article *a lot of.* If we applied it to **a lot + of + Nondef + boys,** we would get the ungrammatical **a lot boys.* A complete grammar would describe this and other subdivisions of pre-articles. Here we will just note that the complexity exists and go on.

151

We rewrote determiner thus: **Det → (pre-article) + Art**. This indicates that the item of the determiner that may, but need not, occur is _____ .

152

We will now add an item to this rule: **Det → (pre-article) + Art + (Demon)**. Before **Art** we may have pre-article. After **Art** we may have _____ .

153

We must be careful not to go too fast. The symbol **Demon** stands for the word *demonstrative*, as you may have guessed, and you may know that such words as *this* and *these* are called demonstratives. However, **Demon** here doesn't stand for *this* or *these*. The situation is a little more complicated. The next rule specifies **Demon**: **Demon** → $\begin{Bmatrix} D_1 \\ D_2 \end{Bmatrix}$ Again, the brackets indicate a choice. If, after **Art**, we choose **Demon**, it will be either ____ or ____ .

154

This is as far as the rules of syntax take us. The rules that we have given would produce, for example, a structure like this: **the + D_1 + table**. Is this structure (1) a noun, (2) a determiner, (3) an article, (4) a noun phrase? ____

155

Now take **the + D_1**. Is this (1) a noun, (2) a determiner, (3) an article, (4) a noun phrase? ____

156

The description **the + D_1 + table** is the end of the *syntactic* description of this particular structure; it doesn't indicate how the structure is pronounced. The rules for pronunciation are contained in another part of grammar, which is called *phonology*. One such rule is the following: **the + D_1 → this**. Does the sentence "This table is expensive" contain a determiner? ____

30   ENGLISH SYNTAX

157

The word *this* results from **the** + **D₁**, which is a case of **Def** + **Demon**, which is one of many possible determiners. Does the sentence "This table is expensive" contain an article? ____

158

The word *this* results from **the** + **D₁**, which is a case of **Def** + **Demon**, and **Def** is one of the articles. Since we are concerned in this text with syntax and not with phonology, we will indicate rules of phonology only occasionally and not in a very rigorous way. Do you think **the** + **D₁** can be *this* when **N** is *tables?* ____

159

The structure **this tables* is clearly ungrammatical. When the **N** of the noun phrase is a plural count noun, **the** + **D₁** is *these*. What word in the sentence "I like these tables" contains the definite article?

____

160

Note that the description again accounts for meaning relationships. The words *the, this, these* are all definite. *The* is the definite article. *This* and *these* are the definite article with demonstrative (pointing out or indicating something) meaning added. How many articles does the sentence "I like these tables" contain? ____

161

The noun phrase *these tables* has the form **the** + **D₁** + **tables**, and *the* is the definite article. The noun phrase *I* has the form **Ø** + **I**, and **Ø** is one form of the nondefinite article. What is the rewrite rule for demonstrative? **Demon** → ____

162

Another phonological rule says that **the** + **D₂** is *that* or *those*, depending on whether **N** is a plural count noun or not. If the **N** is a plural count noun, **the** + **D₂** will be ____ .

163

There is one noun phrase in the sentence "Many of those dishes are broken." What is it? _____

164

What is the determiner in "Many of those dishes are broken"? _____

165

What is the pre-article in "Many of those dishes are broken"? _____

166

Every noun phrase contains an article, unless the noun phrase is a proper noun (or, as we shall note later, an indefinite pronoun). In "Many of those dishes are broken," **Art** is contained in the word _____ .

167

The rewrite of determiner, at this point, is **Det** → **(pre-article) + Art + (Demon)**. Art can be either _____ or _____ .

168

For every noun phrase, we must have **Art**, which can be either **Def** or **Nondef**. We may have **Demon**, which can be either D_1 or D_2. Therefore, one possible construction is **Nondef + D_1**. Let us now add the following phonological rule: **Nondef + D_1** → a certain. Then **Nondef + D_1 + man + came in** describes the sentence _____ .

169

We now add another phonological rule: **Nondef + D_2** → some. Then **Nondef + D_2 + man + came in** describes the sentence _____ _____ .

170

You will remember that we have encountered the word *some* as one of the nondefinite articles, occurring in such noun phrases as *some letters, some meat*—that is, before noncount nouns and plural count nouns. Now pronounce the two sentences "Some men came in" and "Some man came in." Is the *some* pronounced more loudly in the first sentence or the second? _____

171

It is not only pronounced more loudly in the second sentence, it is also pronounced with greater length and with a slightly different vowel sound. It is in fact a different word, and the two words spelled *some* are described by different rules in the grammar. In "Some men came in," *some* is a nondefinite _____ .

172

In "Some man came in," *some* is a nondefinite article plus _____ .

173

In "A certain man came in," *a certain* is **Nondef** plus _____ .

174

In "This man came in," *this* is **Def** plus _____ .

175

In "Those men went out," *those* is **Def** plus _____ .

176

Consider (1) *this man,* (2) *that man,* (3) *a certain man,* (4) *some man.* (1) and (2) are alike in that they both contain the element **Def.** (3) and (4) are alike in that they both contain the element _____ .

177

In (1) *this man,* (2) *that man,* (3) *a certain man,* (4) *some man,* (1) and (3) are alike in that they both contain D_1, and (2) and (4) are alike in that they both contain _____ .

You may have noticed that this description emphasizes certain meanings that recur in the English noun phrase: definiteness (**Def**), lack of definiteness (**Nondef**), nearness (D_1), remoteness (D_2). Thus *the men, several of the men, this man, some of these men* are all definite and all contain the definite article. *A man, some men, men, a certain man, several men* are all not definite and all contain **Nondef**. You should remember, however, that meanings are much more slippery than forms. Given the grammatical description, one can say assuredly whether **Def** occurs or not, though there are certain noun phrases about which one could argue interminably as to whether or not they are nondefinite in meaning. For example, are the subjects of "Men are human beings," "A man is a human being," "He is a human being," "David is a human being" definite or not? It is difficult to say. But we can certainly say that none contains the definite article.

Similarly, D_1 and D_2 in combination with **Def** clearly contain the meanings *nearness* and *remoteness: this* and *that*. In combination with **Nondef**, this meaning contrast is not so clear, though one could perhaps argue that *a certain* is more "near" than *some*.

178

Many of the men has the structure **pre-article** + **Def** + **N**. *A few of those men* has the structure _____ + ____ + ____ + **N**.

179

We will conclude our description of the kernel noun phrase by adding one more item to the rewrite of determiner: **Det** → (pre-article) + **Art** + (**Demon**) + (number). This says that after **Art** we may have a number as well as a demonstrative. The fact that **Demon** and number may, but need not, occur is shown by the _____ .

180

The structure *number* has two possibilities: number → { cardinal number / ordinal number } Ordinal numbers are words like *first, second, third, fourth*. The corresponding cardinal numbers are _____ , _____ , _____ , _____ .

181

Cardinal numbers have already been encountered before *of*, as in *two of, six of*, etc. Along with such forms as *several of, many of*, these were called _____ .

182

Thus cardinal numbers appear both before and after the article in the determiner. Ordinals appear only after the article. Note again the rewrite rule for determiner: Det → (pre-article) + Art + (Demon) + (number). If we have both a number and Demon after the article, which comes first? _____

183

The rules will now provide for such noun phrases as *the three cars* and *the third car*. Here *the* is **Def,** *three* is a cardinal number, and *third* is an _____ .

184

Det → (pre-article) + Art + (Demon) + (number). To have a determiner we must have **Art**. Then we may have **Demon** or number. Or we may have both, if we have them in the order given. In *the third car* and *the three cars,* we have taken the definite article and number but omitted _____ .

185

In *those three cars,* we have taken article, **Demon,** and cardinal number. The word *those* is a case of **Def** + _____ .

186

If the structure of *those three cars* is the + D_2 + cardinal number + **N**, the structure of *this third car* is _____ + _____ + _____ + _____ .

187

In *several of those students,* the determiner is composed of **pre-article + Def + D_2**. What is the determiner composed of in *a lot of these books?* _____ + ____ + ____

188

In *many of those twenty items,* the determiner is composed of **pre-article + Def + D_2 + cardinal number**. What is the determiner composed of in *a few of these third pages?* _____ + ____ + ____ + _____ .

189

The noun phrase *a few books* is composed of **pre-article + Nondef + N**, with the *of* obligatorily omitted and **Nondef** as ∅. *Many books* is composed of _____ + _____ + ___ .

190

The determiner in *men* is the article **Nondef**. What is the determiner in *you?* _____

191

Give the rewrite rule for sentence. S → ___ + ___

192

NP → _____

___ + ___

193

N → _____

_____

194

common noun → _____

_____

195

Det → _____ + _____ + _____ + _____

196

Art → _____

_____

197

Def → ___

198

Nondef → ___

___

___

199

Demon → _____

_____

200

The rules for **NP** that we have given will generate a great many noun phrases. However, they will not account for all of the noun phrases in English. For instance, they will specify *some of the men* and *some men*, but they will not specify *both the men*. For the latter (as for *all the men* and *half the men*) we would need a special rule. We have traced just the main features of the English kernel noun phrase. Much of the detail we must necessarily ignore.

One kind of noun phrase that we have left out altogether is what is called an *indefinite pronoun*. Indefinite pronouns are words like *everybody, anyone, something, nothing*. These are composed of the elements *every-, any-, some-, no-* compounded with *-body, -one,* or *-thing*. They are quite different from the other noun phrases we have examined. No article, pre-article, demonstrative, or number can occur with them. In a sense, they have the determiner built into them, in the *every-, any-, some-, no-* part. This is not entirely a matter of the history of these structures, because these determiners alternate predictably, just as other determiners do. For example, we say "I need some paper" but "I don't need any paper." Similarly we say, "I need something" but "I don't need anything."

If we want to include indefinite pronouns in the description, we must do so at a high level, at the rewrite of noun phrase:

$$NP \rightarrow \left\{ \begin{array}{l} \text{proper noun} \\ \text{indefinite pronoun} \\ \text{Det} + \text{N} \end{array} \right\}$$

The indefinite pronoun is then seen as a particular kind of noun phrase. It is not an **N,** and it is not preceded by a determiner, since, in a way, it contains the determiner.

MAIN POINTS OF LESSON FOUR

Det → (pre-article) + **Art** + (**Demon**) + (number)   A determiner must contain **Art**. It may contain the other items in the order given.

Demonstrative (**Demon**) is either D_1 or D_2, which may be thought of as elements containing the meanings *nearness* and *remoteness* respectively. Phonological rules require that **Def** + D_1 → this, these; **Def** + D_2 →

that, those; Nondef + D_1 → a certain; Nondef + D_2 → some (pronounced differently from the *some* in "Some men were here"). Note that these phonological rules differ in kind from the rewrite rules we have been considering. They are of the type X + Y → Z, not X → Y + Z.

Number is either cardinal number or ordinal number. Cardinal numbers are structures like *one, two, three, four*. Ordinal numbers are structures like *first, second, third, fourth*. Either of these can appear after the article (and after the demonstrative, if there is one) to produce noun phrases like *the three cars, the third cars, those three cars, those third cars*. By a rule not specified here, they can appear together in noun phrases like *those first three cars*.

Lesson Five
THE VERB PHRASE

We turn now to the second main structure of the kernel sentence—the verb phrase that functions as its predicate. Again we use the term *phrase* to include all the different structures that occur in this position. These are often groups of words: *landed the plane, was in the house, walked away, seems pleasant*. Sometimes they are single words: *laughed, winked, sings*.

We will make a fundamental distinction that will probably be unfamiliar to you. We will distinguish between the word class that we call *verbs (walk, seem, laugh, wink)* and the word *be*, which we do not include with the verb class. *Be* (in its various forms, *is, were*, etc.) is just *be*. Like a number of other words in English, *be* is unique. Most of the grammatical rules that apply to verbs do not apply to *be*; most of those that apply to *be* do not apply to verbs. We therefore get a simpler and more explanatory grammar of English if we recognize the special character of *be* at the beginning and do not try to treat it with the verbs, to whose rules it almost always constitutes an exception.

You may very likely continue, from force of habit, to speak of "the verb *be*." There is nothing particularly wrong with doing so. The important thing is to remember that, whatever you call it, *be* is altogether special.

201

The rule S → NP + VP indicates that every English kernel sentence contains a noun phrase plus a verb phrase, in that order. Every verb phrase contains some form of a verb or some form of the word *be*. In the sentence "He is happy," *is* is a form of the word *be*. What word is a form of *be* in "I am happy"? ____

202

What word is a form of *be* in "They are happy"? ____

203

What word is a form of *be* in "She was happy"? ____

204

What word is a form of *be* in "We were happy"? _____

205

We have noted five forms of *be* in addition to *be* itself: *am, is, are, was, were.* There are two other forms, *been* and *being,* which we shall encounter later. Any **VP** contains a form of a verb or a form of ____ .

206

In addition to *be, been,* and *being,* there are five forms of *be.* They are _____ , _____ , _____ , _____ , _____ .

207

Any kernel **VP** which contains a form of *be* must also contain another structure. In "He is happy," the **VP** contains *is* plus the word *happy*. *Happy* belongs to the word class called *adjectives*. What is the adjective in "She is sad"? ____

208

What is the adjective in "The box was heavy"? _____

209

What is the adjective in "The joke was funny"? _____

210

What is the adjective in "The temptation was irresistible"? _____

211

We abbreviate *adjective* **Adj** and begin to define it thus: **Adj** → **happy, sad, heavy, funny, irresistible** . . . Like the rules for pre-article, personal pronoun, etc., the rule is just a list of some of the words that occur as adjectives. A verb phrase may contain a form of *be* plus an _____ .

40 ENGLISH SYNTAX

212

In the sentence "She was a teacher," which word is a form of *be*? ____

213

In "She was a teacher," what kind of structure is *a teacher*? ____

214

In "She was a teacher," what kind of structure is *was a teacher*? ____

215

An English verb phrase may consist of a form of *be* followed by an adjective or a form of *be* followed by a _____.

216

In "Harold was young," what kind of structure is *young*? ____

217

In the sentence "Harold was a child," what kind of structure is *a child*? ____

218

In "They are a few of the hundred rebels," what kind of structure is *a few of the hundred rebels*? ____

219

A verb phrase may consist of a form of *be* followed by either an _____ or a _____.

220

It will prove useful to have a term that includes both *adjective* and *noun phrase*. We will use the term *substantive*.

$$\text{substantive} \rightarrow \left\{ \begin{array}{l} \text{NP} \\ \text{Adj} \end{array} \right\}$$

A verb phrase may consist of *be* followed by a substantive—that is, by either a _____ or an _____.

Like many other terms in grammar, *substantive* is used differently by different grammarians. It is sometimes given the meaning *a noun phrase or anything that can replace a noun phrase*. We are using it here in an older sense, one employed also in grammars of Latin and of Hebrew: a noun phrase or an adjective. We write *substantive* in the formula in just those places where either a noun phrase or an adjective can grammatically occur. There are several such places in English structure.

Many grammars use the term *complement* for what we are calling *substantive*. We cannot use *complement* here, however, because we shall need it for another important structure, one that we will discuss when we come to talk about certain transformations.

221

We can now begin the rule for verb phrase: **VP → be + substantive**. Later we will include the machinery that turns *be* into *am, is, are, was, were*. What is the rule for substantive?   **substantive → ____**

____

222

There is another structure that can follow *be* in the verb phrase. In "Sally was here," *here* is not a substantive but an *adverbial of place*. What is the adverbial of place in "Tom is outside"?   _____

223

We will abbreviate adverbial of place as **Adv-p**. Then **Adv-p → here, outside, upstairs, in the room, on the table, . . .** What is the **Adv-p** in "The kite is on the roof"?   _____

224

What kind of structure follows *be* in "John is inside"?   _____

225

Be may be followed by an **Adv-p** or by a _____ .

226

A substantive is either a _____ or an _____ .

---

42   ENGLISH SYNTAX

227

Now we can add to the rewrite of verb phrase:

$$VP \rightarrow be + \begin{Bmatrix} \text{substantive} \\ \text{Adv-p} \end{Bmatrix}$$

According to this formula, "The child was unhappy" consists of **NP** + **be** + _____ .

228

The sentence "The socks are in the drawer" consists of **NP** + ___ + _____ .

229

The sentence "Several of the newcomers were students" consists of ___ + ___ + ___ .

230

The sentence "Merrill was there" consists of ___ + ___ + _____ .

231

We said that every verb phrase contains either a form of _be_ or a verb. _Verbs_ are words like _arrive, go, think, carry, prepare_. What is the verb in "They hurried"? _____

232

What is the verb in "The plane arrived"? _____

233

What is the verb in "The porter carried the bags"? _____

234

What is the verb in "The mechanic repaired the car"? _____

235

What is the verb in "Harry looked sick"? _____

236

What is the verb in "Mervin became a monk"? _____

237

We need a term which excludes verb phrases with *be* but includes all verb phrases with verbs—that is, which includes *arrived, landed the plane, became a monk,* but excludes *is sick, are here, were students.* We shall use the term *verbal.* The verb phrases *came, carried the bags, ate dinner* are all examples of _____ .

238

Which sentence contains a verbal: (1) Harry was in the office. (2) Harry was a friend of mine. (3) Harry looked sick? _____

239

A verb phrase contains either a verbal or a form of *be.* If it contains *be,* the *be* will be followed by a _____ or an _____ .

240

We now enlarge the **VP** rule as follows:

$$VP \rightarrow \left\{ \begin{array}{l} be + \left\{ \begin{array}{l} \text{substantive} \\ \text{Adv-p} \end{array} \right\} \\ \text{verbal} \end{array} \right\}$$

A **VP** must contain _____ or a _____ .

241

If the **VP** contains *be,* it must also contain _____ or _____ .

242

A substantive is either an _____ or a _____ .

243

A verbal always contains a _____ .

244

In "The box was square," *square* is a substantive. What kind of substantive is it? _____

245

In "The instructions are in this envelope," *be* is followed by an _____ .

246
In "The plane arrived" and "The pilot landed the plane," the verb phrases are both _____ .

247
In "The plane arrived" and "The pilot landed the plane," *arrived* and *landed* are both _____ .

248
In "Many of the losers were underfed," both the subject and the substantive are _____ .

249
Apart from *be, been, being,* what are the forms of *be*? ____ , ____ , ____ , ____ , ____

250
The two general kinds of verb phrases are verbals and verb phrases with *be*. In the next lesson we will examine some kinds of verbals.

MAIN POINTS OF LESSON FIVE

$$\textbf{VP} \rightarrow \left\{ \begin{array}{l} \text{be} + \left\{ \begin{array}{l} \text{substantive} \\ \text{Adv-p} \end{array} \right\} \\ \text{verbal} \end{array} \right\}$$

This is just a preliminary rewriting of **VP**. There are some more items to be added. This rule says that every verb phrase must contain the word *be* or a verbal. If it contains *be*, then it must also contain a substantive or an adverbial of place (**Adv-p**).

$$\text{substantive} \rightarrow \left\{ \begin{array}{l} \textbf{NP} \\ \textbf{Adj} \end{array} \right\}$$

A substantive is either a noun phrase or an adjective. We have already described noun phrases. Adjectives are words like *good, happy, true, oblong*.

Adverbials of place may be either single adverbs (*here, outside, upstairs*) or phrases (*in the house, by the river, behind the door*).

We shall have to spend some time on the rule that rewrites verbal. For the present we can say that verbals are those verb phrases which contain verbs instead of *be*.

Lesson Six
TYPES OF VERBALS

We first encountered noun phrases in the function of subject—that is, as the first **NP** of the rule **S → NP + VP**. Now we identify noun phrases occurring also in the **VP** that functions as predicate. We find the noun phrase as a type of substantive in "He's a student." We find it in use after verbs: *landed the plane, became a monk.*

Having identified the **NP** in the function of subject and described its structure, we have described it everywhere. The same rules obtain, whether the **NP** functions as subject or as part of the **VP**.

$$\mathbf{NP} \rightarrow \begin{Bmatrix} \text{proper noun} \\ \text{indefinite pronoun} \\ \text{Det + N} \end{Bmatrix}$$

Det → (pre-article) **+** Art **+** (Demon) **+** (number)

Both are still true. Only a few special rules need be applied to certain **N**'s (I → me, he → him, she → her, we → us, they → them) when these occur in some parts of the verb phrase. In general, the structure of the **NP** is everywhere just what it is in the function of subject, and having described it there, we don't have to describe it again.

We have also observed noun phrases occurring in certain types of adverbials: *in the house, by the car,* etc. Structures of this type are called *prepositional phrases*. In these examples the words *in* and *by* are *prepositions* (**Prep**), and the noun phrases that follow them are said to function as *objects of the prepositions*. Again, the special rules of the type I → me apply to noun phrases in this function when **N** is a personal pronoun. Apart from these, the structure of the noun phrase is just what has been described. The possibilities are the same. The adverbial *by the car* consists of **Prep + NP**. So does the adverbial *by one of those three cars*.

251

VP's must contain either a verb or the word _____ .

---

46 ENGLISH SYNTAX

252

VP's which contain *be* must also contain either a _____ or an _____ .

253

VP's which contain verbs instead of *be* are called *verbals*. In "The plane arrived," the predicate is several structures in one word. It is a verb phrase, a verb, and a _____ .

254

There are several types of verbs, and so there are several types of verbals. The verb *arrive* in "The plane arrived" is what is called an *intransitive verb*. What word is the verb in "Something occurred"? _____

255

In "Something occurred," the verb is also an intransitive verb. What word is the verb in "Sheila slept"? _____

256

We abbreviate intransitive verb as **VI**. Then we specify the category **VI** as usual by giving the list of words that occur as VI's. VI → **arrive, occur, sleep, . . .** Of course there are many more. What word is the verb in "Something happened yesterday"? _____

257

In "Something happened yesterday" or "Sheila slept late," *happen* and *sleep* are intransitive verbs. Intransitive verbs may be followed by structures like *yesterday* or *late* (adverbials), but they are not followed by ordinary noun phrases or by adjectives. In "The plane arrived," *arrive* is an _____ verb.

258

What is the abbreviation for intransitive verb? ___

259

We can now begin to rewrite verbal: **verbal** → **VI**. What is the intransitive verb in "Samuel laughed loudly"? _____

TYPES OF VERBALS   **47**

260

What word is the verb in "They ate a cookie"? ____

261

In "They ate a cookie," the verb is a *transitive verb*. What kind of structure is *a cookie*? ____

262

In kernel sentences transitive verbs are always followed by noun phrases. Intransitive verbs may be followed by nothing at all. In "Stan saw a movie," the transitive verb is the word ____ .

263

We abbreviate transitive verb **VT**. In "The man died," *die* is a **V**____ .

264

In "George found the money," *find* is a **V**____ .

265

We can now enlarge the rewrite of verbal: **verbal** → $\left\{ \begin{array}{l} \text{VI} \\ \text{VT + NP} \end{array} \right\}$

What must occur after a transitive verb in a kernel sentence? ____

266

In "Tom gasped," the verb is a **V**____ .

267

In "Mary washed the car," the verb is a **V**____ .

268

In "Lou works at night," the verb is a **V**____ .

269

Both intransitive and transitive verbs can be followed by adverbials. In "Randy petted the cat gingerly," the verb is a **V**____ .

270

In "The carpenter repaired the door," the verb is a **V**____ .

271

In "The pilot landed the plane smoothly," the verb is a V____ .

272

Now take the sentence "Kathryn is happy." Here the word *is* is a form of ____ .

273

In kernel sentences *be* is followed by an adverbial of place or by a _____ .

274

There are two kinds of substantives, _____ and _____ .

275

What kind of substantive is *happy* in "Kathryn is happy"? _____

276

What kind of substantive is *a teacher* in "Kathryn is a teacher"? _____

277

In the sentence "Kathryn became a teacher," what word is the verb? _____

278

What kind of word is *sad* in "Kathryn became sad"? _____

279

There are a few verbs in American English which, like *be,* can be followed by either noun phrases or by adjectives—in other words, which can be followed by substantives. What kind of substantive is *true,* in "Helen remained true"? _____

TYPES OF VERBALS   49

280

What kind of substantive is *a friend* in "Helen remained a friend"?

_____

281

We shall call a verb which can be followed by a substantive (i.e., by either an adjective or a noun phrase) a verb of the *become* class. In "Helen remained true," *remain* is a verb of the _____ class.

282

In "Randy became a general," the verb is a verb of the _____ class.

Remember that we use the term *substantive* only for those places where both a noun phrase and an adjective can occur. In "Helen ate a cookie," *a cookie* is a noun phrase. However, it is not a substantive, because an adjective cannot occur in that pattern. (*"Helen ate sad" is ungrammatical.)

283

We abbreviate verb of the *become* class as **Vb**. Note that we use a small letter **b**, in contrast with the capitals of **VI** and **VT**. The reason is that **VI** and **VT** must be further subdivided, but **Vb** and the other types we will describe will not be. We can again enlarge the rewrite of verbal:

$$\text{verbal} \rightarrow \begin{Bmatrix} \text{VI} \\ \text{VT} + \text{NP} \\ \text{Vb} + \text{substantive} \end{Bmatrix}$$

A **VI** need not be followed by anything. A **VT** is followed by an **NP**, and a **Vb** by a _____ .

284

Vb → become, remain ... One hardly knows whether to put ... or not. Many speakers of American English have only these two verbs in the *become* class. Most speakers of British English have many more. In addition to the class of verbs **Vb**, we have noted the classes V___ and V___ .

285

Now take the sentence "It tasted good." What kind of word is *good?*
_____

286

What kind of word is *true* in "It seemed true"? _____

287

What kind of word is *beautiful* in "She looked beautiful"? _____

288

Some verbs are followed by adjectives, though not by noun phrases. We will call them, arbitrarily, verbs of the *seem* class and abbreviate them **Vs**. In "He appeared calm," the verb is a V____ .

289

In "They sold the house," the verb is a V____ .

290

In "He remained an apprentice," the verb is a V____ .

291

There is no practical problem in distinguishing **Vs** from **Vb**. For our purposes, the only **Vb**'s are *become* and *remain*. Other verbs which are followed by adjectives belong to the class V____ .

292

In "He felt silly," the verb is a V____ .

293

A **VP** consists of *be* plus a substantive or an adverbial of place or a _____ .

294

$$\text{verbal} \rightarrow \begin{Bmatrix} \text{VI} \\ \text{VT + NP} \\ \text{Vb + substantive} \\ \text{Vs + Adj} \end{Bmatrix}$$

A **Vs** is a verb of the _____ class.

TYPES OF VERBALS

295

A **Vb** is a verb of the _____ class.

296

VI is an abbreviation of _____.

297

VT is an abbreviation of _____.

298

A **VT** is followed by a _____.

299

A **Vs** is followed by an _____.

300

There are a good many complications in the verb phrase in addition to those we have noted. The **VT** is a particularly complicated class, with many subdivisions. However, we will not examine most of these until we have considered transformation.

MAIN POINTS OF LESSON SIX

$$\text{verbal} \rightarrow \begin{Bmatrix} \text{VI} \\ \text{VT + NP} \\ \text{Vb + substantive} \\ \text{Vs + Adj} \end{Bmatrix}$$

This is a preliminary description of verbals. There are other items to be added, and the transitive and intransitive verb classes must be divided into several subclasses.

VI → arrive, occur, sleep, . . . These are intransitive verbs. Unlike other verb types, they do not have to be followed by other structures, though they sometimes may be.

VT → see, find, help, . . . These are transitive verbs. They are always followed, in kernel sentences, by noun phrases.

Vb → become, remain, . . . There are some others for some speakers in certain contexts. For example, some people might say "He appeared a failure" along with "He appeared calm." However, the list is short for

American English. **Vb**'s are verbs of the *become* class. They are followed by substantives—i.e., by either noun phrases or adjectives.

Vs → **seem, taste, look,** . . . These are verbs of the *seem* class. They are followed by adjectives, but not by noun phrases.

Lesson Seven
VERBS OF THE *HAVE* CLASS, ADVERBIALS

We have now reached one point where we must qualify a rule of the grammar by saying "in American English." We said that the list of **Vb** verbs is a short one in American English. It is longer in British English. For example, in British English the verbs *look* and *feel* and many others belong to this class; the British say "He looked a fool," "He felt a fool," along with "He looked foolish," "He felt foolish." In other words, English grammar isn't quite the same thing for everyone who speaks English.

As we get to more and more specific matters, we find more differences among speakers of English. At some point we encounter rules that are true for Massachusetts English but untrue for Maryland or Texas English, and then rules that are true for some people in Massachusetts but not others. Finally we come to a level where everybody's English differs from everybody else's.

The term *level* is an important one. We can think of the general rules that we began with, like **S → NP + VP** and **NP → Det + N**, as high-level rules. They deal with the larger structures of the sentence. Rules like **Vb →** become, remain, ... are relatively low-level rules. They deal with specific elements in the sentence. In general, speakers of English, even those whose English is quite different, differ only in low-level rules. In the high-level rules, English is the same for everybody. This explains how we can readily understand people whose English seems quite different from ours.

Notice that we do not at this point make any statement about the superiority or inferiority of different kinds of English. We do not say that **Vb →** become, remain is a better or worse rule than **Vb →** become, remain, look, feel, seem. We have spoken of *grammatical* and *ungrammatical*, and we shall have much more to say about these concepts as we go along. By *ungrammatical* we mean "not corresponding to the grammar of English." Both **Vb** rules correspond to grammars of English, though to grammars which differ on low levels. It is possible for users of English to speak or write ungrammatically—that is, in ways that do not correspond to any grammar of English, including their own. But they generally do not do so in kernel sentences.

301

In "John worked," the verb is a V_____ .

302

In "Alice looked beautiful," the verb is a V_____ .

303

In "Sally saw a lady," the verb is a V_____ .

304

In "Sally became a lady," the verb is a V_____ .

305

"Sally saw a lady" and "Sally became a lady" have almost the same structure. In both cases the verb is followed by a _____ .

306

However, the two structures are rather obviously different. In "Sally became a lady," the two noun phrases refer to the same person. In "Sally saw a lady," they don't. We have also noted a formal difference in the two structures: *became* can be followed by a substantive (that is, by an adjective or a noun phrase), and *saw* cannot. We shall see other formal differences between the **VT** and **Vb** structures later on. In "Sally saw a lady," the noun phrase *Sally* functions as _____ .

307

The noun phrase after a **VT** functions as *object* of the **VT**. In "Sally saw a lady," *a lady* functions as object of the verb. What noun phrase functions as object in "Henry lifted the lid"? _____

308

What noun phrase functions as object in "Somebody broke a window"?

_____

VERBS OF THE *HAVE* CLASS, ADVERBIALS

309

In "Sheila slept," the verb is a V____ .

310

In "Tom looked indignant," the verb is a V____ .

311

All of the verbs we have so far described—VI, VT, Vb, Vs—may, but need not, be followed by an *adverbial of manner*. The word *peacefully* is an adverbial of manner in "Sheila slept peacefully." What is the adverbial of manner in "Alice laughed happily"? _____

312

What is the adverbial of manner in "John worked carelessly"?
_____

313

What is the adverbial of manner in "Henry lifted the lid quickly"?
_____

314

In "Sally became a lady unwillingly," *unwillingly* is an _____
_____ .

315

What is the adverbial of manner in "Tom looked indignant playfully"?
_____

316

What is the adverbial of manner in "Tom looked foolish on purpose"?
_____

317

What is the adverbial of manner in "Henry lifted the lid with a jerk"?
_____

56   ENGLISH SYNTAX

318

Adverbials of manner may, but need not, occur in verbals containing the following types of verbs: V____ , V____ , V____ , V____ .

319

We abbreviate adverbial of manner **Adv-m**. Then we can write:

$$\text{verbal} \rightarrow \begin{Bmatrix} \text{VI} \\ \text{VT + NP} \\ \text{Vb + substantive} \\ \text{Vs + adjective} \end{Bmatrix} + \text{(Adv-m)}$$

The fact that an adverbial of manner may occur but need not is indicated by the _____ .

320

Now take the sentence "Tom has a car." Like a **VT**, the verb *have* is followed by a _____ .

321

The sentence "Tom has a car" seems to have the same structure as "Tom drives a car." However, there are formal differences. One is that adverbials of manner do not occur in verbals when the verb is *have*. Which of these is ungrammatical: (1) Tom drove the car recklessly. (2) Tom had the car recklessly? ____

322

Which of these is ungrammatical: (1) Henry lifted the lid on purpose. (2) The lid weighed ten pounds on purpose? ____

323

Which of these is ungrammatical: (1) Sally slept peacefully. (2) The dress cost. (3) She bought a dress? ____

324

Verbs like *have, cost, weigh* are different from the others we have noted. Like transitive verbs and verbs of the *become* type, they are followed by **NP**'s. But the **NP** is not an object for either the *have* type or the *become*

VERBS OF THE *HAVE* CLASS, ADVERBIALS   57

type, and the *have* type will not take an adverbial of manner. In "Harry drank some milk," the noun phrase *some milk* functions as _____

325

But *some milk* does not function as object in "Harry had some milk." We shall not give a name to its function but simply say that it doesn't function as an object. We shall abbreviate verb of the *have* type as **Vh**. In "The milk cost twenty cents," the verb is a **V**____.

We might say, loosely, that a **VT** shows some sort of thing done to the following noun phrase by the subject, whereas a **Vh** does not. This is a loose thing to say, because it is simply an appeal to our feeling for the meaning of the construction rather than to formal characteristics of the structure itself. However, we have noted one formal distinction between the **VT** and the **Vh** constructions: the **VT** construction can be followed, after the noun phrase, by an adverbial of manner, and the **Vh** cannot. We shall see other formal differences later on. We shall find that the important differences in meaning that we perceive in grammatical structures will usually be supported in this way by formal differences.

326

In "The lid weighed ten pounds," the verb is a **V**____.

327

Vh is the last main verb type we shall note. We now have:

$$\text{verbal} \rightarrow \left\{ \begin{Bmatrix} \text{VI} \\ \text{VT + NP} \\ \text{Vb + substantive} \\ \text{Vs + Adj} \\ \text{Vh + NP} \end{Bmatrix} + (\text{Adv-m}) \right\}$$

This shows that an **Adv-m** may occur in verbals with **VI, VT, Vb, Vs**. It does not occur when the verb is a **V**____.

328

When the verbal contains a noun phrase, the verb will be either a **V**____, a **V**____, or a **V**____.

---

58   ENGLISH SYNTAX

329

When the verbal contains an adjective, the verb will be either a V____ or a V____ .

330

When nothing follows the verb, the verb is a V____ .

331

If only an **Adv-m** follows the verb, the verb is a V____ .

332

It is easy enough to distinguish intransitive verbs from all the others: they are not followed by noun phrases or adjectives. **Vb**'s are different from **Vs**'s because noun phrases occur only after V____ .

333

What is the term that includes both **Adj** and **NP**? _____

334

What structure in the verb phrase besides **Vb** can be followed by a substantive, that is, by either a noun phrase or an adjective? ____

335

One can easily see a similarity between sentences with *be* and those with either **Vb** or **Vs:** "Sally was a lady," "Sally became a lady"; "The pie was good," "The pie tasted good." A verb that thus relates the subject to what follows the verb is a **Vb** or a **Vs**. The only **Vb**'s we have noted for American English are _____ and _____ .

336

Other verbs showing this relationship must be **Vs**'s. Apart from **Vb**, noun phrases occur after V____ and V____ .

337

A **VT,** but not a **Vh,** can be followed, after the noun phrase, by an _____ .

338

We have so far named only three **Vh**'s: *have, cost, weigh*. There are many others. What is the **Vh** in "The bill totaled five dollars"? _____

339

What is the **Vh** in "John stood six feet"? _____

340

The **NP** that follows a **VT** functions as its _____ .

341

In "Evelyn replied quietly," the verb is a **V**____ .

342

In "The first man paid the bill," the verb is a **V**____ .

343

In "The idea sounded good," the verb is a **V**____ .

344

In "The girls remained quiet," the verb is a **V**____ .

345

In "Henry closed the door with a bang," the verb is a **V**____ .

346

In "Henry closed the door with a bang," the prepositional phrase *with a bang* is an _____ .

347

In "Josephine has several sisters," the verb is a **V**____ .

348

In "Mary replied graciously," the verb is a **V**____ .

349

In "Sally felt fine," the verb is a **V**____ .

350

Every verb phrase in the kernel contains *be* or a verbal. If *be*, it also contains a substantive or an adverbial of place. The principal types of verbals are those we have described: **VI, VT + NP, Vb + substantive, Vs + Adj, Vh + NP**. Of these, we shall have to return to the **VI** and **VT** later on to describe some of their complexities. The others present no particular problems.

MAIN POINTS OF LESSON SEVEN

$$VP \rightarrow \left\{ \begin{array}{l} be + \left\{ \begin{array}{l} \text{substantive} \\ \text{Adv-p} \end{array} \right\} \\ \text{verbal} \end{array} \right\}$$

$$\text{verbal} \rightarrow \left\{ \left\{ \begin{array}{l} \text{VI} \\ \text{VT + NP} \\ \text{Vb + substantive} \\ \text{Vs + Adj} \\ \text{Vh + NP} \end{array} \right\} + (\text{Adv-m}) \right\}$$

These rules specify most, but not all, of the main features of the English verb phrase in kernel sentences. More needs to be said about adverbials. **VI** and **VT** need to be subdivided to account for such sentences as "He glanced up," "He relied on the the evidence," "He gave John a book," "He thought John a fool," and others. The most important missing feature is that which accounts for the tense of verbs and *be* and for various auxiliaries that may accompany verbs and *be*.

Lesson Eight
THE AUXILIARY

We have now accounted for the main types of English kernel sentences. Specifically, we have accounted for seven types differing in the verb phrase. These might be illustrated by such sentences as the following:

1. John is heroic (a hero).   NP + be + substantive
2. John is in the room.   NP + be + Adv-p
3. John worked.   NP + VI
4. John paid the bill.   NP + VT + NP
5. John became a hero (heroic).   NP + Vb + substantive
6. John felt sad.   NP + Vs + Adj
7. John had a car.   NP + Vh + NP

Most of the structure of any of these sentences could be shown by a kind of branching diagram. For example, we could represent the number 4 type as follows:

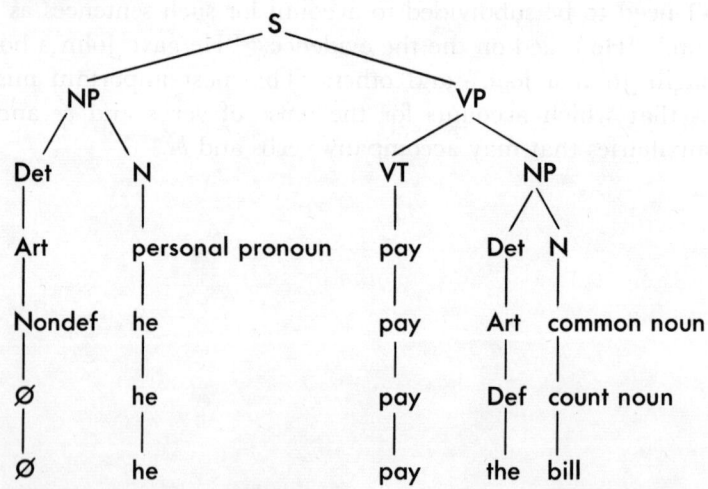

```
                    S
             /             \
           NP                VP
          /  \              /  \
        Det   N            VT   NP
         |    |            |   /  \
        Art   personal    pay Det  N
         |    pronoun      |   |   |
       Nondef   he        pay Art common noun
         |      |          |   |   |
         Ø      he        pay Def count noun
         |      |          |   |   |
         Ø      he        pay the bill
```

A diagram of this sort is called a tree of derivation, because it shows, in branches like those of a tree, the larger (or higher-level) structures

62   ENGLISH SYNTAX

from which the smaller (or lower-level) structures derive. We shall make considerable use of trees of derivation in the lessons that follow.

You may have noticed that one important part of the sentence "He paid the bill" is missing from the diagram above, which gives in fact the ungrammatical sentence * "He pay the bill." We will now study the mechanism which, among other things, turns *pay* into *paid*.

351

What are the verbs in the sentences "They walk," "He walks," and "He walked"? _____ , _____ , _____

352

Walk, walks, and *walked* are three different forms of the verb *walk*. What are the three corresponding forms of the verb *talk*? _____ , _____ , _____

353

Walk and *walks* are *present tense* forms. *Walked* is a *past tense* form. Which of the following is a past tense form: (1) *dream,* (2) *thinks,* (3) *helped*?

_____

354

Both *walked* and *helped* consist of two elements: the simple verb plus the ending *-ed*. The ending spelled *-ed* is one form of what is called the *past morpheme*. The past morpheme stands for whatever is done to a verb to make it past. We make the verb *scream* past by adding the ending spelled

_____ .

Morpheme is an important word in grammar, and we shall use it often. Roughly, it means the smallest meaningful units into which a sentence can be sensibly divided. A morpheme is often the same as a word; for example, *sad* is both a word and a morpheme. Sometimes a word is made up of several morphemes; *kindliness* consists of three morphemes: *kind, -ly* (or *-li*), and *-ness*. A morpheme is not necessarily the same thing as a syllable. *Happy* is a word of two syllables but is a single morpheme. It cannot be sensibly broken into *hap-* and *-py,* since neither of these has any separate significance.

Some morphemes, like the *-ed* introduced in 354, are not so much

THE AUXILIARY

parts of words as generalizations of grammatical categories: past tense, plural, possessive, etc. Thus we speak of the *past* morpheme, the *plural* morpheme, and so on.

355

A morpheme may have several forms. The morpheme *past* represents whatever is done to a verb to make it past. Some verbs are made past by adding the ending spelled *-ed,* and some are not. *Shouted* consists of the verb *shout* plus the ending *-ed.* The ending *-ed* is one form of the morpheme _____ .

356

Past means whatever is done to a verb to make it past. The irregular past tense *saw* consists of the verb *see* plus the morpheme *past.* The irregular past tense *sang* consists of *past* plus the verb _____ .

357

Left consists of *leave* plus *past. Gave* consists of _____ plus _____ .

358

Help plus *past* is _____ . *See* plus *past* is _____ . *Find* plus *past* is _____ .

359

Walked is the past tense form of *walk.* What are the present tense forms?

_____ , _____

360

The word *walks* in "He walks slowly" consists of *walk* plus *present.* In "He helps his mother," the word *helps* consists of what verb plus *present*?

_____

361

When *present* is added to verbs, it consists of an *s*-like sound when the subject is *he, she, it,* or a singular noun. Verbs do not add this sound, however, when the subject is *I, you,* or any plural. What is the tense of the verb in "They walk slowly"? Is it present or past? _____

---

64 ENGLISH SYNTAX

362

Observe this closely. In "They walk away," we say that *walk* consists not of the verb *walk* alone but of *walk* plus *present*. *Present* means whatever you do to a verb to form the present tense. When the subject is *they*, you don't do anything, so here *present* means *nothing*. In "They help the teacher," *help* consists of the verb _____ plus *present*.

363

In "She sings beautifully," *sings* consists of the verb _____ plus *present*.

364

In "They sing beautifully," *sing* consists of the verb _____ plus _____ .

365

In "Maria sang beautifully," *sang* consists of the verb _____ plus _____ .

366

In "Joe repaired the car," *repaired* consists of the verb _____ plus _____ .

367

English has two tenses: _____ and _____ .

You may have encountered other grammatical explanations of English that speak of more than two tenses, adding, for example, the future tense *will go* and the perfect tense *has gone*. Modern linguistics, however, does not extend the term *tense* to these phrasal constructions. As we shall see, there are a large number of such constructions, and it is better to treat them separately and reserve the term *tense* for those expressed in the verb itself.

368

We describe English tenses thus: **tense** → $\left\{ \begin{array}{l} \textbf{present} \\ \textbf{past} \end{array} \right\}$

In "He reads the paper," we have in the predicate a case of _____ + **VT** + **NP**.

THE AUXILIARY   **65**

369

In "He read the paper," we have in the predicate a case of _____ + **VT** + **NP**.

370

When the subject is *you*, what is **present** + **walk**? _____

371

The word *be* is more complicated than verbs. We have seen that *be* has five forms in addition to *be, been,* and *being*. These five forms correspond in use to *walk, walks, walked*. They are _____ , _____ , _____ , _____ , _____ .

372

Depending on the subject, **present** + **be** is *am, is,* or *are*. **Past** + **be** is _____ or _____ .

373

Every English kernel sentence must have a verb phrase, and some word in the verb phrase must have a tense form. We can write a formula for the sentence "David washed the car" in this way: **NP** + **tense** + **VT** + **NP**. Here the **NP**'s stand for what words in the actual sentence? _____ , _____

374

In the formula **NP** + **tense** + **VT** + **NP**, what does **VT** represent for the sentence "David washed the car"? _____

375

Washed is, strictly speaking, a wrong answer. **VT** represents only the verb *wash* in "David washed the car." The word *washed* consists of two elements: the verb *wash* and the morpheme _____ .

376

The morpheme *past* would be one possible product of which element in the formula **NP** + **tense** + **VT** + **NP**? _____

66   ENGLISH SYNTAX

377

Tense is part of what we call the *auxiliary*. The abbreviation of auxiliary is **Aux**. The **Aux** includes all the different changes that must or may be made on the verb or *be* of a verb phrase that functions as predicate. Since tense is part of **Aux**, and since every predicate must have tense, every predicate must also have ____ .

378

Notice that in such a formula as **NP + tense + VT + NP**, the tense comes before the verb, instead of after, as one might expect. The reason is that whatever word comes first in the predicate shows the tense. It may be the verb, but it also may not be. What is the verb phrase in "Jeff may wash the car"? _____

379

In "Jeff may wash the car," *wash* is the verb. *May* belongs to a small class of words called *modals*. Other modals are *will, shall, can, must*. What is the modal in "Jeff can wash the car"? ____

380

The modals are *may, must, shall,* _____ , and _____ .

381

Unlike verbs, modals do not add an *s*-like sound when the subject is singular. They have the same form in the present tense, whatever the subject is. Four modals have past tense forms, however. The past tense form of *will* is *would*, of *may* is *might*, of *shall* is *should*. What do you think the past tense form of *can* is? _____

382

The formula for "David would help willingly" is **NP + past + M + VI + Adv-m**. What do you think **M** is an abbreviation for? _____

383

In "David would help willingly," *would* is the past tense form of what modal? _____

THE AUXILIARY 67

384

The formula for "Evelyn should be here" is **NP + past + M + be + Adv-p**. Here **M** represents the modal *shall*. What is **shall + past**?

_____

385

When a modal occurs in a verb phrase, the tense applies to the modal. That is, the modal is either present or past: *can* or *could*, *may* or *might*, etc. The modal is followed by the simple, or base, form of a verb or *be*. The base forms of verbs are *walk, wash, talk, give, drive,* ... What do you think the base form of *be* is? _____

386

Like tense, modals are part of the auxiliary. Tense must occur, but modals may or may not. We represent this situation as follows: **Aux →
tense + (M)**. Here **M** stands for any of the words *shall, will,* _____ , _____ , or _____ .

387

In any predicate in which tense is *past*, the modals *can, may, will, shall* become _____ , _____ , _____ , _____ .

388

The modal *must* has no past tense. What is **may + present**? _____

389

What is **shall + past**? _____

390

What is **must + present**? _____

391

We can now nearly complete the rewrite of verb phrase:

$$VP \rightarrow Aux + \left\{ \begin{array}{l} be + \left\{ \begin{array}{l} substantive \\ Adv\text{-}p \end{array} \right\} \\ verbal \end{array} \right\}$$

This says that in any verb phrase in a kernel sentence we must first have _____ .

68   ENGLISH SYNTAX

392

After the **Aux** we must have either a _____ or a _____ .

393

If we have *be,* we must also have either a _____ or an _____ .

394

$$\text{verbal} \rightarrow \left\{ \begin{Bmatrix} \text{Vl} \\ \text{VT + NP} \\ \text{Vb + substantive} \\ \text{Vs + Adj} \\ \text{Vh + NP} \end{Bmatrix} + \text{(Adv-m)} \right\}$$

All verbals contain an intransitive verb, a transitive verb, or a verb of the *become, seem,* or *have* types. Most contain other structures too. All may be followed by an adverbial of manner except verbals containing a V_____ .

395

Every **VP** functioning as a predicate must contain an _____ .

396

Aux → tense + (M). This says that every **Aux** must contain a _____ .

397

An **Aux** may also contain a _____ .

398

The tenses of English are _____ and _____ .

399

The tense will apply to whatever follows it. This will be a modal, a verb, or a _____ .

400

The formulas that specify the structures that make up noun phrases and verb phrases may seem complicated. But they enable us to display, with just a few generalizations, the structure of a great many English sentence types and of innumerable actual sentences.

THE AUXILIARY   69

MAIN POINTS OF LESSON EIGHT

$$VP \rightarrow Aux + \left\{ \begin{array}{l} be + \left\{ \begin{array}{l} \text{substantive} \\ \text{Adv-p} \end{array} \right\} \\ \text{verbal} \end{array} \right\}$$

Except for the inclusion of certain optional adverbs, this completes the rewrite rule for the verb phrase. It says that every **VP** must contain first an **Aux**. Then it must have either *be* or a verbal. If it has *be*, it must have either a substantive or an adverbial of place.

Aux → tense + (M). This is a preliminary rule for **Aux**. More is to be added. It says that every **Aux** must contain tense. The **Aux** may, but need not, contain an **M**.

$$\text{tense} \rightarrow \left\{ \begin{array}{l} \text{present} \\ \text{past} \end{array} \right\}$$ There are two tenses in English, present and past. Tense applies to whatever follows it in the verb phrase. This may be *be*, a verb, or a modal, depending on what choices are made.

M → can, may, will, shall, must. These are the English modals.

Note that the addition of tense does not always change the actual form of the item to which tense is added. **Shout + past** is *shouted*, and **sing + past** is *sung*, but **put + past** is *put*. **Walk + present** may be *walks* or *walk*, depending on the subject. **Can + present** is always *can*.

Lesson Nine
THE REST OF THE AUXILIARY

With the addition of **Aux**, we can represent such a sentence as "He should pay the bill" with a tree of derivation as follows:

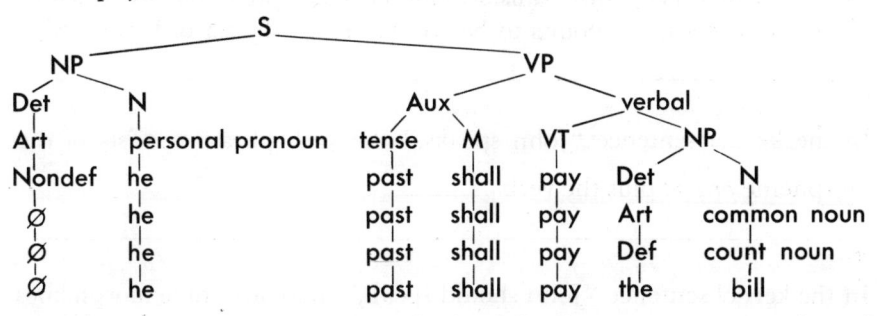

```
                          S
         NP                              VP
   Det        N                  Aux           verbal
   Art    personal pronoun    tense    M    VT        NP
  Nondef       he             past   shall  pay    Det       N
    ∅          he             past   shall  pay    Art    common noun
    ∅          he             past   shall  pay    Def    count noun
    ∅          he             past   shall  pay    the       bill
```

We come out at the bottom with the following sequence or string of elements:

∅ + he + past + shall + pay + the + bill

We call the items between plus signs *morphemes*. We use this term with reference to grammatical categories like tense, speaking of the morpheme *present* and the morpheme *past*. It applies also to the other elements derived from the rules given. It means something like *a unit of form*. We might also think of it, rather loosely, as a unit of meaning.

If the sentence above were actually pronounced, some of the morphemes would emerge as words and some would not. For example, *the* and *pay* would come out as words. However, *past* and *shall* combine to give the word *should*. Thus we note again that the terms *morpheme* and *word* are not identical.

The representation ∅ + he + past + shall + pay + the + bill is as far as we can go with the kind of rule we have been studying to this point—that is, with rules like **S → NP + VP; M → can, may, will, shall, must**. Rules of this type describe all the basic relationships of the language—what we have called the kernel. We refer to them, therefore, as *kernel rules*. In forming any particular sentence, when we have applied all the rules that apply, we get a string of morphemes like the string illustrated above. Since this is an end or terminal product, we call it a *terminal string*. Since it is the end product of the set of kernel rules, we call it a **K**-*terminal string*.

A **K**-terminal string is of course not a sentence. It is a representation of the structure of a sentence on a rather high level. The **K**-terminal string **Ø + he + past + shall + pay + the + bill** gives the morphemes of "He should pay the bill" in a certain order, but it doesn't tell anything about how the sentence is pronounced. The full description of the sentences of a language requires two other sets of rules: *transformation rules* and *phonological rules*. We have already had a few examples of phonological rules: **Def + D₁ → this, these; past + sing → sang**. We shall be concerned with transformational rules presently. Meanwhile, there are a few more points to be considered in the set of kernel rules.

401

In the kernel sentence "John speaks," the verb phrase consists of the morpheme *present* plus the verb _____ .

402

In the kernel sentence "John should speak," there are three morphemes in the verb phrase. One is *past*. The others are the modal _____ and the verb _____ .

403

What is the verb phrase in the kernel sentence "John had spoken"?

_____

404

In "John had spoken," *had* is part of the auxiliary. Is *had* present or past?

_____

405

In "John had spoken," *had* consists of the morpheme *have* plus the morpheme _____ .

406

Tense would not be an exact answer for 405. *Past* and *present* are morphemes, but tense is not. In "John had spoken," a part of *spoken* also belongs to the auxiliary. *Spoken* is what is called a *past participle*. A past

72   ENGLISH SYNTAX

participle consists of the simple form of a verb or *be* plus what we will call the morpheme **part**. **Part** means whatever is done to a verb or *be* to make it a past participle. *Spoken* consists of **part** plus the verb _____ .

407

In "John had eaten," *eaten* is a past participle. It consists of **part** plus _____ .

408

In "John had left," *left* is a past participle. It consists of _____ + _____ .

409

In "John had arrived," *arrived* is a past participle. It consists of _____ + _____ .

410

In "John arrived," *arrived* is not a past participle but a past tense form. It therefore consists of the morpheme *past* plus _____ .

411

Most verbs are like *arrive:* they have the same form for the past tense and the past participle. For these verbs **verb** + **past** and **verb** + **part** are identical. Many verbs, however, most of them very common ones, have different forms. **Eat** + **part** is *eaten*. What is **eat** + **past**? _____

412

Now compare "John ate" and "John had eaten." Both contain the verb *eat* and the morpheme *past*. In "John ate," *past* goes with *eat*. In "John had eaten," *past* goes with the word *have*. "John had eaten" contains all the elements of "John ate," and in addition, *have* and the morpheme _____ .

413

The formula for the predicate of "John ate" is **past** + **eat**. The formula for the predicate of "John had eaten" is **past** + **have** + **part** + **eat**. "John had eaten" contains the new elements _____ and _____ .

THE REST OF THE AUXILIARY 73

414

In **past** + **have** + **part** + **eat,** the morpheme *past* goes with the morpheme *have*. The morpheme **part** goes with the morpheme _____ .

415

The morphemes *have* and *part* belong to the auxiliary. They go together in the sense that whenever we have a **part** in a kernel sentence we also have a **have**. We can show this tentatively by rewriting auxiliary as follows: **Aux → tense + (M) + (have + part)**. What term does **M** stand for? _____

416

Aux → tense + (M) + (have + part). We must have an **Aux** for any kernel verb phrase. The **Aux** must contain tense and may contain a modal. It may also contain a _____ + _____ .

417

If the **Aux** contains a *have*, it must also contain _____ .

418

If an **Aux** contains both a modal and a **have + part**, which comes first? _____

419

We have so far noted four elements occurring in the auxiliary: *tense, modal, have, part*. Which of these does the sentence "Georgia spoke" contain? _____

420

Which of the elements *tense, modal, have, part* does the sentence "John typed rapidly" contain? _____

421

The sentence "John might help us" contains two elements of the auxiliary. What are they? _____ , _____

74 ENGLISH SYNTAX

422

"John will help us" also contains two of the four elements of the auxiliary—*tense, modal, have, part*. What are they? _____ , _____

423

In "John will help us," we have the two auxiliary elements tense and modal. The formula for the sentence is **NP + present + will + help + NP**. **Present + will** is *will*. What is **past + will**? _____

424

The four elements of the auxiliary so far given are *tense, modal, have, part*. The sentence "John has left" contains three of these. What are they? _____ , _____ , _____

425

In "John has left," tense is contained in the word _____ .

426

In "John has left," **part** is contained in the word _____ .

427

What is **present + have** when the subject is *Tom?* _____

428

What is **past + have**? _____

429

What is **past + shall**? _____

430

What is **present + shall**? _____

431

What is **part + speak**? _____

432

In "John had eaten," the form *eaten* is called a past _____ .

THE REST OF THE AUXILIARY   75

433

How many elements of the auxiliary are contained in the sentence "John should have eaten"? _____

434

"John should have eaten" contains all of the elements of the auxiliary so far given: *tense, modal, have, part.* The tense occurs in the word _____ , the **part** in the word _____ .

435

Which elements of the auxiliary occur in the sentence "John should be here"? _____ , _____

436

Which elements of the auxiliary occur in the sentence "John has been here"? _____ , _____ , _____

437

In "John has been here," *been* is a past _____ .

438

What is **part** + **be**? _____

439

"John should have been here" contains all four elements of the auxiliary. What are they? _____ , _____ , _____ , _____

440

Can you remember the rewrite of the auxiliary as so far given? **Aux** →
_____

441

The auxiliary in English contains just two more elements. Like *have* and **part** they go together. What is the verb phrase in the kernel sentence "John was speaking"? _____

76 ENGLISH SYNTAX

442

In "John spoke," tense is contained in the word *spoke*. In "John was speaking" tense is contained in the word _____.

443

Was is a past tense form of the word _____.

444

The verb phrase in "John spoke" contains *past* and the verb *speak*. The verb phrase in "John was speaking" also contains *past* and the verb *speak*. In addition, "John was speaking" contains *be* and the morpheme *-ing*. If we compare "John spoke" and "John was speaking," we see that the second contains all the elements of the first plus _____ and _____.

445

In the kernel sentence, *be* and *-ing* go together. Whenever we have an *-ing* in a kernel sentence, we have a *be*, just as whenever we have a *part* we have a _____.

446

Be + ing is also part of the auxiliary. We can add this to the rewrite rule: Aux → tense + (M) + (have + part) + (be + ing). Tense, part, and ing always go with whatever follows. In *should have walked*, tense is contained in the word _____, part in the word _____.

Forms like *walking, speaking, going* are called *present participle* forms, or simply present participles. Unlike past participle forms, present participle forms are completely regular. They always consist of the base form of the verb plus the syllable that we spell *-ing*. Even the present participle form of *be* is regular—*being*.

447

In *should be walking*, tense is contained in the word _____, ing in the word _____.

448

The verb phrase *should have been walking* contains all of the elements of the auxiliary. Tense is contained in the word _____, part in the word _____, and ing in the word _____.

THE REST OF THE AUXILIARY

449

Write the formula for auxiliary. Aux → _____

_____

450

In the next lesson we shall revise this formula slightly, presenting the same facts in a slightly different way.

MAIN POINTS OF LESSON NINE

Aux → tense + (M) + (have + part) + (be + ing). Every verb phrase that functions as a predicate must contain an **Aux**. Every **Aux** must contain at least a tense. That is, something in the verb phrase must be a form that carries the meaning *past* or *present*. In addition, the verb phrase may contain a modal, it may contain a **have + part,** it may contain a **be + ing,** or it may contain any combination of these, taking them in the order given.

The form that follows *have* in the verb phrase, when *have* is part of the auxiliary, is called the past participle. **Part** is an arbitrary symbol meaning "whatever is done to a verb or *be* to make it a past participle." The forms *driven, eaten, come, left, walked, hurried* are all past participle forms. For most verbs—*leave, walk, hurry,* etc.—the past tense form and the past participle form are identical. For some common verbs—*drive, eat, come,* etc.—the past participle form is different from the past tense form.

The symbol **ing** means "whatever you do to a verb or *be* to make it a present participle." What you always do is add the sound spelled *-ing*.

Lesson Ten
PRACTICE WITH THE AUXILIARY

We have had, among others, the following kernel rules:

S → NP + VP

VP → Aux + $\begin{Bmatrix} be + \begin{Bmatrix} substantive \\ Adv\text{-}p \end{Bmatrix} \\ verbal \end{Bmatrix}$

Aux → tense + (M) + (have + part) + (be + ing)

verbal → $\begin{Bmatrix} VI \\ VT + NP \\ Vb + substantive \\ Vs + Adj \\ Vh + NP \end{Bmatrix} + (Adv\text{-}m)$

This describes most of the basic structure of the verb phrase of an English kernel sentence. To have a kernel sentence, we must have a noun phrase and a verb phrase. The verb phrase must have an auxiliary and either *be* or a verbal. If it has *be*, then it must also have a substantive or an adverbial of place. If it has a verbal, then it can have any of the variety listed in the rewrite of verbal.

The auxiliary must consist of at least tense, present or past. It may also contain a modal or a **have + part** or a **be + ing**. Or it may have any combination of these, provided it has them in the order given. First comes the modal, then the **have + part,** then the **be + ing.**

Any permitted combination in the auxiliary can be applied to any permitted following structure. Here are some of the possible verb phrases in which the auxiliary consists of just past tense and the rest of the verb phrase is **be + substantive; VI; VT + NP;** or **Vb + substantive.**

> was happy
> arrived
> washed the car
> became a monk

Now we might add the modal *shall*.

>should be happy
>should arrive
>should wash the car
>should become a monk

We add have + part in place of the modal.

>had been happy
>had arrived
>had washed the car
>had become a monk

We add be + ing in place of have + part.

>was being happy
>was arriving
>was washing the car
>was becoming a monk

We add the modal *may* and have + part.

>might have been happy
>might have arrived
>might have washed the car
>might have become a monk

We add the modal *may* and be + ing.

>might be being happy
>might be arriving
>might be washing the car
>might be becoming a monk

We add have + part and be + ing.

>had been being happy
>had been arriving
>had been washing the car
>had been becoming a monk

We add the modal *may* and have + part and be + ing.

>might have been being happy
>might have been arriving

ENGLISH SYNTAX

might have been washing the car
might have been becoming a monk

These kernel rules are both simple and powerful. They are simple in the sense that they are short and compact and there aren't very many of them. They are powerful in the sense that they produce or generate or describe the structure of a great number of grammatical English kernel sentences. They display most of the essential structure of the English kernel.

451

Native speakers of English seldom have trouble producing the correct past tense and past participle forms of verbs. (People who learn English as a second language often have trouble.) The past participle form is simply the form that goes with *have*, as in "They have spoken" or "John had gone." What is the past participle form of *eat*? _____

452

In "He had driven the car," *driven* is a past participle form. It consists of the two morphemes _____ and _____ .

453

What is the past participle form of *leave*? _____

454

Many verbs, like *leave*, have the same form for the past tense and the past participle. What is the past participle form of *scream*? _____

455

The past participle form is the form that goes with *have*. What is the past participle form of *find*? _____

456

What is the past participle form of *grow*? _____

457

Be isn't a verb, but like verbs it has a past participle form. What is it?
_____

PRACTICE WITH THE AUXILIARY

458

What is the past participle form of *fall?* _____

459

The past tense form of a verb is that form which would occur in such a structure as "John _____ yesterday": "John spoke yesterday," "John worked yesterday," "John was here yesterday," "John washed the car yesterday." What is the past tense form of *return?* _____

460

In "John had returned," *returned* consists of the verb *return* plus the morpheme _____ .

461

In "John returned yesterday," *returned* consists of the verb *return* plus the morpheme _____ .

462

What is the past tense form of the verb *throw?* _____

463

What is the past participle form of the verb *put?* ____

464

Write the past tense and past participle forms (in that order) of *speak.*

_____ , _____

465

Write the past tense and past participle forms of *fall.* _____ , _____

466

Write the past tense and past participle forms of *hope.* _____ , _____

467

Write the past tense and past participle forms of *go.* _____ , _____

468

Ran consists of the morphemes *run* and *past*. *Went* consists of the morphemes ____ and _____ .

469

Gone consists of the morphemes ____ and _____ .

470

Whenever **part** occurs in a verb phrase, what else must occur? _____

471

According to the rules so far given, whenever **ing** occurs in a verb phrase, what else must occur? ____

472

According to the rules so far given, can *be* occur without **ing**? ____

473

Be can come in as part of the auxiliary in the unit **be + ing**. But it is also one of the two choices *after* the auxiliary. In the rewrite of **VP**, we have an **Aux** and then a choice between ____ and _____ .

474

If we choose *be*, we get sentences like "John's here," "John's a boy," in which *be* is not part of the auxiliary. **Part** cannot occur without *have* in a kernel sentence. Can *have* occur without **part**? ____

475

We have sentences like "John has a job," in which there is no past participle and in which *have* is not part of the auxiliary. Here it is a verb. What kind of verb is it? V____

476

We have rewritten **Aux** as a sequence of four units: **Aux → tense + (M) + (have + part) + (be + ing)**. Of these four units, which one must occur in a verb phrase that functions as a predicate? _____

PRACTICE WITH THE AUXILIARY

477

Of the other three, the modal (like tense) can occur *only* in a verb phrase that functions as a predicate. The other units (have + part and be + ing) can occur in verb phrases that function in other ways. The two items that can occur only in verb phrases that function as predicates are _____ and _____ .

478

The units have + part and be + ing can occur in verb phrases with other functions. Therefore, it is best to take them together as a special part of the auxiliary. We will give them the term *aspect* and revise the rewrite of the auxiliary as follows: Aux → tense + (M) + (aspect). Aspect includes the items (_____ + _____) and (_____ + _____).

479

Aspect is a grammatical term used to refer to forms tnat give a particular meaning to verbs—for example, the meaning that distinguishes "John is speaking English" from "John speaks English." So we have Aux→ tense + (M) + (aspect). Of these three units, the two that may, but need not, occur in a VP that functions as a predicate are _____ and _____ .

Like all grammatical terms, aspect is essentially defined only by its rewrite rule: aspect → (have + part) + (be + ing). That is, aspect "means" the meaning imparted to a verb phrase by the addition of have + part or be + ing, whatever that meaning is. For instance, it is the meaning we find in "John has worked" or "John is working" in comparison with "John works." In "John has worked," the time of the action is set indefinitely in the past. In "John is working," it is suggested as going on in the present. These meanings differ somewhat according to particular contexts and sometimes according to particular verbs or verb classes. Although one can never be perfectly clear and concrete in discussing meanings, one *can* be in discussing the forms that convey the meanings.

480

Aux → tense + (M) + (aspect). Of these three the two that occur *only* in verb phrases that function as predicates are _____ and _____ .

---

84   ENGLISH SYNTAX

481

In English we have such constructions as "Having been working for a long time, John grew tired," in which *having been working for a long time* contains no tense or modal but does contain both parts of aspect. The two parts of aspect are (_____ + _____) and (____ + ____).

482

We must keep the parentheses, because these items need not occur. We then complete the auxiliary rules of the kernel as follows: **Aux → tense + (M) + (aspect); aspect → (have + part) + (be + ing)**. What part of **Aux** does the sentence "The Dodgers lost the game" contain? _____

483

If the formula for "David returned" is **NP + past + VI**, what is the formula for "The plane arrived"? ____ + _____ + ____

484

If the formula for "We might come" is **NP + past + may + VI**, what is the formula for "We may go"? ____ + _____ + ____ + ____

485

If the formula for "Tom is going" is **NP + present + be + ing + VI**, what is the formula for "Lou has gone"? ____ + _____ + _____ + _____ + ____

486

If the formula for "David sold the car" is **NP + past + VT + NP**, what is the formula for "Henry bought a book"? ____ + _____ + ____ + ____

487

What is the formula for "Joan should buy the book"? ____ + _____ + _____ + V____ + ____

PRACTICE WITH THE AUXILIARY

488

What is the formula for "Joan had bought the book"? ___ + _____ + _____ + _____ + V___ + _____

489

What is the formula for "Joan was buying the book"? ___ + _____ + ___ + ___ + ___ + V___ + ___

490

What is the formula for "Sally felt ill"? ___ + _____ + _____ + V___ + **Adj**

491

What is the formula for "Mervin had a cold"? ___ + _____ + _____ + V___ + ___

492

What is the formula for "Mervin had had a cold"? ___ + _____ + _____ + _____ + V___ + ___

493

What is the formula for "Mervin must have had a cold"? ___ + **present** + _____ + _____ + _____ + V___ + ___

494

What is the formula for "Mervin must have been having a cold"? ___ + _____ + _____ + _____ + _____ + ___ + ___ + V___ + ___

495

What is the formula for "Helen was in the room"? ___ + _____ + ___ + **Adv-p**

496

What is the formula for "Helen had been in the room"? ___ + _____ + _____ + _____ + ___ + _____

86 ENGLISH SYNTAX

497

What is the formula for "Helen might have been in the room"? ___ + _____ + ___ + _____ + _____ + ___ + _____

498

What is the formula for "The children had been teasing the cat"? ___ + _____ + _____ + _____ + ___ + ___ + V___ + ___

499

What is the formula for "Some of those tomatoes are in the refrigerator"? ___ + _____ + ___ + _____

500

We shall be using formulas of this kind in working with the transformation rules with which we shall presently be concerned.

MAIN POINTS OF LESSON TEN

Aux → tense + (M) + (aspect)
aspect → (have + part) + (be + ing)

This revision of the auxiliary rule concludes our description of the auxiliary. It is best to take the last two units of the auxiliary—have + part and be + ing—separately, because there are some constructions in which either or both of them can occur but in which neither tense nor modal can occur.

Aspect is a traditional grammatical term which is applied to forms that change the meaning of verbs in respect to the action. Like all grammatical terms, it means simply what is indicated for it on the right of the arrow. It means (have + part) + (be + ing).

Lesson Eleven
ADVERBIALS AGAIN

Let us make a tree of derivation for the kernel sentence "She had written the answer quickly."

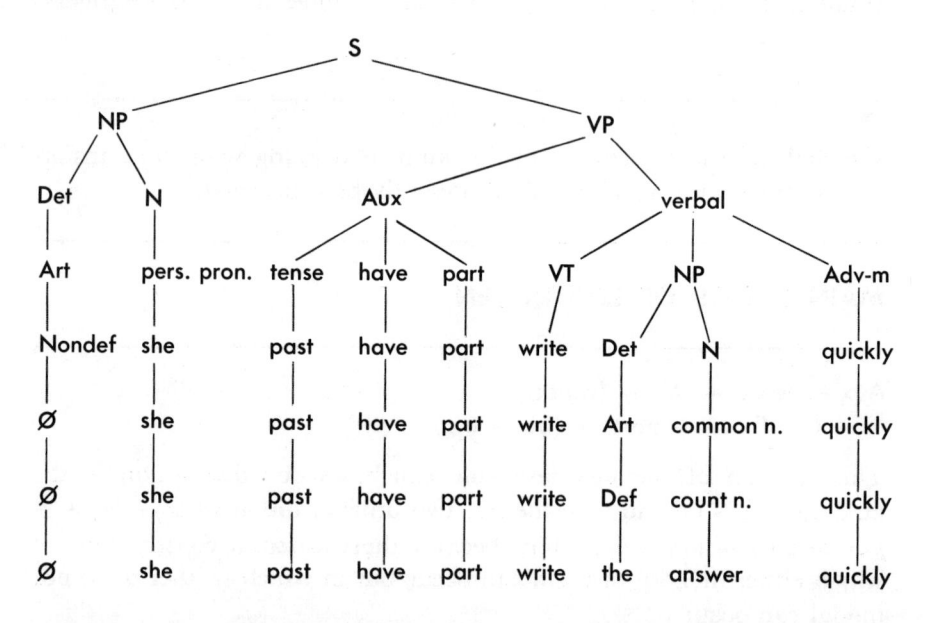

```
                            S
             ┌──────────────┴──────────────┐
            NP                             VP
          ┌──┴──┐              ┌───────────┼───────────┐
         Det    N             Aux                    verbal
          │     │           ┌──┴──┐         ┌──────────┼──────┐
         Art  pers. pron.  tense have part  VT        NP     Adv-m
          │     │            │    │    │    │      ┌───┴──┐    │
       Nondef  she          past have part write  Det     N  quickly
          │     │            │    │    │    │      │      │    │
          Ø    she          past have part write  Art  common n. quickly
          │     │            │    │    │    │      │      │    │
          Ø    she          past have part write  Def  count n. quickly
          │     │            │    │    │    │      │      │    │
          Ø    she          past have part write  the  answer  quickly
```

If we ask "What is the formula for 'She had written the answer quickly'?" we get several answers, all of them correct. Any string of symbols or morphemes read from left to right in the tree is a correct formula for the sentence on some level or on some mixture of levels. For example, all of the following accurately describe the structure of this sentence, each more specifically as you go down the list.

    NP + VP
    Det + N + Aux + verbal
    personal pronoun + Aux + verbal
    personal pronoun + tense + have + part + VT + NP + Adv-m
    She + past + have + part + write + the + answer + quickly

88   ENGLISH SYNTAX

If we ask for the formula of the sentence, we must indicate the level or levels the formula should describe. We did this in the last section by example: "If **NP** + **past** + **sell** + **NP** is the formula for 'David sold the car,' what is the formula for 'The children found a spider'?" The answer would be **NP** + **past** + **find** + **NP**. We could also indicate the level wanted in the formula by giving specific directions, like "indicate any noun phrase as **NP**."

Notice that only the last line in the tree of derivation is a K-terminal string. For this sentence the K-terminal string is the following:

she + past + have + part + write + the + answer + quickly

In this string there is no symbol to which any kernel rule can apply, for all symbols have been turned into particular morphemes. The set of kernel rules has been exhausted for this sentence.

501

In "The girl responded quietly," *quietly* is an adverbial of manner. What is the adverbial of manner in "Jack left in a hurry"? _____

502

The term *adverbial* thus covers single words like *quietly* and groups of words like *in a hurry*. We call words like *quietly* adverbs and groups like *in a hurry* prepositional phrases. In "Rita replied in a fury," *in a fury* is both a prepositional phrase and an _____ .

503

In "Rita replied angrily," *angrily* is both an adverbial and an _____ .

504

Adv-m stands for *adverbial of manner* and thus includes certain adverbs as well as certain prepositional phrases. We shall see that it also includes certain noun phrases. For the moment we shall concern ourselves only with adverbs of manner—single words. What is the adverb of manner in "Georgia worked quickly"? _____

505

Most adverbs of manner, though not quite all, consist of an adjective plus the morpheme *-ly*. What is the adjective corresponding to *quickly*?

ADVERBIALS AGAIN   89

506

What is the adverb of manner in "Georgia worked fast"? _____

507

Fast is one of a few forms which occur both as an adverb of manner ("He worked fast") and as an adjective ("He is fast"). Others are *straight* and *hard*. In "Georgia answered the question honestly," *honestly* is an adverb of _____ .

508

In "George stayed here," *here* is an adverb. It is an adverb (and also an adverbial) of place. We have already encountered adverbials of place in the verb-phrase pattern **Aux** + ____ + **Adv-p**.

509

In "Georgia remained outside reluctantly," *outside* is an adverb of _____ and *reluctantly* is an adverb of _____ .

510

In "George left yesterday," *yesterday* is an adverb of *time*. It is also an adverbial of time. What is the adverbial of time in "Georgia leaves tomorrow"? _____

511

We have so far encountered three kinds of adverbials—adverbials of _____ , _____ , and _____ .

512

In "Ed remained below today," *below* is an adverb of _____ , *today* an adverb of _____ .

513

In "Sally played the piano beautifully yesterday," *beautifully* is an adverb of _____ , *yesterday* an adverb of _____ .

514

In "Sally played the piano well," *well* is an adverb of _____ .

515

In "Peter laughed occasionally," *occasionally* is an adverb (and adverbial) of *frequency*. Adverbials of frequency have something to do with time, but they behave a little differently from words like *today* and *tomorrow*. "In Derek visited us sometimes," *sometimes* is an adverb of _____ .

516

In "Peter lived here happily then," *here* is an adverb of _____ , *happily* an adverb of _____ , and *then* an adverb of _____ .

517

It is possible to have all four adverb types in a single verb phrase following the verb: "Tommy played outside happily sometimes yesterday." Here the adverbs occur in the order place, _____ , _____ , _____ .

Notice that we must follow certain rules of order in using adverbs and other adverbials. It would be ungrammatical, for example, to say *"Tommy played yesterday happily sometimes outside."

In the classification of adverbials, as in other classifications we have made, we begin by simply distinguishing meanings. But the further we go, the more we find these differences in meaning supported and conveyed by differences in form. Ultimately it is the formal differences that make us aware of the meaning differences. For the adverbials, one formal difference is the rules of order or position just mentioned. Another is the relation of the different adverbial groups to different transforms. As we shall see further on, adverbials of place transform into questions with *where,* those of time into questions with *when,* and so on.

518

In "Derek laughed frequently," *frequently* is an adverb of _____ .

519

Frequently is also an adverb of frequency in "Derek frequently laughed." This position before the verb is more common for adverbs of frequency than the position after. In "Herbert often stayed home," *often* is an adverb of _____ .

520

The word *never* behaves in some ways like the adverb of frequency group. We say, "Herbert never stayed home." Can *never* occur after the verb also? ____

521

*"Herbert stayed never home" and *"Herbert stayed home never" are ungrammatical. *Never* has some but not all of the characteristics of adverbs of frequency. In "Chris willingly helped us," *willingly* is an adverb of _____ .

522

Adverbs of manner also occur before the verb, but not so commonly as adverbs of frequency do. "Chris helped us willingly" is probably more common than "Chris willingly helped us." Adverbs of place never occur before the verb, and adverbs of time seldom do. In "They seldom occur there," *seldom* is an adverb of _____ .

523

In "Chris was upstairs," the verb phrase consists of **Aux** + _____ + **Adv-p**.

524

In "Chris was often upstairs," *often* is an adverb of _____ .

525

When the verb phrase contains *be* instead of a verbal, the most common position for adverbs of frequency is immediately after the *be*. In "Chris is usually happy," *usually* is an adverb of _____ .

526

Adverbials of manner do not ordinarily occur in verb phrases with *be*. They also do not occur in verb phrases with verbals when the verbal is the type containing **V**____ .

527

We have noted four main types of adverbials, distinguished partly by the positions they take in sentences. The four types are _____ , _____ , _____ , _____ .

92   ENGLISH SYNTAX

528

English has some other adverbial types—for example, direction ("He went *to the store*"), duration ("He stayed there *for several days*"). However, we will confine our attention to adverbials of place, manner, frequency, and time. Remember that *adverbial* includes prepositional phrases as well as adverbs. In "Judith was in the house," the prepositional phrase *in the house* is an adverbial of _____ .

529

A prepositional phrase consists of a preposition followed by a noun phrase. In "The piano was near the door," *near* is a _____ , and *the door* is a _____ .

530

In "Sue arrived yesterday" and "Sue arrived on Saturday," both *yesterday* and *on Saturday* are adverbials of _____ .

531

In "Sue arrived on Saturday," *on Saturday* is a _____ phrase, and *on* is a _____ .

532

Compare "Sue worked willingly" and "Sue worked with a will." *Willingly* and *with a will* are both _____ of _____ .

533

In "Sue worked with a will," *with* is a _____ .

534

A prepositional phrase consists of a _____ plus a _____ .

535

In "Sue travels by plane," *by plane* is an adverbial of _____ .

536

In "The cat is under the desk," *under the desk* is an adverbial of _____ , and *under* is a _____ .

ADVERBIALS AGAIN   93

537

In "He'll be here in a jiffy," *here* is an adverbial of _____, and *in a jiffy* is an adverbial of _____ .

538

Compare "Sue left yesterday" and "Sue left this morning." In the first sentence, *yesterday* is an adverbial of _____ .

539

In "Sue left this morning," *this morning* is also an adverbial of time. In form it is a noun phrase, consisting of the determiner *this* and the noun *morning*. In "Sue leaves next week," *next week* is a _____ phrase used as an adverbial of _____ .

540

In "Don visits us frequently" and "Don visits us every day," *frequently* and *every day* are both adverbials of _____ .

541

In "Mrs. Caspar cleaned the kitchen each morning," *each morning* is a _____ used as an adverbial of _____ .

542

Some adverbs occur in positions where prepositional phrases and noun phrases cannot occur. "Don visits us often" and "Don visits us every day" both contain an adverbial of frequency. Which one may also occur before the verb? _____

543

The sentence "Don often visits us" is grammatical, but *"Don every day visits us" is not. In general, prepositional phrases and noun phrases used as adverbials come only after the verb. Adverbs of frequency and manner may also occur before the verb. In "Evelyn replied graciously," *graciously* is an adverb of _____ .

544

In "Don sometimes stayed home," *sometimes* is an adverb of _____, and *home* is an adverbial of _____.

545

In "He slept heavily last night," *heavily* is an adverb of _____, and *last night* is an adverbial of _____.

546

In "He slept in the car," *in the car* is a _____ phrase used as an adverbial of _____.

547

In "He sleeps in the car on Tuesdays," *in the car* and *on Tuesdays* are both _____ phrases.

548

In "He works at the office in shirt sleeves at night," there are three prepositional phrases. They are, in order, adverbials of _____, _____, and _____.

549

In "Don comes here every day," *here* is an adverb of _____, and *every day* is an adverbial of _____.

550

Notice that we have classified adverbials in two different ways: (1) according to function—place, manner, frequency, time; (2) according to form—adverb, prepositional phrase, noun phrase.

MAIN POINTS OF LESSON ELEVEN

Verb phrases may include structures called *adverbials*. Adverbials are of three formal types: adverbs (single words), prepositional phrases, and noun phrases. Any of these may function as adverbials of place, manner, frequency, and time. This classification of the functions of adverbials depends ultimately on formal features of the grammar, such as the positions which the adverbials can grammatically occupy and the words that substitute for them in transforms.

Not all adverbial functions are possible in all verb phrases. Adverbials of manner do not occur in verb phrases with *be* or in verb phrases with verbals containing **Vh**.

All adverbials may occur at the end of verb phrases. Adverbs of frequency most commonly occur, however, before verbs and immediately after *be*. Adverbs of manner may occur before verbs. The regular position for other adverbials is at the end of the verb phrase.

When several adverbials occur in a single verb phrase, the normal order is place, manner, frequency, time.

Lesson Twelve
TRANSFORMATION

We have now completed what we have to say about English kernel sentences. This is of course not a complete description; many particulars have been omitted. However, the main features of the syntax of the English kernel sentence have been described. We began by saying that a sentence consists of a noun phrase and a verb phrase, the noun phrase functioning as the subject and the verb phrase as the predicate. We then specified the features of the noun phrase and the verb phrase, concluding the latter with a description of the adverbials that may occur in the verb phrase.

The kernel is the part of English that is basic and fundamental. It is the heart of the grammar, the core of the language. All other structures of English can be thought of as deriving from this kernel. All the more complicated sentences of English are derivations from, or transformations of, the K-terminal strings. For example, the question "Can John go?" is easily seen to be related to the statement "John can go." Given the K-terminal string for any sentence like "John can come," we can make it into a corresponding question by applying the rule for question-making. Such a rule is called a transformation rule. It tells us how to derive something from something else by switching things about, putting things in or leaving them out, and so on. Thus we derive "Can John go?" and "Did John go?" from "John can go" and "John went." But we can't derive "John can go" and "John went" from anything. There are no sentences underlying them. They are basic and fundamental, a part of the kernel.

It is in terms of kernel structures that *all* grammatical relations are defined. The kernel gives all the grammatical relations of the language. These grammatical relations are then carried over into transforms, so that they will hold among words which are arranged in many different ways and which may actually be widely separated.

For example, the sentence "The dog barked" indicates a certain relationship between the noun *dog* and the verb *bark*. We find exactly the same relationship in such transforms as "The barking dog frightened me," "The barking of the dog kept us awake," "I hate dogs that are always barking." The relationship shown between *dog* and *sad* in the kernel sentence "The dog is sad" carries over in the transforms "The sad dog wailed," "The dog's sadness was apparent," "I don't like dogs that are too sad."

We shall see that there are two kinds of transformation rules: *obligatory rules* and *optional rules*. An obligatory rule is one that must be applied to produce a grammatical sentence. An optional rule is one that may be applied but doesn't have to be. Some obligatory rules apply only when certain elements occur in the sentence. Sometimes the elements do not occur, so the rule does not apply. One rule, however, applies to all kernel sentences, and we shall begin with that one. It is a rule for putting the elements of the auxiliary in their proper order.

551

The rule that rewrites auxiliary is **Aux → tense + (M) + (aspect)**. What is the rule that rewrites aspect? **aspect → (_____ + _____) + (___ + ___)**

552

We can represent "Bob laughed" in this way: **NP + tense + VI**. We must put tense first, because it is part of the auxiliary, and the auxiliary comes before everything else in the rewrite of **VP**. The sentence "John might laugh" contains two elements of the auxiliary. What are they?

_____ , _____

553

"John might laugh" can be represented as **NP + tense + M + VI**. Let us consider **tense, M, have + part**, and **be + ing** each as single elements. "John was laughing" contains two of these elements. What are they?

_____ , _____

554

"Bob should laugh" contains the two auxiliary elements _____ and _____ .

555

"John had laughed" contains the two auxiliary elements _____ and _____ .

98   ENGLISH SYNTAX

556

"John had laughed" is **NP + tense + have + part + VI**. "John may be laughing" contains three of the four elements of the auxiliary. They are _____ , _____ , _____ .

557

"John has been laughing" contains the three auxiliary elements _____ , _____ , _____ .

558

"John has been laughing" is **NP + tense + have + part + be + ing + VI**. "John must have been laughing" contains all of the elements of the auxiliary. In order, they are _____ , _____ , _____ , _____ .

559

The formula for "John must have been laughing" is **NP + tense + M + have + part + be + ing + VI**. When we make this into a sentence, the tense goes with the **M**, the **part** with the _____ , the **ing** with the _____ .

560

If **NP + tense + have + part + be + ing + VT + NP** is made into a sentence, the tense will go with the _____ , the **part** with the _____ , the **ing** with the _____ .

561

Tense, part, and ing always go with whatever follows them in the formula. What follows may be an **M**, a *have*, a *be*, or a verb. Tense, **part**, and **ing** are called *affixes*. Affixes change words in various ways. In English they are mostly endings. Which of the three affixes occurs in "Mary prayed"? _____

562

Which of the affixes—tense, **part**, **ing**—occur in "Mary was praying"? _____ , _____

TRANSFORMATION 99

563

Which of the affixes occur in "Mary has failed"? _____ , _____

564

Which affixes occur in "Mary has been sleeping"? _____ , _____ , _____

565

The affixes generally appear in sentences at the ends of words. But in the formulas they appear before the words they go with. The formulas must be written this way. If we tried to put the affixes directly into their proper place, we would run into large complications in the kernel rules, as you might prove to yourself by experiment. What part of the auxiliary is contained in "John was laughing" but not in "John laughed"?

_____

566

Be + ing is a unit of the auxiliary. The two elements *be* and **ing** are added simultaneously. We don't have the **ing** unless we have the *be*. Yet in an actual sentence, the **ing** goes at the end of whatever follows, whereas the *be* remains where it is. What unit of the auxiliary is contained in "John had laughed" but not in "John laughed"? _____

567

Again, in an actual sentence, *have* stays put, and **part** goes on whatever follows. Our formulas show all the elements of the kernel sentence, but not always in the proper order. To put them in the proper order, we apply a transformation rule. What is the term that means "any tense or part or ing"? _____

568

We shall use the abbreviation **Af** to mean any of the affixes—tense, **part**, or **ing**. We shall use the small letter **v** to mean any **M** or *have* or *be* or verb.

Then **part** is a case of _____ , and *have* is a case of _____ .

569

Past is a case of _____ , and *go* is a case of _____ .

---

100   ENGLISH SYNTAX

570

The **Af**'s are any _____ or _____ or _____ .

571

The **v**'s are any ____ or _____ or ____ or _____ .

572

This is the transformation rule: whenever the combination **Af** plus **v** occurs, change it to **v** plus **Af**. We might express this rule in formula as follows: **Af** + **v** ⇒ ____ + ____ .

573

We use a double arrow as an indication that this is a different kind of rule from the kernel rules we have been studying. It doesn't just indicate that something consists of something else, like **NP** → **Det** + **N**. Instead, it switches items around. What does **past** + **Vl** become by this rule?

____ + _____

574

What does **past** + **M** + **Vl** become?   ____ + _____ + ____

It is understood that this transformation is applied only once to any one affix. If, for example, we have **John** + **past** + **can** + **go**, we apply it and get **John** + **can** + **past** + **go**. We now have, in **past** + **go**, another sequence of **Af** + **v**. But we can't apply the transformation again and get **John** + **can** + **go** + **past**, because this would give us the ungrammatical sentence *"John can went."

To avoid this conclusion, grammarians sometimes write the rule as follows: **Af** + **v** ⇒ **v** + **Af** + **#**, where the symbol **#** marks the end of a word. Thus **John** + **past** + **can** + **go** becomes **John** + **can** + **past** + **#** + **go**. There is now no sequence of **Af** + **v**, since **#** intervenes between *past* and *go*. We do not, however, have very much need of the symbol **#** in describing the syntax, and we can omit it if we understand that the affix transformation applies only once to any one affix.

575

What does **present** + **be** + **ing** + **Vl** become?   ____ + _____ + ____ + ____

TRANSFORMATION   **101**

576

What does present + have + part + be become? _____ + _____ + ____ + _____

577

What does past + M + have + part + be become? ____ + _____ + _____ + ____ + _____

578

What does past + M + have + part + be + ing + VI become? ____ + _____ + _____ + ____ + _____ + ____ + ____

579

Af + v $\Rightarrow$ v + Af is a transformation rule. Furthermore, it is an *obligatory* transformation rule, which means that it must be applied in any terminal string that contains a sequence of Af + v. Since it has to do with affixes, we shall call it the affix transformation and abbreviate it

T-af. Here T stands for _____ .

580

T-af is Af + v $\Rightarrow$ v + Af. Does every K-terminal string contain an Af? ____

581

Which of the three Af's must occur in every sentence? _____

582

Part and ing may occur or may not, but tense must occur. Does every K-terminal string contain a v? ____

583

Every kernel sentence contains at least a *be* or a verb. *Be* and verbs are v's. Therefore every K-terminal string must contain a v. Will every K-terminal string contain the sequence Af + v? ____

102   ENGLISH SYNTAX

584

Every K-terminal string will contain at least one sequence of **Af + v**. Therefore, **T-af (Af + v ⇒ v + Af)** will be applied at least once in the production of any kernel sentence. What are the three **Af**'s? _____ , _____ , ____

585

What are the four **v**'s? ____ , _____ , ____ , _____

586

In he + past + see + the + boy, which two elements constitute a sequence of **Af + v**? _____ + ____

587

By T-af, he + past + see + the + boy becomes he + see + past + the + boy and ultimately the English sentence "He saw the boy." In he + past + may + see + the + boy, which two elements are a case of **Af + v**? _____ + ____

588

By T-af, he + past + may + see + the + boy becomes he + may + past + see + the + boy and finally the actual sentence "He might see the boy." The string he + present + have + part + see + the + boy contains two sequences of **Af + v**. What are they? _____ + _____ , _____ + ____

589

By T-af, he + present + have + part + see + the + boy becomes he + have + present + see + part + the + boy. What is the actual sentence represented by this formula? _____

590

The string he + present + will + be + ing + see + the + boy contains two sequences of **Af + v**. What are they? _____ + _____ , ____ + ____

591

By T-af, he + present + will + be + ing + see + the + boy becomes he + will + present + be + see + ing + the + boy. Will + past is *would*. What is will + present? _____

592

What actual sentence is represented by he + will + present + be + see + ing + the + boy? _____

593

What does he + past + be + ing + pet + the + cat become by T-af? ___ + ___ + _____ + ___ + ___ + ___ + ___

594

What is be + past when the subject is *he?* ____

595

What actual sentence is represented by the string of morphemes he + be + past + pet + ing + the + cat? _____

596

He + shall + past + stay + here is a string to which T-af has (1) already (2) not yet been applied. ____

597

What sentence is represented by the string he + shall + past + stay + here? _____

598

He + present + must + have + part + be + ing + joke contains three sequences of Af + v. What are they? _____ + _____, _____ + ___, ___ + _____

599

After T-af has been applied, what actual sentence will be produced by he + present + must + have + part + be + ing + joke? _____

_____

_____

600

This way of presenting the elements of English kernel sentences no doubt will seem cumbersome at this point. But we shall see that, beginning with this description, we will be able to make rather simple and economical explanations of many other structures of English.

MAIN POINTS OF LESSON TWELVE

Af stands for *affix*. The three affixes that we are presently concerned with are tense, **part,** and **ing**. **Af** therefore means any tense or **part** or **ing**.

The small letter **v** stands for any modal, *have, be,* or verb.

Our first transformation rule is this: **Af** + **v** ⟹ **v** + **Af**. We call this rule **T-af,** in which **T** stands for *transformation*. The double arrow will be regularly used for transformation rules, distinguishing them from kernel rules.

T-af is an obligatory transformation rule. This means that it must be applied to every sequence of **Af** + **v** before a grammatical sentence can be produced. Every **K**-terminal string will contain at least one sequence of **Af** + **v**.

Lesson Thirteen
YES/NO QUESTIONS

There are two main kinds of questions in English: those that can be answered by the words *yes* or *no* and those that can't. For example, one can answer the question "Are you going home?" by saying "Yes" or "No." But one cannot answer the question "Where are you going?" by saying "Yes" or "No." "Are you going home?" is a *yes/no* question. "Where are you going?" is not. (It is what we will call, when we come to explain its structure, a *wh* question.)

All questions in English are transforms. That is, they all derive from and are related to underlying structures. The transform "Are you going home?" is related to the kernel sentence "You are going home." It is obviously simpler to describe "Are you going home?" as a sentence related to "You are going home" than it would be to describe the two structures separately, as if there were no connection between them. We have already described the structure of statements like "You are going home." Instead of doing this all over again for questions, we simply give the rules by which statements are transformed into questions.

The mechanism for making questions out of statements is closely connected with the auxiliary that we have just been studying. We have seen that the auxiliary always provides the sentence with a tense. There may also be a modal, a *have* (plus **part**), or a *be* (plus **ing**). If the predicate begins with a tense plus modal, a tense plus *have*, or a tense plus *be*, these sequences reverse with the subject to form the *yes/no* question. We shall study this mechanism in this lesson. When there is no modal, *have*, or *be*, the question is constructed in a quite different way, as we shall see later.

601

The *yes/no* question corresponding to "John can leave" is "Can John leave?" What is the *yes/no* question corresponding to "John could leave"? _____

602

What is the *yes/no* question corresponding to "John will leave"?

_____

603

Can, could, and *will* are all cases of _____ plus tense.

604

The *yes/no* questions "Can John leave?," "Could John leave?," and "Will John leave?" all begin with _____ + _____ .

605

The form *could* consists of the modal *can* plus _____ tense.

606

The form *will* consists of the modal _____ plus _____ tense.

607

What is the *yes/no* question corresponding to "John should leave"?

_____

608

We see that *yes/no* questions may begin with modals plus tense. What is the *yes/no* question corresponding to "John has left"? _____

609

What is the *yes/no* question corresponding to "John had left"? _____
_____

610

Has and *had* both consist of _____ plus tense.

611

A *yes/no* question may begin with a modal plus tense or with _____ plus tense.

YES/NO QUESTIONS   107

612

What is the *yes/no* question corresponding to "Bruce is studying"?

_____

613

Is consists of the word ____ plus present tense.

614

Are consists of the word ____ plus _____ tense.

615

Had consists of the word _____ plus _____ tense.

616

What is the *yes/no* question corresponding to "Bruce was studying"?

_____

617

Was consists of the word ____ plus _____ tense.

618

Look at these *yes/no* questions: "Should Bruce study?," "Had Bruce studied?," "Was Bruce studying?" They all begin with a form of modal, a form of _____, or a form of ____.

619

Look at them again: "Should Bruce study?," "Had Bruce studied?," "Was Bruce studying?" They all begin with a modal, *have*, or *be* plus _____ tense.

620

"Carl should go away" might be written **NP + past + shall + go + away**. What would be the corresponding formula for "Leslie could come in"? ____ + _____ + ____ + _____ + ____

108 ENGLISH SYNTAX

621

Both NP + past + shall + go + away and NP + past + can + come + in contain a sequence of **Af** + **v**. In the first sentence it is **past** + **shall**. What is it in the second sentence? _____ + ____

622

Af stands for affix. It includes three elements. One is tense. What are the other two? _____ , ____

623

The letter **v** stands for any of four elements. One is modal. What are the other three? _____ , ____ , _____

624

The first obligatory transformation rule, **T-af**, requires that whenever we have a sequence of **Af** + **v** we change it to ____ + ____ .

625

Every K-terminal string will contain at least one sequence of **Af** + **v**, because the kernel verb phrase must contain at least tense, which is an **Af**, and at least *be* or a verb, which are **v**'s. **T-af** applied to **NP** + **past** + **shall** + **go** + **away** gives **NP** + _____ + _____ + ____ + _____ .

626

However, before we apply **T-af**, we have the option, or choice, of applying one of the many other transformations. For example, we can change **NP** + **past** + **shall** + **go** + **away** to **past** + **shall** + **NP** + **go** + **away**. Here we have switched the structures ____ and _____ + _____ .

627

We now have **past** + **shall** + **NP** + **go** + **away**. We still have a sequence of **Af** + **v**, and **T-af** must apply before we can arrive at an actual English sentence. This is why we apply the obligatory transformations only after the optional transformations have been applied. By **T-af, past + shall + NP + go + away** becomes _____ + _____ + **NP + go + away**.

628

We have applied an optional transformation and then an obligatory one, **T-af**, and we have arrived at **shall + past + NP + go + away**. If the **NP** is the proper noun *Bruce*, this will give the actual sentence _____ .

629

Let's start now with **NP + present + have + part + go**. This contains two sequences of **Af + v**. What are they? _____ + _____ , _____ + _____

630

If we apply the optional *yes/no* question transformation to **NP + present + have + part + go**, we get **present + have + NP + part + go**. To this we apply **T-af: Af + v ⟹ v + Af**. We apply it twice, because there are two sequences of **Af + v**. This gives us _____ + _____ + **NP + _____ + _____** .

631

We now have **have + present + NP + go + part**. If the **NP** is *Leslie*, the actual sentence will be _____ .

632

Let us now take the formula **NP + past + be + ing + play**. The optional *yes/no* question transformation will reverse the positions of the **NP** and the **past + be**. This will give us _____ + ___ + ___ + ___ + ___ .

633

Past + be + NP + ing + play contains two sequences of **Af + v**. What are they? _____ + ___ , ___ + _____

110 ENGLISH SYNTAX

634

From **past + be + NP + ing + play**, we get **be + past + NP + play + ing** by application of **T-_____** .

635

If the **NP** of **be + past + NP + play + ing** is *the children*, what will the actual sentence be? _____

636

In producing the questions "Should Bruce go away?," "Has Leslie gone?," and "Were the children playing?," we have reversed the **NP** and (1) **tense + M**, (2) **tense + have**, (3) **tense + be**. Does this happen before or after the application of the rule **T-af?** _____

637

The transformation that produces *yes/no* questions is an optional transformation. We may apply it to get an English sentence, but we can get English sentences without applying it. The abbreviation of *yes/no* question transformation is **T-yes/no**. Is **T-yes/no** optional or obligatory?

_____

638

So far, **T-yes/no** reads thus:
1. **NP + tense-M   + X ⇒ tense-M   + NP + X**
2. **NP + tense-have + X ⇒ tense-have + NP + X**
3. **NP + tense-be + X ⇒ tense-be + NP + X**

Tense will always be either _____ or _____ .

639

T-yes/no:
1. **NP + tense-M   + X ⇒ tense-M   + NP + X**
2. **NP + tense-have + X ⇒ tense-have + NP + X**
3. **NP + tense-be + X ⇒ tense-be + NP + X**

Here **X** means "whatever occurs after the **M**, *have*, or *be*." In **John + present + can + go**, what is the **X**? _____

YES/NO QUESTIONS   111

640

T-yes/no:
1. NP + tense-M + X ⟹ tense-M + NP + X
2. NP + tense-have + X ⟹ tense-have + NP + X
3. NP + tense-be + X ⟹ tense-be + NP + X

In Anne + past + be + ing + go, the X is ____ + ____ .

641

What is the X in Anne + past + shall + have + part + go? ____ + ____ + ____

642

What is the X in Anne + past + have + part + come + in? ____ + ____ + ____

643

What is the X in Anne + present + must + have + part + see + Jim? ____ + ____ + ____ + ____

644

If we apply T-yes/no to John + past + shall + have + part + go, we get ____ + ____ + John + have + ____ + ____ .

645

If we apply T-af to past + shall + John + have + part + go, we get ____ + ____ + ____ + ____ + ____ + ____ .

646

Shall + past + John + have + go + part represents the actual sentence _____ .

647

Apply T-yes/no to Andy + past + be + ing + wait. ____ + ____ + ____ + ____ + ____

---

112   ENGLISH SYNTAX

648

Apply **T-af** to past + be + Andy + ing + wait. ____ + _____ + _____ + _____ + ____

649

What actual sentence will we get from **Andy + present + have + part + be + ing + sleep** after the application of **T-yes/no** and **T-af**?

650

So far, **T-yes/no** tells us how to make a *yes/no* question when the sentence contains a modal, a *have,* or a *be.* What happens when it contains none of these, as in **Andy + past + sleep,** we shall see in the next section.

MAIN POINTS OF LESSON THIRTEEN

T-yes/no:
1. NP + tense-M   + X ⇒ tense-M   + NP + X
2. NP + tense-have + X ⇒ tense-have + NP + X
3. NP + tense-be   + X ⇒ tense-be   + NP + X

This rule is not yet complete, because it does not indicate what happens when tense is followed by a verbal, instead of **M,** *have,* or *be.*

X means whatever follows the **M,** *have,* or *be.* The rule works in the same way no matter what follows.

T-yes/no is an optional rule. If applied, it comes before **T-af.** After **T-yes/no** is applied, then **T-af** is applied to put the morphemes in their proper order.

Lesson Fourteen

THE *DO* TRANSFORMATION

We shall make quite a lot of use of such symbols as **X**, as in the transformation given on page 111. It means whatever occurs in the position indicated. If nothing occurs there, **X** means nothing. In the *yes/no* transformation, for example, all sorts of structures can follow a *be:*

John + past + be + a student
John + past + be + happy
John + past + be + here
John + past + be + in school
John + past + be + ing + wait
John + past + be + ing + be + a pest

T-yes/no works on all of these in the same way. *John* reverses with the following **past** + **be**. Then, after **T-af** has been applied, we get the following questions:

Was John　a student?
Was John　happy?
Was John　here?
Was John　in school?
Was John　waiting?
Was John　being a pest?

The structures *a student, happy, here, in school,* **ing** plus *wait,* **ing** plus *be a pest* are all **X**'s for the purposes of **T-yes/no**.

The fourth part of **T-yes/no** takes care of sentences which do not contain a modal, a *have*, or a *be*. It permits us to begin with "John worked" and derive "Did John work?" or with "John works" and derive "Does John work?" or with "They work" and derive "Do they work?" This and similar uses of *do, does, did* are central and very important in English grammar.

114　ENGLISH SYNTAX

651

The *yes/no* question corresponding to "John left" is "Did John leave?" What is the *yes/no* question corresponding to "Samuel went away"?

_____

652

The *yes/no* question corresponding to "John lives here" is "Does John live here?" What is the *yes/no* question corresponding to "Samuel eats here"? _____

653

The *yes/no* question corresponding to "The men like mush" is "Do the men like mush?" What is the *yes/no* question corresponding to "The children prefer spinach"? _____

654

Did, do, and *does* are forms of the word *do. Did* is _____ + **past.**

655

Depending on the subject, **do** + **present** is _____ or _____.

656

The formula for "Samuel eats here" is **NP** + **present** + **eat** + **Adv-p.** The formula for "Does Samuel eat here?" is **do** + **present** + **NP** + **eat** + **Adv-p.** The statement contains all of the elements of the question except _____ .

657

Compare the statement **NP** + **present** + **eat** + **Adv-p** and the question **do** + **present** + **NP** + **eat** + **Adv-p.** What item of the statement has reversed with the **NP** to form the question? _____

658

Leaving aside for a moment the word *do*, we can say that whenever the K-terminal string does *not* contain a modal, a *have*, or a *be*, the tense alone reverses with the subject. Then **John** + **past** + **laugh** (forgetting about the *do*) becomes what? _____ + _____ + _____

THE DO TRANSFORMATION

The effect of T-yes/no applied to the sequence **NP + tense + verbal** is to eliminate the sequence **Af + v**. **John + past + go** contains a sequence **Af + v**, but **past + John + go** does not. Therefore, in structures of this type, **T-af** cannot apply.

659

We have had so far the following parts of **T-yes/no**:
    1. NP + tense-M   + X ⟹ tense-M   + NP + X
    2. NP + tense-have + X ⟹ tense-have + NP + X
    3. NP + tense-be   + X ⟹ tense-be   + NP + X

Thus **John + present + will + come** becomes, by the first line of **T-yes/no**, _____ + _____ + _____ + _____ .

660

By the second line of **T-yes/no**, **John + past + have + part + go** becomes _____ + _____ + _____ + _____ + ____ .

661

By which line of **T-yes/no** does **John + present + be + here** become **present + be + John + here**? _____

662

Here is the fourth part of **T-yes/no**: **NP + tense + verbal ⟹ tense + NP + verbal**. Tense alone reverses with the subject when tense is followed, not by an **M**, a *have*, or a *be*, but by a _____ .

663

Remember that we rewrote verbal as **VI, VT + NP, Vb + substantive**, etc., so verbal stands for any of these. Whenever a tense is not followed by a modal, a *have*, or a *be* in a **K**-terminal string, it must be followed by a _____ .

664

Here is the whole of **T-yes/no**:
    1. NP + tense-M   + X ⟹ tense-M   + NP + X
    2. NP + tense-have + X ⟹ tense-have + NP + X

3. NP + tense-be + X ⇒ tense-be + NP + X
4. NP + tense + verbal ⇒ tense + NP + verbal

Which line applies to John + past + be + here? _____

665

1. NP + tense-M + X ⇒ tense-M + NP + X
2. NP + tense-have + X ⇒ tense-have + NP + X
3. NP + tense-be + X ⇒ tense-be + NP + X
4. NP + tense + verbal ⇒ tense + NP + verbal

Which line applies to John + past + have + part + go? ____

666

1. NP + tense-M + X ⇒ tense-M + NP + X
2. NP + tense-have + X ⇒ tense-have + NP + X
3. NP + tense-be + X ⇒ tense-be + NP + X
4. NP + tense + verbal ⇒ tense + NP + verbal

Which line applies to John + past + wash + the + car? _____

667

By the fourth line of T-yes/no, John + past + wash + the + car becomes _____ + _____ + _____ + ___ + ___ .

668

By T-yes/no, Edith + present + seem + angry becomes _____ + _____ + _____ + _____ .

669

By T-yes/no, he + past + shall + be + here becomes _____ + _____ + ___ + ___ + _____ .

670

By T-yes/no, they + past + be + here becomes _____ + ___ + _____ + _____ .

671

By T-yes/no, John + present + have + part + finish becomes _____ + _____ + _____ + _____ + _____ .

THE DO TRANSFORMATION

672

By T-yes/no, John + past + laugh becomes _____ + _____ + _____ .

673

Consider the sequence past + John + laugh. Here we have a tense that has nothing to be a tense for. *Past* cannot be added to the noun phrase *John*. *Past* can be added only to a modal, a _____ , a _____ , or a _____ .

674

Now whenever we have a tense with nothing to be a tense for—that is, with no **M** or *have* or *be* or verb following it—there is a transformation rule that must be applied: tense ⇒ do + tense. By this rule, past + John + laugh becomes ____ + _____ + John + laugh.

675

What is do + past? _____

676

Do + past + John + laugh gives the actual sentence _____ _____ .

677

We will call the rule tense ⇒ do + tense the *do* transformation and abbreviate it **T-do**. This is our second obligatory transformation rule. What is the first? T-____

678

T-af is Af + v ⇒ v + Af. Af means any of the three elements _____ , _____ , ____ .

679

The symbol v means any of the four elements _____ , _____ , ____ , _____ .

118   ENGLISH SYNTAX

680

By T-yes/no, Samuel + past + be + ing + eat + the + fish becomes

_____ + ___ + _____ + ___ + _____ + ___ + _____ .

681

By T-af, past + be + Samuel + ing + eat + the + fish becomes ___ +

_____ + _____ + ___ + ___ + ___ + _____ .

682

By T-yes/no, we + past + meet + John becomes _____ + ___ +

_____ + _____ .

683

By T-do, past + we + meet + John becomes ___ + _____ + ___

+ _____ + _____ .

684

By T-yes/no, the + boys + past + eat + the + fish becomes _____

+ ___ + _____ + ___ + ___ + _____ .

685

By T-do, past + the + boys + eat + the + fish becomes _____ +

_____ + _____ + _____ + eat + the + fish.

686

Do + past + the + boys + eat + the + fish represents the actual sentence _____ .

687

Af stands for affix and means any _____ , _____ , _____ .

688

T-af says that whenever we have a sequence of **Af** + **v** we must change it to ___ + ___ .

689

The symbol **v** means any _____ , _____ , _____ , or _____ .

THE DO TRANSFORMATION   **119**

690

T-do says that whenever we have a tense with nothing following it that it can be a tense for—that is, with no **v** following it—we must rewrite tense as _____ + _____ .

691

When tense is followed by an **M** in the **K**-terminal string, what reverses with the subject by **T-yes/no?** _____

692

When tense is followed by a *be* in the **K**-terminal string, what reverses with the subject by **T-yes/no?** _____

693

When tense is followed by a verbal in the **K**-terminal string, what reverses with the subject by **T-yes/no?** _____

694

When tense is followed by a *have* in the **K**-terminal string, what reverses with the subject by **T-yes/no?** _____

695

In the sentence **John + past + do + the + work,** *the work* is an object. *Do* is a **V** ___ .

696

Apply **T-af** to **John + past + do + the + work.** _____ + _____ + _____ + _____ + _____

697

John + do + past + the + work represents the sentence "John did the work." Now let's go back to **John + past + do + the + work.** Apply **T-yes/no** to this. _____ + _____ + _____ + _____ + _____

120   ENGLISH SYNTAX

698

Apply T-do to past + John + do + the + work. _____ + _____ + _____ + _____ + _____ + _____

699

Do + past + John + do + the + work represents the sentence _____ .

700

In the string do + past + John + do + the + work, the second *do* is a transitive verb, like *finish* in *finish the work*. But the first *do* is not a transitive verb. In our terminology it is not a verb at all. It is just a *do,* as *be* is just a *be*. Similarly, in "He had had a cold," the second *have* is a verb, a **Vh,** but the first *have* is just a *have*. The *do* of **T-do** and the *have* that comes from **Aux** are unique forms. We cannot put them in any word classes, because the statements we have to make about them are special. *Be* is always unique. There is no verb *be* corresponding to the verb *do (did the work)* or the verb *have (had a cold)*. *Be* always behaves in its special way whether it comes from the auxiliary or the rewrite of the verb phrase.

MAIN POINTS OF LESSON FOURTEEN

T-yes/no:
  1. NP + tense-M + X ⇒ tense-M + NP + X
  2. NP + tense-have + X ⇒ tense-have + NP + X
  3. NP + tense-be + X ⇒ tense-be + NP + X
  4. NP + tense + verbal ⇒ tense + NP + verbal

T-do: tense ⇒ do + tense. T-do is obligatory whenever tense is not followed by a **v**—that is, by a modal, *be, have,* or verb.

Lesson Fifteen
OTHER OCCURRENCES OF THE DO TRANSFORMATION

We have described at considerable length **T-yes/no** and the *do* transformation which must accompany it when tense alone reverses with the subject. We need to become very familiar with this machinery, because it is central to English grammar. We shall find several other optional transformations very similar to **T-yes/no,** with the obligatory *do* transformation always coming along in the same way. Seeing this, we begin to view the language as a real system and not as just a loose collection of structures. It is because it *is* a system that children learn to manage it in a relatively short time and that we are able to use it to create new sentences which are grammatical and which we have never specifically learned.

```
        1            2         3                 2            1      3
     NP + tense-M  + X      ⟹ tense-M     + NP + X
     NP + tense-have + X    ⟹ tense-have  + NP + X
     NP + tense-be + X      ⟹ tense-be    + NP + X
     NP + tense    + verbal ⟹ tense       + NP + verbal
```

Columns 1 and 2 reverse to form the *yes/no* question, so that columns 1-2-3 appear in the order 2-1-3. For the first three lines, **T-af** then applies as usual: tense-**M,** tense-*have,* tense-*be* become **M**-tense, *have*-tense, *be*-tense. If, however, the structure is that of the fourth line, where the tense is not followed by a modal, a *have,* or a *be,* then the tense alone reverses with the subject. We then have what we might call a "floating" tense—a tense that doesn't have anything following it that it can be a tense for.

In that case, English employs the peculiar device of the *do* transformation: **tense** ⟹ **do** + **tense.** We put in the word *do* to carry the tense, as it were. *Do* has no meaning here except as a tense carrier. It simply expresses past or present. If present, it indicates whether the subject is third person singular or not.

We have now had examples of two kinds of rules: kernel rules (like

NP → Det + N) and transformation rules (like Af + v ⟹ v + Af). Transformation rules are of two kinds: optional and obligatory. **T-yes/no** is optional; we don't have to apply it to any particular string of morphemes. This is another way of saying that not every sentence we utter must be a *yes/no* question. **T-af** and **T-do**, however, are obligatory. We must put the affixes and the v's in the proper order, and we must put in a *do* whenever tense is not followed by a v.

Notice that these rules apply in a certain order in the specification of the structure of any particular sentence: first the kernel rules, then the optional transformations if any, then the obligatory transformations. When all obligatory transformation rules have been applied, we have what we will call a T-terminal string. Thus the syntactic structure of the sentence "Did the man laugh?" would be specified in this way:

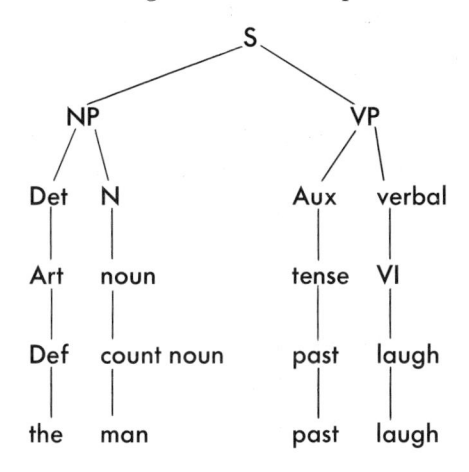

```
                    S
            ／            ＼
          NP                VP
         ／  ＼            ／  ＼
       Det    N          Aux   verbal
        |     |           |      |
       Art   noun        tense   Vl
        |     |           |      |
       Def  count noun   past   laugh
        |     |           |      |
       the   man         past   laugh
```

past + the + man + laugh   (by T-yes/no)

do + past + the + man + laugh   (by T-do)

The line at the end of the tree of derivation—**the + man + past + laugh** is a K-terminal string. The very last line is a T-terminal string.

A T-terminal string is, of course, not a sentence but the representation of the arrangement of the morphemes of a sentence. We would still have to apply phonological rules—e.g., convert **do + past** to *did* and show how *the, man,* and *laugh* are pronounced.

701

A negative sentence is one that contains some form of the word *not*. If the negative of "John should go" is "John should not go," what is the negative of "John would go"? _____

OTHER OCCURRENCES OF THE DO TRANSFORMATION   123

702

Usually, instead of "John should not go," we say or write "John shouldn't go." We call *shouldn't* the *contracted form* of *should not*. What is the contracted form of *would not?* _____

703

What are the contracted forms of *could not, cannot,* and *must not?*
_____ , _____ , _____

704

Be sure that you get the spelling right for these contracted forms. What is the contracted form of *will not?* _____

705

Shall not, may not, and *might not* do not occur so commonly as the other modals in the contracted form. A sentence that contains some form of the word *not* is a _____ sentence.

706

We can write the formula for "John shouldn't go" in this way: **NP + past + shall + not + go**. Write the corresponding formula for "John wouldn't go." _____ + _____ + _____ + _____ + _____

707

If the formula for "John won't go" is **NP + present + will + not + go**, what is the formula for "John will go"? _____ + _____ + _____ + _____

708

When the K-terminal string has the form **NP + tense + M + X**, we make the sentence negative by adding the word *not* after the _____ .

709

This is the first part of the negative transformation, which we will abbreviate T-neg: **NP + tense-M + X ⇒ NP + tense-M + not + X**. Apply

124   ENGLISH SYNTAX

T-neg to the string **John + past + shall + have + part + go. John +** _____ + _____ + _____ + _____ + **part + go**

710

T-neg applied to **John + past + shall + have + part + go** gives us **John + past + shall + not + have + part + go.** This string contains two sequences of **Af + v**, so we must apply the obligatory transformation **T-____** .

711

Apply **T-af** to **John + past + shall + not + have + part + go. John +** _____ + _____ + _____ + _____ + _____ + _____

712

Having applied **T-neg** and **T-af**, we now have **John + shall + past + not + have + go + part**. What actual sentence does this T-terminal string represent? (Use the contracted form.) _____

713

T-neg says to rewrite **NP + tense-M + X** as _____ + _____ + _____ + _____ .

714

T-yes/no says to rewrite **NP + tense-M + X** as _____ + _____ + _____ .

715

We see that in **T-yes/no** and **T-neg** we begin with the same structure, though we do different things to it. The negative of "John has gone" is "John hasn't gone." What is the negative of "They have gone"?
_____

We are omitting negative questions, like "Hasn't John gone?," "Didn't John go?" from our description. These could be added by altering the description of either **T-yes/no** or **T-neg,** depending on which it seemed best

OTHER OCCURRENCES OF THE *DO* TRANSFORMATION

to apply first. That is, we could have the sequence "John has gone" → "Has John gone?" → "Hasn't John gone?" or the sequence "John has gone" → "John hasn't gone" → "Hasn't John gone?"

716

Hasn't is the contracted form of *has not*. *Haven't* and *hadn't* are the contracted forms of _____ and _____ .

717

If the formula for "John has gone" is **NP + present + have + part + go**, what is the formula for "John hasn't gone"? **NP +** _____ **+** _____ **+** _____ **+** _____ **+ go**

718

To make **NP + present + have + part + go** negative, we add *not* after _____ .

719

The second part of **T-neg** is this: **NP + tense-have + X ⟹ NP + tense-have + not + X**. When the K-terminal string contains an **M** or a *have*, we add *not* after the **M** or *have*. As you might guess, if the word after tense is *be*, we add *not* after _____ .

720

The negative of "John was here" is "John wasn't here." The negative of "Archibald is going" is "Archibald isn't going." What is the negative of "They are teachers"? _____

721

The formula for "They are teachers" is **they + present + be + teachers**. What is the formula for "They aren't teachers"? _____ **+** _____ **+** _____ **+** _____ **+** _____

722

So far, **T-neg** reads as follows:

    NP + tense-M   + X ⟹ NP + tense-M   + not + X
    NP + tense-have + X ⟹ NP + tense-have + not + X
    NP + tense-be   + X ⟹ NP + tense-be   + not + X

The part to the left of the arrows is the same as in **T-**_____.

723

The negative of "John worked" is "John didn't work." What is the negative of "John left"? _____

724

The formula for "John worked" is **John + past + work**. The one for "John didn't work" is **John + do + past + not + work**. Apart from the *do*, we make **John + past + work** negative by adding *not* after _____ .

725

Here is the last part of **T-neg**: **NP + tense + verbal** ⇒ **NP + tense + not + verbal**. According to this, **the + girls + past + help + us** becomes **the + girls +** _____ **+** _____ **+** _____ **+ us**.

726

Now look at **the + girls + past + not + help + us**. Once again we have a floating tense. *The girls* can't be *past*, and neither can *not*. The rule says that whenever we have a floating tense, we must add the word _____ .

727

By **T-do**, **the + girls + past + not + help + us** becomes **the + girls +** _____ **+** _____ **+** _____ **+** _____ **+ us**.

728

Here is all of **T-neg**:

    NP + tense-M   + X   ⇒ NP + tense-M   + not + X
    NP + tense-have + X   ⇒ NP + tense-have + not + X
    NP + tense-be   + X   ⇒ NP + tense-be   + not + X
    NP + tense   + verbal ⇒ NP + tense   + not + verbal

If the subject is followed by an **M**, *have*, or *be*, the word *not* is added after the **M**, *have*, or *be*. Otherwise, *not* is added after _____ .

729

When *not* is added after tense, the tense floats, because it is not tied to an **M**, *have*, *be*, or verb. Therefore we must apply **T-do**, which says rewrite tense as _____ **+** _____ .

730

The structure on the left side of the arrows is exactly the same for **T-yes/no** and **T-neg**. It is exactly the same also for **T-affirm,** which is the *affirmation* transformation. Ordinarily, which word in the sentence "He's here" do we pronounce loudest? _____

731

Ordinarily, when we say the sentence "He's here," the adverb *here* has the loudest pronunciation or, as we say, the loudest *stress*. What do you think ordinarily has the loudest stress in "She may come"? _____

732

But we may say, instead of "He's here," "He IS here," putting the loudest stress on *is*. Instead of "She may come," we could say "She MAY come," with the loudest stress on *may*. What word in "She's gone" usually has the loudest stress? _____

733

If, however, we want to emphasize the *has,* we can say "She HAS gone," with loudest, or affirmation, stress on *has*. This affirms the statement and denies the contrary. Let us use the letter **A** to mean *affirmation stress on the preceding word,* the word before the **A**. Then **John** + **present** + **will** + **A** + **come** means that which word will be pronounced loudest? _____

We might note the difference between what we have called the affirmation transformation and a simple emphatic one. Any word in a sentence can be emphasized by being pronounced with primary stress. For example, the sentence "A boy left it" is normally pronounced with the primary stress on *left,* but we can also have

    A boy left it. (not several)
    A *boy* left it. (not a girl)
    A boy left *it*. (not something else)

Or we can put an extra heavy stress on the verb:

    A boy LEFT it. (didn't take it away)

All of these contrast a word in the sentence with some other word that might occur in its place. However, the effect of the affirmation transformation is to assert the truth of the whole utterance against a statement to the contrary:

        A boy *can* leave it. (Why do you deny it?)
        A boy *did* leave it. (Why do you deny it?)

734

Here is T-affirm, the affirmation transformation:

NP + tense-M   + X   ⇒ NP + tense-M   + A + X
NP + tense-have + X   ⇒ NP + tense-have + A + X
NP + tense-be   + X   ⇒ NP + tense-be   + A + X
NP + tense   + verbal ⇒ NP + tense   + A + verbal

The structures to the left of the arrows are exactly the same as those for T-_____ and T-_____.

735

NP + tense-M   + X   ⇒ NP + tense-M   + A + X
NP + tense-have + X   ⇒ NP + tense-have + A + X
NP + tense-be   + X   ⇒ NP + tense-be   + A + X
NP + tense   + verbal ⇒ NP + tense   + A + verbal

According to this, **John + past + be + ing + go** becomes **John + past + _____ + _____ + _____ + go.**

736

By T-af, **John + past + be + A + ing + go** becomes **John + _____ + _____ + A + _____ + _____ .**

737

When *John* is subject, what is **past + be**? _____

738

We can write a word in capital letters to show that it has affirmation stress. So **was + A** is _____ .

739

John + past + be + A + go + ing represents the sentence _____ .

OTHER OCCURRENCES OF THE DO TRANSFORMATION

740

NP + tense-M + X ⇒ NP + tense-M + A + X
NP + tense-have + X ⇒ NP + tense-have + A + X
NP + tense-be + X ⇒ NP + tense-be + A + X
NP + tense + verbal ⇒ NP + tense + A + verbal

Which line—first, second, third, or fourth—describes the structure **John + past + write + the + letter?** _____

741

The structure **John + past + write + the + letter** is described by the fourth line of **T-affirm—NP + tense + verbal ⇒ NP + tense + A + verbal**. Therefore, if we apply **T-affirm** to this structure, we get **John + _____ + _____ + _____ + the + letter.**

742

In **John + past + A + write + the + letter**, we again have a floating tense—a tense with nothing next to it that it can be a tense for. Therefore, **T-do** must be applied, and we get **John + _____ + _____ + _____ + write + the + letter.**

743

What is **do + past?** _____

744

Did + A means that *did* will be the loudest word in the sentence, as it always is in a sentence like "John did write the letter." Apply **T-affirm** to **Annie + present + can + write.** _____ + _____ + _____ + _____ + _____

745

By **T-af, Annie + present + can + A + write** becomes **Annie + can + present + A + write.** When this is spoken, what word will have loudest stress? _____

746

"Annie CAN write" derives from "Annie can write" by **T-affirm**. By the same transformation, "Annie DID write" derives from _____ .

747

Complete this series: "She's waiting," "Is she waiting?"; "She waited," _____ .

748

Complete this series: "She's given up," "She hasn't given up," "She HAS given up"; "She gave up," _____ , _____ _____ .

749

Complete this series: "She should come home," "Should she come home?," "She shouldn't come home," "She SHOULD come home"; "She came home," _____ , _____ , _____ .

750

Notice that, while "She should COME" and "She SHOULD come" are both grammatical English sentences, "She did COME" is not grammatical. We don't say it. We use the *did* in a sentence of this type only when we have the stress of affirmation. Then we must use it.

MAIN POINTS OF LESSON FIFTEEN

T-yes/no, T-neg, and T-affirm all operate on structures of the following description:

NP + tense-M   + X
NP + tense-have + X
NP + tense-be   + X
NP + tense   + verbal

T-yes/no switches the first two columns. The other two transformations insert the morpheme *not* or the morpheme **A** after the second column.

When any of these three transformations is applied to a structure described by the fourth line, where tense is immediately followed by a verbal, the effect is to separate the tense from the verb contained in the verbal. The *do* transformation then automatically applies to provide a carrier for the tense.

OTHER OCCURRENCES OF THE DO TRANSFORMATION

Lesson Sixteen
WH QUESTIONS

We have not by any means described all of the applications of the *do* transformation and the optional transformations related to it. They occur in many parts of the English grammar. Let us look again at the structures to which the optional transformations **T-yes/no, T-neg,** and **T-affirm** apply:

     NP + tense-M + X
     NP + tense-have + X
     NP + tense-be + X
     NP + tense   + verbal

If we immediately apply the obligatory transformation **T-af (Af + v ⇒ v + Af)**, we get such sentences as these:

     John should go.
     John has gone.
     John is going.
     John went.

But there is another transformation we might apply to get a *yes/no* question of a type different from the one we have studied:

     NP + tense-M + X ⇒
     NP + tense-have + X ⇒
     NP + tense-be + X ⇒
     NP + tense   + verbal ⇒

  NP + tense-M + X, tense-M + not + pronoun
  NP + tense-have + X, tense-have + not + pronoun
  NP + tense-be + X, tense-be + not + pronoun
  NP + tense   + verbal, tense + not + pronoun

Here we understand the tense, **M,** *have,* and *be* that occur after the commas to be the same ones that occur before the commas. We understand *pronoun* to mean the personal pronoun that refers to the **NP**: if the **NP** is *John*, the pronoun will be *he*; if the **NP** is *Sally*, the pronoun will be *she*; if the **NP** is *the boys*, the pronoun will be *they*. Then, with obligatory transformations **T-af** and **T-do** applied wherever the structures require them, the formulas will automatically produce such questions as

John should go,   shouldn't he?
John has gone,   hasn't he?
John is going,   isn't he?
John went,   didn't he?

In the last example, we again had a floating tense, so *do* was put in to carry it.

If the structure to the left of the arrow already contains the negative, as in "John shouldn't go," then the transformation contains the direction to drop the negative. We thus get

John shouldn't go,   should he?
John hasn't gone,   has he?
John isn't going,   is he?
John didn't go,   did he?

The concept of transformation can be used to describe many particular features of the language which would be quite hard to describe with kernel rules. We listed the personal pronouns as simply *I, you, he, she, it, we,* and *they*. But personal pronouns can occur in object positions, and clearly we must exclude such ungrammatical sentences as *"John bought they." Probably the best way to do it is to introduce an object transformation, **T-obj**, which adds the symbol m after **NP** in certain positions when **NP** is a personal pronoun or the word *who*. The transformation could be shown as follows:

VT + NP ⟹ VT + NP + m
Vh + NP ⟹ Vh + NP + m
Prep + NP ⟹ Prep + NP + m

Then the following phonological rules apply:

I + m → me
you + m → you
he + m → him
she + m → her
it + m → it
we + m → us

WH QUESTIONS   **133**

$$\text{they} + m \rightarrow \text{them}$$
$$\text{who} + m \rightarrow \text{whom}$$

We shall use this, along with the machinery described in Lessons Fourteen and Fifteen, in the description of *wh* questions, to which we now turn.

751

Wh questions are questions introduced by words called *interrogatives*. In the sentence "Where does John live?" *where* is an interrogative. What is the interrogative in "When did Sally leave?" _____

752

Wh questions cannot be answered by *yes* or *no* but only by some bit of information. What is the interrogative in "Who was speaking"?

_____

753

What is the interrogative in "What did Mr. Wheeler do"? _____

754

Most interrogatives begin with the letters *wh*. That is why we call these questions *wh* questions. However, not all interrogatives are spelled this way. What is the interrogative in "How is John going"? _____

755

Take the sentences "John lives here" and "John lives in Arroyo Grande." The adverb *here* and the prepositional phrase *in Arroyo Grande* are both adverbials of _____ .

756

Both "John lives here" and "John lives in Arroyo Grande" can be expressed in the formula **John + present + live + Adv-p**. If we apply **T-yes/no** to this formula, we get _____ + _____ + _____ + **Adv-p**.

---

134   ENGLISH SYNTAX

757

The *wh* transformations are applied only to structures produced by the optional transformation **T-yes/no**. Has **present + John + live + Adv-p** been produced by **T-yes/no**? _____

758

Present + John + live + Adv-p is produced by **T-yes/no**, so *wh* transformations can be applied to it. The first *wh* transformation rule we will call **T-wh-adv-p**. It is this: **X + Adv-p + Y ⟹ where + X + Y**. Here X means everything in the sentence that occurs before the adverbial of place. In **present + John + live + Adv-p**, X stands for _____ + _____ + _____ .

759

In formulas of the type **X + Adv-p + Y**, X and Y mean *anything or nothing*. Y means anything that follows **Adv-p**, if anything follows it, or nothing, if nothing follows it. In **present + John + live + Adv-p**, the Y of **X + Adv-p + Y** stands for _____ .

760

In **present + John + live + Adv-p**, the X of **T-wh-adv-p** stands for **present + John + live**—in other words, for everything before the **Adv-p**. The Y in this case stands for nothing, since nothing follows the **Adv-p**. **T-wh-adv-p** is **X + Adv-p + Y ⟹ where + X + Y**. So **present + John + live + Adv-p** becomes _____ + _____ + _____ + **live**.

761

Where + present + John + live contains a floating tense, so **T-do** must be applied. **T-do** rewrites tense as _____ + _____ .

762

Applying this, we get **where + do + present + John + live** and the finished sentence "Where does John live?" Try one with a modal: **John + past + shall + live + Adv-p**. Application of **T-yes/no** gives _____ + _____ + _____ + _____ + _____ .

WH QUESTIONS   **135**

763

Since past + shall + John + live + Adv-p is a result of T-yes/no, we can apply to it our rule T-wh-adv-p: X + Adv-p + Y ⟹ where + X + Y. Again, Y stands for nothing. X stands for _____ + _____ + _____ + _____.

764

X + Adv-p + Y ⟹ where + X + Y changes past + shall + John + live + Adv-p into _____ + _____ + _____ + _____ + _____.

765

After T-af reverses past + shall, where + past + shall + John + live will give us the actual sentence _____.

766

In "John lived there in 1963," what is the Adv-p? _____

767

We can write "John lived there in 1963" as follows: John + past + live + Adv-p + in 1963. T-yes/no applied to this gives _____ + _____ + _____ + Adv-p + in 1963.

768

T-wh-adv-p is X + Adv-p + Y ⟹ where + X + Y. What is the Y in past + John + live + Adv-p + in 1963? _____

769

Application of T-wh-adv-p to past + John + live + Adv-p + in 1963 gives us where + past + John + live + in 1963. After T-do is applied to provide a *do* for the floating tense, we get the actual sentence _____.

770

In "John lived there in 1963," the prepositional phrase is an adverbial of _____.

771

The *wh* rule that can be applied when the K-terminal string contains an adverbial of time is this: X + Adv-t + Y ⟹ when + X + Y. We call this **T-wh-adv-t**. **T-yes/no** must be applied first. By **T-yes/no**, John + past + live + there + Adv-t becomes _____ + _____ + _____ + there + Adv-t.

772

By **T-wh-adv-t** (X + Adv-t + Y ⟹ when + X + Y), past + John + live + there + Adv-t (in which Y is nothing) becomes _____ + _____ + _____ + live + there.

773

When + past + John + live + there becomes when + do + past + John + live + there by **T-do**, and the finished sentence "When did John live there?" We have seen that in these two *wh* transformations *where* replaces an adverbial of _____, *when* an adverbial of _____.

774

There is a *wh* rule that applies when a noun phrase is to be replaced by an interrogative. We take the noun phrase to be replaced as either *someone* or *something*. (This specification permits us to reconstruct the K-terminal string from the transform.) *Someone* and *something* are both _____ pronouns.

775

Here is the rule: X + { someone / something } + Y ⟹ { who / what } + X + Y. Since this rule applies to the noun phrases *someone* and *something*, we will call it **T-wh-NP**. A *wh* transformation can apply only to a string that is a result of **T-** _____ .

776

T-wh-NP (X + { someone / something } + Y ⟹ { who / what } + X + Y) gives two possible replacements for the **NP** of the K-terminal string. We take *who* if the **NP** is *someone*, *what* if it is *something*. **Past + someone + see + Samuel** is a string to which **T-wh-NP** can apply, because it is a result of **T-yes/no**, and it contains the **NP** *someone*. What interrogative will replace *someone*?

777

Applying X + {someone / something} + Y ⟹ {who / what} + X + Y to past + someone + see + Samuel, we get _____ + _____ + _____ + _____ .

778

Who + past + see + Samuel, after T-af, gives the sentence _____ .

779

Applying X + {someone / something} + Y ⟹ {who / what} + X + Y to past + something + happen, we get _____ + _____ + _____ .

780

What + past + happen represents the question "What happened?" Had we applied T-do instead of T-wh-NP to past + something + happen, we would have got the sentence _____ .

781

T-wh-NP also applies when the indefinite pronoun *someone* or *something* is an object instead of a subject. Let us take John + past + see + someone + last night. By T-yes/no, this becomes _____ + _____ + _____ + someone + last night.

782

Past + John + see + someone + last night is a case of X + someone + Y. The X is _____ , and the Y is _____ .

783

Apply T-wh-NP (X + {someone / something} + Y ⟹ {who / what} + X + Y) to past + John + see + someone + last night. _____ + _____ + _____ + _____ + _____ .

138   ENGLISH SYNTAX

784

We now have **who + past + John + see + last night**. But the object transformation described in the introduction to this lesson says that when an **NP** is an object and either a personal pronoun or *who*, **NP ⇒ NP + m**. So we get **who + m + past + John + see + last night**. A phonological rule will convert **who + m** into the word _____ .

785

In **who + m + past + John + see + last night**, we again have a floating tense, so **T-do** must apply. This gives us **who + m + do + past + John + see + last night** and the actual sentence _____ _____ .

786

In conversation the object transformation which introduces **m** after *who* in the object position is optional for most speakers. That is, we often say "Who did John see last night?" But for the present we will confine ourselves to the more literary *whom*. Apply **T-wh-NP** to **past + John + find + something + yesterday**. _____ + _____ + _____ + _____ + _____ .

787

After **T-do** has been applied, **what + past + John + find + yesterday** will give us the actual sentence _____ .

788

There is an interesting rule-proving exception to **T-wh-NP**: It will not produce the question "With whom did John go?" from "John went with someone." The latter sentence has the K-terminal string **John + past + go + with + someone**. **T-yes/no** applied to this gives _____ + _____ + _____ + _____ + _____ .

789

Past + John + go + with + someone is a case of **X + someone + Y**. Here the **Y** stands for _____ .

WH QUESTIONS   139

790

If we apply **T-wh-NP** to **past + John + go + with + someone,** we get
_____ + m + _____ + _____ + _____ + _____ .

791

This will give the sentence "Whom did John go with?" (If **T-obj** is taken as optional and omitted, the sentence is "Who did John go with?") It takes a special rule to produce "With whom did John go?" This probably explains the tendency to avoid this structure, except in rather formal style, in favor of the one with the preposition at the end. **T-wh-NP** applied to "John gave it to someone" would give the sentence "Who(m) _____ ?"

792

English also has a *wh*-article transformation, in which an interrogative replaces an article of the K-terminal string. This is the rule:

$$X + \text{article} + N + Y \Rightarrow \left\{ \begin{array}{c} \text{which} \\ \text{what} \end{array} \right\} + N + X + Y$$

Applying **T-yes/no** to **John + past + buy + the + car,** we get **past + John + buy + the + car.** Here the **X** of **X + article + N + Y** stands for _____ + _____ + _____ .

793

In **past + John + buy + the + car,** the article of **X + article + N + Y** stands for *the*. What does **N** stand for? _____

794

T-wh-article is $X + \text{article} + N + Y \Rightarrow \left\{ \begin{array}{c} \text{which} \\ \text{what} \end{array} \right\} + N + X + Y$. In this transformation we can choose either *which* or *what* and still get a grammatical sentence. Let us choose *which*. Then **past + John + buy + the + car** becomes _____ + _____ + _____ + **John + buy.**

795

After **T-do** has been applied, **which + car + past + John + buy** gives us the sentence "Which car did John buy?" Now apply **T-yes/no** to the

+ boy + past + buy + the + car. _____ + _____ + _____ + _____ + _____ + _____ .

796

Now we can apply **T-wh-article** so that the interrogative *which* or *what* replaces the first *the* or so that it replaces the second *the*. Let article be the first *the* in **past + the + boy + buy + the + car**. Then the Y of X + article + N + Y is buy + the + car. The X is _____, and the N is _____.

797

Applying **T-wh-article** (X + article + N + Y ⇒ $\left\{ \begin{array}{c} \text{which} \\ \text{what} \end{array} \right\}$ + N + X + Y) to **past + the + boy + buy + the + car**, letting article be the first *the* and choosing the interrogative *which*, we get _____ + _____ + _____ + _____ + _____ + _____ .

798

After **T-af**, **which + boy + past + buy + the + car** gives us "Which boy bought the car?" Now apply X + article + N + Y ⇒ $\left\{ \begin{array}{c} \text{which} \\ \text{what} \end{array} \right\}$ + N + X + Y to **past + the + boy + buy + the + car**, letting article stand for the second *the* and using *which* again. _____ + _____ + _____ + _____ + _____ + _____ .

799

Which + car + past + the + boy + buy, after the application of the *do* transformation, will give the sentence _____.

800

Notice again the replacements in the *wh* transformations. In **T-wh-adv-p**, *where* replaces an adverbial of place in the kernel. In **T-wh-adv-t**, *when* replaces an adverbial of time. In **T-wh-NP**, *who* or *what* replaces the indefinite pronouns *someone* or *something*. In **T-wh-article**, *which* or *what* replaces an article.

WH QUESTIONS   141

MAIN POINTS OF LESSON SIXTEEN

T-wh-adv-p: $X + \text{Adv-p} + Y \Rightarrow \text{where} + X + Y$

T-wh-adv-t: $X + \text{Adv-t} + Y \Rightarrow \text{when} + X + Y$

T-wh-NP: $X + \begin{Bmatrix} \text{someone} \\ \text{something} \end{Bmatrix} + Y \Rightarrow \begin{Bmatrix} \text{who} \\ \text{what} \end{Bmatrix} + X + Y$

T-wh-article: $X + \text{article} + N + Y \Rightarrow \begin{Bmatrix} \text{which} \\ \text{what} \end{Bmatrix} + N + X + Y$

The interrogatives *where, when, who, whom, what, which* replace items of the **K**-terminal string as indicated. The order of the underlying string is changed, so that the interrogative comes first in the *wh* question. The *wh* transformations can be applied only to strings which result from **T-yes/no**. This relates the two main kinds of English questions in a systematic way. After the *wh* transformation, **T-af** or **T-do** is applied to produce the T-terminal string.

An object transformation, **T-obj,** introduces the morpheme **m** after **NP**'s in object position when the **NP** is a personal pronoun or *who*. Phonological rules then rewrite I + m as *me*, he + m as *him*, who + m as *whom*, etc. **T-obj** is generally obligatory for personal pronouns. It is optional for *who* except in rather formal style.

Lesson Seventeen
POSSESSIVES

We have used the technical term **K**-terminal string for sequences of morphemes which result after all kernel rules have been applied and **T**-terminal string for sequences which result after all transformation rules have been applied. Since more than one transformation rule may be applied in the generation of a sentence, there will be some strings in between which are neither **K**-terminal nor **T**-terminal. For example, consider this generation:

1. John + past + laugh
2. past + John + laugh   (resulting from **T-yes/no**)
3. do + past + John + laugh   (resulting from **T-do**)

Number 1 is a **K**-terminal string and 3 is a **T**-terminal string, but 2 is neither. Thus **T-do** in this generation is applied to a string which is not a **K**-terminal string because it is itself the result of transformation. It will be useful to have a term which applies to any underlying string of morphemes, whether **K**-terminal or not. We will use the term *base string*. A base string is simply any string of morphemes to which some transformation is applied. In the generation above, 1 is the base of 2, and 2 is the base of 3.

801

The *possessive* morpheme is a set of forms added to noun phrases to give various meanings, of which the most important is possession—having or owning something; it is added to noun *phrases*, not just nouns. What is the noun phrase in "John went away"?   _____

802

What is the noun phrase in "The men went away"?   _____

POSSESSIVES   143

803

In "The men went away," *the men* is a noun phrase containing the count noun _____ .

804

In "He went away," *he* is a pronoun functioning as subject. It is also a _____ .

805

We will abbreviate possessive morpheme as **Pos**. **Pos** is added to a noun phrase to make it possessive. **NP + Pos** gives a possessive _____ phrase.

806

In "John's brother went away," *John's* is a possessive noun phrase. It consists of a noun _____ plus _____ .

807

What is the possessive noun phrase in "A student's books were on the table"? _____

808

Note that in *a student's books*, the article *a* goes with *student*. It can't go with *books*, because *books* is plural, and *a* is not used with plural nouns. **Pos** is here added to the whole noun phrase *a student*. This is different from *a men's store*, where the possessive noun phrase *men's* is embedded in the noun phrase *a store*. The stress is different too: In *a student's books*, the principal stress is on *books*, but in *a men's store*, it is on *men's*. What is the possessive noun phrase in "I saw that student's books"? _____

809

Compare "The brother went away" and "John's brother went away." The word *the* in the first sentence is a definite _____ .

144   ENGLISH SYNTAX

810

A possessive noun phrase substitutes for the definite article *the* in a base, or underlying, string. In general wherever we have *the* in a base string, we can substitute a _____ phrase plus _____ .

811

In the base string I + past + buy + the + car, we can substitute **John + Pos** for the word _____ .

812

Tom + Pos is *Tom's*. What is **John + Pos**? _____

813

Watch the apostrophe (') and get it in the right place; it is an important part of the spelling. What is **the boy + Pos**? _____

814

Apply the possessive transformation to "John found the bicycle," using *the boy's*. _____

815

What is **a man + Pos**? _____

816

Apply the possessive transformation to "John did the work," using *a man's*. _____

817

Apply the possessive transformation twice to "The brother did the work," using *John's* for the first *the* and *a man's* for the second. _____

818

To what is the possessive morpheme added? _____

POSSESSIVES 145

819

Earlier we mentioned singulars and plurals in talking about forms like *boy* and *boys, man* and *men*. Like the possessive, the plural is a morpheme. Like the possessive, it is added to noun phrases, not to nouns. We will abbreviate plural as **Plur**. What is **the boy + Plur**? _____

820

Earlier we spoke of three kinds of nouns. Count nouns are one kind. What are the other two? _____ , _____

821

Count nouns are nouns that refer to things that can be counted. Therefore, they can form plurals. Noncount nouns and proper nouns ordinarily do not form plurals. What kind of noun is *Pat* in "Pat plays basketball"? _____

822

In "The men ate the mush," *men* is a _____ noun, *mush* a _____ noun.

823

To what are the possessive and plural morphemes added? _____

824

With what kind of noun does the nondefinite article *a* occur—count, noncount, or proper? _____

825

The article *a(n)* is one of two words that occur as nondefinite articles. What is the other one? _____

826

What is the product of **a student + Pos**? _____

---

146   ENGLISH SYNTAX

827

The nondefinite article *some* occurs with plural count nouns and with noncount nouns, but *a* occurs only with singular count nouns. When a noun phrase with the nondefinite article *a*—like *a student*—adds the plural morpheme, the *a* is dropped. What is the product of **a student + Plur**?

_____

828

What is the product of **the teacher + Pos?** _____

829

Apply the possessive transformation to "I have the pencil," using *the teacher's*. _____

830

The definite article *the* is not dropped when the plural morpheme is added. What is the product of **the teacher + Plur?** _____

831

Are the noun phrases *the teacher's* and *the teachers* pronounced the same way? _____

832

Count nouns in English are either regular or irregular. Regular nouns are those that form their plurals according to the general system: *boy, chair, lady, dog*. Irregular nouns form plurals in some special way: *man, foot, woman, mouse*. What is **the man + Plur?** _____

We are using the terms *regular* and *irregular* to refer to sound, not spelling. Words like *lady* and *hero* are slightly irregular in spelling, since their plurals are spelled *ladies* and *heroes*. However, they are regular as far as sound goes. There is no difference in the pronunciation of the endings of *heroes* and *pianos*.

833

The noun phrases *the teacher's* and *the teachers* are identical in sound, though different in spelling. This is true of all regular nouns. The noun phrase *the teacher's* is composed of **NP** + _____ .

834

You can tell that *the teacher's* is composed of **NP** plus the possessive morpheme because of the apostrophe. However, if you only heard it, you couldn't tell whether it was **NP** + **Pos** or **NP** + **Plur**. The man + Pos is *the man's*. What is **the men** + **Pos**? _____

835

The plurals and possessives of irregular noun phrases differ in sound as well as in spelling. **The woman** + **Plur** is *the women*. What is **the woman** + **Pos**? _____

836

Plur and **Pos** may be added to the same noun phrase. If this happens, **Plur** is added first, and **Pos** is added second. What is **the woman** + **Plur**? _____

837

Notice the spelling of the singular *the woman* and the plural *the women*. Many people misspell these. *The women* consists of **NP** + _____ .

838

If we now add **Pos** to *the women*, the product is *the women's*. **The woman** + **Plur** is *the women*. What is the product of **the woman** + **Plur** + **Pos**? _____

839

What is the product of **the man** + **Plur** + **Pos**? _____

840

Are the nouns *man* and *woman* regular or irregular? _____

---

148   ENGLISH SYNTAX

841

Student is a regular noun. **The student + Plur** is *the students*. **The student + Pos** is *the student's*. **The student + Plur + Pos** is *the students'*. Are *the students, the student's,* and *the students'* all pronounced in the same way? _____

842

For regular nouns, there is no difference in pronunciation between **NP + Plur, NP + Pos,** and **NP + Plur + Pos.** They do, however, differ in spelling. Which of them has an apostrophe before the letter *s*? _____

843

All singular noun phrases plus possessive end with the spelling *'s*. All regular noun phrases plus plural end with the letter *s* and no apostrophe. All regular noun phrases plus plural plus possessive end with the spelling *s'*. The noun phrase *the teachers'* consists of _____ + **Plur + Pos.**

844

Is *the man's* a case of (1) **NP + Plur,** (2) **NP + Pos,** (3) **NP + Plur + Pos**? (Give the number.) _____

845

Is *the rabbits'* a case of (1) **NP + Plur,** (2) **NP + Pos,** (3) **NP + Plur + Pos**?
_____

846

Is *the mice's* a case of (1) **NP + Plur,** (2) **NP + Pos,** (3) **NP + Plur + Pos**?
_____

847

Apply the possessive transformation to "We found the books," using **Mr. Cane + Pos.** _____

848

Apply the possessive transformation to "The books are inside," using **the student + Plur + Pos.** _____

POSSESSIVES 149

849

Apply the possessive transformation to "Steve stole the candy," using the child + Plur + Pos. _____

850

Remember that the terms *regular* and *irregular* refer to the formation of the plural. They also refer to sound, not spelling. *Lady,* for example, is a regular noun, because, so far as sound goes, it forms its plural in the regular way.

MAIN POINTS OF LESSON SEVENTEEN

The possessive morpheme and the plural morpheme may be added to noun phrases. The possessive morpheme (**Pos**) makes the noun phrase possessive. The plural morpheme (**Plur**) makes it plural. If both **Plur** and **Pos** are added to the same noun phrase, they are added in that order.

If the possessive morpheme is added to a noun phrase consisting of a noun (not a pronoun) or a determiner plus noun, **Pos** is an *s*-like sound, spelled *'s*. The plural morpheme is identical for regular nouns but is spelled without the apostrophe. For regular nouns, **NP** + **Plur** + **Pos** results in the spelling *s'*.

The unit **NP** + **Pos** replaces the definite article *the* of the base string in the possessive transformation.

Lesson Eighteen
MORE POSSESSIVES

You may have noticed that we have talked about the possessive transformation but have not actually given it as a formula. It is considerably more complicated than the transformations we have been dealing with, and we are not yet ready to cope with all its details. We might, however, observe something of its general nature.

The possessive transformation is of a type that we call a double-base transformation. That is, instead of having a single base string, as do **T-yes/no, T-af,** etc., it has two. One string supplies the structure to be used, and the other string uses it. The first string is called the *insert* string and the second the *matrix* string. Thus, with the strings given in final sentence form, we have such relationships as these:

insert: John has a hat.
matrix: The hat is on the table.
result: John's hat is on the table.

If we want to know something about the meaning of the possessive morpheme, we look at the insert string from which it derives. As we have already noted, all meaning relationships in the language are contained in the kernel, and it is often only by going back to the kernel that we can clearly understand the meanings in transforms. So far as the possessive goes, its most common meaning is *having*. That is, for the most part it derives from kernel strings containing the verb *have:*

KERNEL	TRANSFORM
John has a hat.	John's hat
John has a car.	John's car
John has a mother.	John's mother
John has an idea.	John's idea

However, not all possessives derive from kernel strings with *have*. *Shakespeare's plays* does not come from "Shakespeare had plays." *A year's work* does not come from "A year has work." These transforms come from quite different kernel sentences:

KERNEL	TRANSFORM
Shakespeare wrote the plays.	Shakespeare's plays
The work will last a year.	a year's work
A man can do the job.	a man's job
The store is for men.	a men's store
Boys attend the school.	a boys' school

What we call the possessive morpheme has many meanings besides possession, though possession, or *having*, is its most common meaning. In any particular expression containing the possessive morpheme, we find its meaning in the kernel from which it derives.

851

To what is the possessive morpheme added? _____

852

What is the noun phrase in "He went away"? _____

853

In "He went away," *he* is a noun phrase that functions as a subject. It is also a _____ pronoun.

854

The possessive morpheme is regular for all nouns but irregular for all personal pronouns. **He + Pos** is *his*. We said that we could substitute **NP + Pos** for the word _____ in a base string.

855

If we apply the possessive transformation to "The mother is here," using **he + Pos**, we get _____ .

856

Some personal pronouns have two possessive forms. We shall give them both, but for the present, use the first one only. **I + Pos** is *my, mine*. Applying the possessive transformation to "That's the book," and using **I + Pos**, we get _____ .

857

She + Pos is *her, hers*. Applying the possessive transformation to "The cat is sick" and using she + Pos, we get _____ .

858

What is I + Pos? _____ , _____

859

What is she + Pos? _____ , _____

860

What is he + Pos? _____

861

What actual sentence is represented by the formula do + past + John + find + I + Pos + book? _____

862

They + Pos is *their, theirs*. What actual sentence is represented by the formula they + Pos + books + be + present + on the desk? _____

863

You + Pos is *your, yours*. What actual sentence is represented by the formula this + be + present + you + Pos + desk? _____

864

What is they + Pos? _____ , _____

865

What is she + Pos? _____ , _____

866

What is you + Pos? _____ , _____

MORE POSSESSIVES

867

We + Pos is *our, ours*. Applying the possessive transformation to "We sold the car," and using **we + Pos**, we get _____.

868

It + Pos is *its*. What sentence is represented by the string **be + present + this + it + Pos + cover**? _____

869

For the pronouns *I, she, they, you,* and *we,* we have shown two different possessive forms: *my* and *mine, her* and *hers, their* and *theirs, your* and *yours, our* and *ours*. The second forms are used when the noun following **NP + Pos** is omitted. What word could be omitted from the sentence "This is John's book"? _____

870

We have already encountered, briefly, the process of omission, or deletion, in sentence formation. What word could be omitted from the sentence "This coat looks good"? _____

871

The transformation that omits or deletes items in sentences is very common and important in the grammars of all languages. We will call it **T-del,** where **del** stands for *deletion*. We get "This is John's" from "This is John's book" by T- _____ .

872

By **T-del,** "This pie tastes good" becomes _____ .

873

The word *this* is a case of **the + D₁**. We can state a rule that **the + D₁ + N** becomes, optionally, **the + D₁ + Ø**, by T-del. By this rule "I'll take this coat" would become _____ .

874

Could we have the rule **the + N ⇒ the + Ø** by **T-del**? _____

154 ENGLISH SYNTAX

875

Such a rule would convert "I'll take the coat" to the ungrammatical *"I'll take the." Obviously not just anything can be deleted from a sentence, though a great many structures can. Could we have the rule **NP + Pos + N ⟹ NP + Pos + Ø** by **T-del**? _____

876

If you answered "No" to 875, it shouldn't be held against you, because you may have been seeing unexpectedly far into the problem. Actually, the rule **NP + Pos + N ⟹ NP + Pos + Ø** is valid, though there is a complication. What words in the sentence "I took John's book" represent the sequence **NP + Pos + N**? _____

877

NP + Pos + N ⟹ NP + Pos + Ø applied to "I took John's book" gives _____ .

878

What words in the sentence "John took my book" are a case of **NP + Pos + N**? _____

879

The word *my* is composed of **I + Pos** and therefore is a case of **NP + Pos**. So *my book* is a case of **NP + Pos + N**. If we apply **NP + Pos + N ⟹ NP + Pos + Ø** to the string **John + past + take + I + Pos + book**, we get **John + past + take +** _____ **+** _____ **+** _____ .

880

The sentence *"John took my" is of course ungrammatical. But we don't have *my* at the end of this sentence. We have *my* (that is, **I + Pos**) plus **Ø**. We then have the phonological rule **my + Ø → mine**. Therefore the string **John + past + take + I + Pos + Ø** will give, after **T-af**, the actual sentence _____ .

881

Similarly, we have the phonological rules **her + Ø → hers; their + Ø → theirs; our + Ø → ours**. What do you suppose **your + Ø** is? _____

MORE POSSESSIVES 155

882

With these rules, **T-del** applied to "Her dress cost forty dollars" will give the sentence _____ .

883

Only the personal pronouns *I, she, we, they,* and *you* have two possessive forms and require the special rules involving Ø. Ø has no effect on other possessive noun phrases. **T-del** applied to "I borrowed the teacher's motorcycle" gives _____ .

884

Apply the possessive transformation to "I borrowed the book," using **the brother + Pos.** _____

885

The possessive transformation can be applied to a *the* in any base string, not just in a K-terminal string. Apply it to "I borrowed the brother's book," using **the friend + Pos.** _____

_____

886

Now apply the possessive transformation to "I borrowed the friend's brother's book," using **I + Pos.** _____

_____

887

In "I borrowed my friend's brother's book," the possessive transformation has been applied three times. We cannot apply it a fourth time, because the last transformation did not put in another _____ .

888

Apply **T-del** to "I borrowed my friend's brother's book." _____

_____

889

Apply the possessive transformation to "Samuel bought the car," using **someone + Pos.** _____

890

There is a *wh* transformation that can be applied to any sentence containing **someone + Pos**. It is **X + someone + Pos + N + Y ⟹ whose + N + X + Y**. Here, as usual, **X** and **Y** stand for anything or _____.

891

Suppose we take "Samuel bought someone's car." The formula would be **Samuel + past + buy + someone + Pos + car**. This contains the sequence **someone + Pos + N**. The **N** of this sequence is _____.

892

Before any *wh* transformation can be applied, the *yes/no* transformation must first be applied. **T-yes/no**, applied to **Samuel + past + buy + someone + Pos + car** gives _____ + _____ + _____ + _____ + _____ + _____.

893

Now apply the *wh* possessive transformation (**T-wh-pos**) to **past + Samuel + buy + someone + Pos + car**. **T-wh-pos** is **X + someone + Pos + N + Y ⟹ whose + N + X + Y**. (Note that here **Y** is nothing.) _____ + _____ + _____ + _____ + _____

894

Is there another transformation that must be applied to **whose + car + past + Samuel + buy?** _____

895

The string **whose + car + past + Samuel + buy** contains a floating tense, so **T-do** must be applied. *Past* becomes **do + past**. When this is done, we have a **T-terminal** string representing the actual sentence _____.

896

Suppose we start with "Someone's uncle bought the car." **T-yes/no** gives us **past + someone + Pos + uncle + buy + the + car**. This also contains a sequence **someone + Pos + N**. The **N** of the sequence is _____.

MORE POSSESSIVES 157

897

Applying T-wh-pos (X + someone + Pos + N + Y ⇒ whose + N + X + Y) to past + someone + Pos + uncle + buy + the + car, where X is past and Y is buy + the + car, we get _____ + _____ + _____ + _____ + _____ + _____ .

898

One transformation must be applied to whose + uncle + past + buy + the + car. This is T-af. This gives us whose + _____ + _____ + _____ + _____ + _____ .

899

Whose + uncle + buy + past + the + car represents the actual sentence _____ .

900

The important thing to notice about these transformations is their close relationship to one another and to the kernel. Of course, we do not talk in formulas or consciously go through the steps indicated in forming sentences. But the fact that so much of English can be reduced to formulas which can be mechanically applied to produce sentences cannot be some kind of accident or coincidence. It shows that the grammar of English is not a set of unconnected facts but a tight mechanism in which all the parts work together to produce the whole.

MAIN POINTS OF LESSON EIGHTEEN

There is a general deletion transformation in the grammar, **T-del**, which permits various structures to be omitted in sentences and the sentences to be produced in shorter forms. Thus a noun following a demonstrative can be omitted: "That coat looks nice" ⇒ "That looks nice." Traditionally, one would say that in this case the noun is "understood."

The noun following **NP + Pos** can be omitted by **T-del**. "This is John's car" ⇒ "This is John's." Strictly speaking, however, anything deleted by **T-del** is not simply left out but is replaced by ∅. John + Pos + car ⇒ John + Pos + ∅. Usually ∅ will mean that nothing is pronounced in

158   ENGLISH SYNTAX

this position. Sometimes, however, Ø becomes a functioning unit in later rules. Thus my + car ⇒ my + Ø. Then, by a phonological rule my + Ø → mine. Similarly, her + Ø → hers; their + Ø → theirs; our + Ø → ours; your + Ø → yours.

The possessive transformation can be repeated indefinitely many times, so long as each application of the transformation puts in another definite article for NP + Pos to replace: the son ⇒ the brother's son ⇒ the friend's brother's son ⇒ my friend's brother's son.

T-wh-pos: X + someone + Pos + N + Y ⇒ whose + N + X + Y. Thus, "Alice took someone's book" ⇒ "Whose book did Alice take?" Then, by T-del, we can have "Whose did Alice take?"

Lesson Nineteen
VI and VT

In all the examples we have had so far, **T-del,** the deletion transformation, has been optional. Both "This dress is pretty" and "This is pretty" are grammatical English sentences. There are many cases, however, in which **T-del** is obligatory. For example, the kernel and transformation rules we have studied would permit us to generate the sentence *"This dress is Alice's dress." This sentence, however, is ungrammatical. When in such a sentence the two **N**'s are identical, one or the other or both must be deleted to give "This dress is Alice's," "This is Alice's dress," or "This is Alice's." We say that for such a construction **T-del** is obligatory.

In the discussion of verbals, we said that **VT** contained several complications that could not yet be explained. Now that we have become familiar with various types of transformation rules, we are in a position to return to **VT** and see what some of these complications are.

901

You will remember that we rewrote verbal in this fashion:

$$\text{verbal} \rightarrow \left\{ \begin{matrix} \text{VI} \\ \text{VT + NP} \\ \text{Vb + substantive} \\ \text{Vs + Adj} \\ \text{Vh + NP} \end{matrix} \right\} + \text{(Adv-m)} $$

Here **VI** stands for _____ verb.

902

We used capital **I** and **T** for intransitive and transitive verbs because these classes must be subdivided further. There are several subclasses. The simplest kind of **VI**'s are those intransitive verbs which are followed by nothing or by an adverbial of manner: "He laughed," "He slept," "He wept quietly." We will call these verbs Vi_1. In "David relaxed," *relax* is a **VI** of the subtype **V**____ .

---

160   ENGLISH SYNTAX

903

Many intransitive verbs, however, are followed by something other than an adverb of manner. For example, we do not ordinarily say *"He glanced" but "He glanced up" or "He glanced out." Here, *up* and *out* belong to a class of words called *particles*. What is the particle in "He sat down"? _____

904

What is the particle in "He walked in"? _____

905

We will give intransitive verbs followed by particles the designation Vi_2. We then rewrite **VI** as follows:

$$VI \rightarrow \begin{Bmatrix} Vi_1 \\ Vi_2 + Prt \end{Bmatrix}$$

The abbreviation **Prt** stands for the word _____ .

906

Some **VI**'s require some structure other than a particle to complete their meaning. For example, we don't say *"He relied," but "He relied on the evidence" or "He relied on Tom." We will call structures which complete meanings in this way *complements*. After **VI**'s, complements are generally prepositional phrases of some sort. What is the complement in "It lasted for an hour"? _____

907

We now add a third group of **VI**'s:

$$VI \rightarrow \begin{Bmatrix} Vi_1 \\ Vi_2 + Prt \\ Vi_3 + Comp \end{Bmatrix}$$

The abbreviation **Comp** stands for _____ .

908

Many intransitive verbs will occur in two of these groups or all three: "He walked" (Vi_1), "He walked away" (Vi_2), "He walked to the beach" (Vi_3). However, there is not complete freedom of occurrence. *Glance* does not occur as Vi_1; *laugh* does not occur as Vi_2. In "He gnawed at the bone," the verb is a Vi___ .

909

In "Several of the fellows dropped in," the verb is a Vi____ .

910

VT can be subdivided in a parallel way. All VT's are followed by an ____ which functions as the _____ .

911

A VT construction can have (1) nothing between the verb and the NP, (2) a particle between them, (3) a complement between them. Thus we can rewrite VT as we rewrote VI:

$$VT \rightarrow \begin{Bmatrix} Vt_1 \\ Vt_2 + Prt \\ Vt_3 + Comp \end{Bmatrix}$$

Since these are all VT's, each must be followed by a noun phrase. We have already had many examples of the Vt_1 construction—*see the car, find the book,* etc. In the sentence "Mary cleaned out the desk," we have an example of Vt_2. Here the Vt_2 is the verb *clean*. The particle is the word _____ .

912

In "Henry put away the newspaper," the Vt_2 is _____ , the particle is _____ , and the VT is _____ .

913

Notice that in "Henry put away the newspaper," *the newspaper* is not the object of *put*. *"Henry put the newspaper" is ungrammatical. The VT is not *put* but *put away*. Notice that both "Henry put away the newspaper" and "Henry put the newspaper away" are grammatical sentences. If the formula for the first is NP + Aux + Vt_2 + Prt + NP, the formula for the second is NP + Aux + ____ + ____ + ____ .

914

The kernel rule for VT is

$$VT \rightarrow \begin{Bmatrix} Vt_1 \\ Vt_2 + Prt \\ Vt_3 + Comp \end{Bmatrix}$$

Does this rule describe the structure of (1) "Henry put away the newspaper" or (2) "Henry put the newspaper away"? ____

915

Therefore "Henry put away the newspaper" is a kernel sentence, whereas "Henry put the newspaper away" is a transform. We can say that, given a K-terminal string containing a Vt_2, we can optionally transpose the following particle and object, putting the object first and the particle second. We might express this change in this way: Vt_2 + Prt + NP $\Rightarrow$ ___ + ___ + ___ .

916

Let us call this transformation T-VT. For the present we will describe T-VT as the transposition of some part of a VT and a following object. For the K-terminal string John + past + take + off + the + coat, is T-VT optional or obligatory? _____

917

Which of the following sentences is *not* grammatical: (1) "John put away the books." (2) "John put the books away." (3) "John put away them." (4) "John put them away"? ____

918

In the base string John + past + put + away + them, the NP which functions as object of the VT *put away* is a _____ pronoun.

919

The sentences *"John put away them," *"John looked up him," *"John took off it" are all ungrammatical, whereas "John put them away," "John looked him up," "John took it off" are all grammatical. When the NP following Vt_2 + Prt is a personal pronoun, is T-VT optional or obligatory? _____

920

For the sequence Vt_2 + Prt + NP, T-VT is optional unless the NP is a personal pronoun. If the NP is a personal pronoun, T-VT is obligatory. By T-VT, the string John + past + hang + up + it must become John + past + _____ + _____ + _____ .

VI AND VT   163

921

For a Vt₂ construction, T-VT is optional unless the object is a _____ _____ .

922

$$VI \rightarrow \begin{Bmatrix} Vi_1 \\ Vi_2 + Prt \\ Vi_3 + Comp \end{Bmatrix} \qquad VT \rightarrow \begin{Bmatrix} Vt_1 \\ Vt_2 + Prt \\ Vt_3 + Comp \end{Bmatrix}$$

The possibilities for transitive verbs parallel those for intransitive verbs. The difference is that VT's are followed by objects and VI's are not. Both VT's and VI's may include complements. In "He fled to Chicago," *flee* is a Vi₃. The prepositional phrase *to Chicago* is a _____ .

923

Now consider the sentence "He sent to Chicago the painting that he had discovered in Germany." Here the object is the noun phrase *the painting that he had discovered in Germany*, a noun phrase expanded in ways we have not yet described. The prepositional phrase *to Chicago* is a complement, as it is in "He fled to Chicago." The verb *send* is a Vt ____ .

924

In "He dropped in the box a letter that he would later regret very much," the object is the noun phrase *a letter that he would later regret very much*. The verb *drop* is here a Vt₃. The complement is the prepositional phrase _____ .

925

T-VT can be applied optionally to such sentences as "He sent to Chicago the painting that he had discovered in Germany," reversing the complement and the object. That is, "He sent the painting that he had discovered in Germany to Chicago" is also grammatical. If we apply the same transformation to "He dropped in the box a letter that he would later regret very much," we get the sentence _____ _____ .

926

However, T-VT is optional for the structure Vt₃ + Comp + NP only when the NP is expanded and long, as in the examples we have taken. When the **NP** is short, **T-VT** is obligatory. That is, the **Comp** and **NP** must be reversed. Which of the following sentences is grammatical: (1) "He sent to Chicago the painting." (2) "He sent the painting to Chicago"? ____

927

The kernel string **he sent + to Chicago + the painting** must be changed by **T-VT** to **he sent + the painting + to Chicago**. **He dropped + in the box + the letter** must be changed to **he dropped +** _____ **+** _____ .

928

We can write **T-VT** as follows:
$$Vt_2 + Prt + NP \Rightarrow Vt_2 + NP + Prt$$
$$Vt_3 + Comp + NP \Rightarrow Vt_3 + NP + Comp$$

The particle or complement of the **VT** reverses with the object. For the particle construction, this is obligatory when the object is a _____ pronoun.

929

For the construction $Vt_3 +$ **Comp + NP**, the transformation **T-VT** is optional when the **NP** is expanded in certain ways and long. When the **NP** is unexpanded, the transformation is obligatory. The string **he left + on the piano + his hat** must become **he left +** _____ **+** _____ .

930

So far, the complements after Vi_3 and Vt_3 in our examples have all been adverbial prepositional phrases: *to Chicago, in the box, on the piano*. Structures of other types can occur as complements after Vt_3. In "He thought a fool anyone who disagreed with him," *think* is a Vt_3, and the object is *anyone who disagreed with him*. The complement is the noun phrase _____ .

931

In "He thought a fool anyone who disagreed with him," *anyone who disagreed with him* is not the object of the Vt_3 *think*. *"He thought anyone who disagreed with him" is ungrammatical. It is the object of the **VT**—

VI AND VT   165

that is, of *think* plus its complement, *a fool*. Which of the following is *not* grammatical: (1) "He thought a fool anyone who disagreed with him." (2) "He thought anyone who disagreed with him a fool." (3) "He thought a fool Sam." (4) "He thought Sam a fool"? ____

932

There is nothing new here. When the NP of Vt₃ + Comp + NP is expanded in certain ways and long, T-VT is optional; when it is short, T-VT is obligatory. The string **we considered + a hero + Morris** must become **we considered +** _____ **+** _____ .

933

In "We considered Morris a hero," the object is *Morris*. The complement is _____ .

934

In "I believed Sally my friend," the object is _____ , and the complement is _____ .

935

In "He sent the painting to Chicago," the object is _____ , and the complement is _____ .

936

The structure of "I believed Sally my friend" is a bit more complicated than that of "He sent the painting to Chicago." There is only one base string underlying the second sentence, but there are two underlying the first. Take the sentences "Sam is a fool" and "John considers Sam a fool." Both sentences contain the noun phrases _____ and _____ .

937

"John considers Sam a fool" is a case of NP + Aux + Vt₃ + NP + Comp. T-VT, reversing the Comp and the NP, has been obligatorily applied. The object in this sentence is *Sam,* and the complement is _____ .

166   ENGLISH SYNTAX

938

"Sam is a fool" has the K-terminal string **Sam + present + be + a + fool**. The subject of such a string may become the **NP** object of the string **NP + Aux + Vt₃ + Comp + NP**. Then the substantive following *be*—in this case the noun phrase *a fool*—becomes the _____ .

939

This is what we call a *double-base transformation,* because there are two underlying, or base, strings. For "John considers Sam a fool," one base string is **John + present + consider + Comp + Sam**. The other is **Sam + present + be + a + fool**. The noun phrase *a fool* will become the complement of the first string. The subject _____ will become the **NP** object.

940

If "John considers Sam a fool" contains the underlying sentence "Sam is a fool," "They think Edith beautiful" has the underlying sentence

_____ .

941

A double-base transformation involves two underlying strings. One is the *matrix* string, which contains the form of the sentence to be produced. The other is the *insert* string, which contains structures to be inserted in the matrix string. For "They think Edith beautiful," **they + present + think + Comp + Edith** is the matrix string. **Edith + present + be + beautiful** is the _____ string.

942

The adjective *beautiful* of the insert string becomes the **Comp** of the matrix string. This gives **they + present + think + beautiful + Edith**. This contains all the elements of "They think Edith beautiful" but not in the right order. Since the object, *Edith,* is not expanded, the transformation T- _____ is obligatory.

943

They + present + think + beautiful + Edith becomes **they + present + think + Edith + beautiful** by **T-VT** and, after **T-af**, the sentence "They think Edith beautiful." After all transformations have been performed, the matrix string **the + judge + past + suppose + Comp + George** and the insert string **George + past + be + innocent** will yield the sentence _____ .

944

$$VI \rightarrow \begin{Bmatrix} Vi_1 \\ Vi_2 + Prt \\ Vi_3 + Comp \end{Bmatrix} \quad VT \rightarrow \begin{Bmatrix} Vt_1 \\ Vt_2 + Prt \\ Vt_3 + Comp \end{Bmatrix}$$

Both transitive and intransitive verbs may have particles or complements. What must follow every **VT**? _____

945

Any **VT** must have a noun phrase as its object. We have such **VT**'s as *see, hit* (Vt_1); *put away, take off* (Vt_2); *send to Chicago, consider a fool, believe innocent* (Vt_3). What is the **VT** in **he + past + clean + up + it**? _____

946

What is the **VT** in **he + past + recover + some of the money**? _____
_____

947

What is the **VT** in **I + past + find + attractive + Sally**? _____
_____

948

By **T-VT**, "I found attractive Sally" must become _____
_____ .

949

By **T-VT**, "He cleaned up it" must become _____ .

950

We have studied the structure of sentences of the type "John considered Sam a fool" in some technical detail, because the processes that form it are common and important in grammar. In the next section we will look briefly at some structures related to this one.

168   ENGLISH SYNTAX

MAIN POINTS OF LESSON NINETEEN

$$VI \rightarrow \begin{Bmatrix} Vi_1 \\ Vi_2 + Prt \\ Vi_3 + Comp \end{Bmatrix} \qquad VT \rightarrow \begin{Bmatrix} Vt_1 \\ Vt_2 + Prt \\ Vt_3 + Comp \end{Bmatrix}$$

The subclassifications of transitive and intransitive verbs are parallel. The terms **VI** and **VT** refer to structures in which verbs are followed by particles or complements as well as to structures with verbs alone.

Particles are words like *in, up, out, down, on, off*. Some of these forms (not all) appear also as prepositions.

Complements are structures other than particles which complete the meaning of certain intransitive and transitive verbs. These structures may be of several different kinds. Those that occur with intransitive verbs are generally adverbials. We have illustrated prepositional phrases in this function: *rely on the evidence, walk to the beach*. Simple adverbs of certain types can also occur as complements, as *home* in *stay home*. Adverbials of manner, time, and frequency are not considered complements, however, since they do not complete the meaning of verbs; verbs do not depend on them in any way for their essential meanings.

The complement following a Vt_3 may also be an adverbial: *send-to-Chicago the painting*. However, substantives (noun phrases or adjectives) occur as complements also: *consider-a-fool Sam, consider-foolish Sam*. Substantives occurring as complements derive from kernel sentences with *be:* "Sam is a fool," "Sam is foolish." A sentence like "John considered Sam a fool" is therefore formed by a double-base transformation, one with two underlying strings: the matrix string, **John + Aux + consider + Comp + Sam**, and the insert string, **Sam + Aux + be + a + fool**. The matrix string contains the form of the final sentence; the insert string contains material to be inserted in it.

T-VT: Vt_2 + Prt + NP $\Rightarrow$ Vt_2 + NP + Prt
Vt_3 + Comp + NP $\Rightarrow$ Vt_3 + NP + Comp

In certain structures the particle or complement of a **VT** must reverse with the following **NP** object. **T-VT** is obligatory for Vt_2 + **Prt** + **NP** when the **NP** is a personal pronoun; otherwise it is optional. It is optional for Vt_3 + **Comp** + **NP** when the **NP** is expanded in certain ways and long; otherwise it is obligatory.

Lesson Twenty

OTHER VARIETIES OF Vt₃

You may have noticed that part of Lesson Nineteen overlaps the earlier discussion of adverbials. In Lesson Eleven adverbials were illustrated in a general way as occurring in various parts of the verb phrase. Now we see some of these filling the specific function of complements of intransitive and transitive verbs. Not all adverbials occur as complements, however. Adverbials of manner, frequency, and time do not; these add to the meaning of the verb phrase without in any sense completing the meaning of the verb. The adverbials that occur as complements are those of place *(stay in the house)*, direction *(send to Chicago)*, duration *(last for an hour)*, and various others *(rely on the evidence, champ at the bit)*.

There are some sentences in which both a particle and a complement occur in the same **VI** or **VT**. An example for **VI** is *glance up at the clock*, in which *up* is the particle and *at the clock* is the complement. An example for **VT** is *put through the call to Chicago*, in which *through* is the particle, *to Chicago* is the complement, and *the call* is the object. However, the rewrites of **VI** and **VT** given here would not allow for these expressions. A complete grammar would have to revise the rules so as to include them. The best way of doing so is not perfectly clear at the present time.

951

We say that a sentence like "We believed Ellen attractive" is a transform with two underlying strings. One is the matrix string, and one is the insert string. The matrix string provides the general form of the sentence, and the insert string fills it out. For this sentence the insert string is

_____ + **Aux** + **be** + _____ .

952

"We believed Ellen attractive" has the underlying matrix string **we** + **past** + **believe** + **Comp** + **Ellen**. What is the underlying matrix string

170 ENGLISH SYNTAX

of "He thought Sam a patriot"? _____ + _____ + _____ + _____ + _____

953

For the matrix **he + past + think + Comp + Sam,** the insert sentence "Sam was a patriot" replaces the **Comp** with the noun phrase _____.

954

This gives us **he + past + think + a patriot   Sam.** What is the **Vt₃** of this string? _____

955

What is the **VT** of **he + past + think + a patriot + Sam?** _____

956

What is the object of **he + past + think + a patriot + Sam?** _____

957

The sentence *"He thought a patriot Sam" is of course ungrammatical. Given the string **he + past + think + a patriot + Sam,** we must apply the transformation **T-VT.** This gives us _____ + _____ + _____ + _____ + _____.

958

It might be thought simpler to put *Sam* and *a patriot* in their right places at once from the insert string. However, this would complicate the rewrite of **VT** as well as making much trouble in other parts of the grammar. (When one thinks one perceives a simpler way of describing a grammatical construction, it is often profitable to try to work it out. If it really does prove simpler, a new insight into the structure of the language will have been obtained.) The string **he + past + think + Sam + a patriot** contains a sequence of **Af + v.** Therefore, **T-af** must be applied to give **he +** _____ + _____ + _____ + _____ .

959

Now take the sentence "They elected Sally chairman." If *Sam* is the object in "He thought Sam a patriot," what is the object in "They elected Sally chairman"? _____

960

If *a patriot* is the complement of "He thought Sam a patriot," what is the complement of "They elected Sally chairman"? _____

961

If *think a patriot* is the **VT** of "He thought Sam a patriot," what is the **VT** of "They elected Sally chairman"? _____

962

If the underlying insert string of "He thought Sam a patriot" is **Sam + Aux + be + a patriot,** what is the underlying insert string of "They elected Sally chairman"? _____ + ___ + ___ + _____

963

If the underlying matrix string of "He thought Sam a patriot" is **he + past + think + Comp + Sam,** what is the underlying matrix string of "They elected Sally chairman"? _____ + _____ + _____ + _____ + _____

964

Which of the following sentences is ungrammatical: (1) "He thought Sam a patriot." (2) "He thought Sam patriotic." (3) "They elected Sally chairman." (4) "They elected Sally attractive"? ___

965

The word *patriotic* is an adjective. *A patriot* and *chairman* are noun phrases. What is *attractive*? _____

966

What is the term that includes both **NP** and **Adj**? _____

172   ENGLISH SYNTAX

967

Vt₃'s of the type *consider* or *think* and Vt₃'s of the type *elect* are very similar. Both are followed by a **Comp,** with which they make up a **VT,** and then an object. However, the **Comp** that follows a Vt₃ like *consider* or *think* is a substantive. That is, it can be either an **NP** or an adjective. The **Comp** that follows a Vt₃ like *elect* can only be a _____ .

968

"We chose Tom our spokesman" is grammatical. *"We chose Tom polite" is ungrammatical. Is *choose* like *consider* or like *elect?* _____

969

"We found Tom an angel" and "We found Tom angelic" are both grammatical. Is *find* like *consider* or like *elect?* _____

970

Vt₃'s of the type *consider* are followed by complements which may be either _____ or _____ .

971

We could easily distinguish these types of Vt₃'s by some such notation as Vt₃₋c (*consider* type) and Vt₃₋e (*elect* type). But we wouldn't use the notation often enough to make it worthwhile. The insert string for "They elected Sam president" is _____ + **Aux** + **be** + _____ .

972

Notice that there is no such grammatical sentence as *"They elected Sam leadership," because there is no such insert sentence as *"Sam is leadership." In "They elected Sam president," the **Comp** of Vt₃ + **Comp** + **NP** is _____ , and the **NP** object is _____ .

973

We have encountered such **VT**'s as *see, clean up, send to Chicago, consider a fool, elect president.* The first verb is a Vt₁, the second a Vt₂, and the others are Vt₃'s. What is the Vt₃ in the sentence "He put it in the corner"?

OTHER VARIETIES OF Vt₃   **173**

974

The sentence "He put it in the corner" has the underlying structure "He put in the corner it." This consists of **NP + Aux + Vt₃ + Comp + NP**. The **NP** object is *it*. What is the complement? _____

975

What words make up the **VT** in "He put it in the corner"? _____

976

The prepositional phrase *in the corner* is an adverbial of place. The abbreviation for adverbial of place is _____ .

977

The rewrite of verb phrase contains two possibilities after *be*. One is *substantive*. The other is _____ .

978

The sentence "It is in the corner" is a case of **NP + Aux + be +** _____ .

979

Kernel sentences with **be + Adv-p** like "It is in the corner" can be considered insert sentences for transforms like "He put it in the corner." What is the **Adv-p** in "He left there the pencil"? _____

980

"He left there the pencil" is a case of **NP + Aux + Vt₃ + Comp + NP**. In this sentence the **Comp** is the word _____ .

981

In "He left there the pencil," the object is the noun phrase _____ .

982

Is the sentence "He left there the pencil" grammatical? ____

174   ENGLISH SYNTAX

983

The string he + past + leave + there + the pencil must be transformed, by T-VT, into _____ + _____ + _____ + _____ + _____ .

984

T-VT is obligatory for most sequences of Vt_3 + Comp + NP. The exceptions are those structures in which the object is long and complicated, like "He left in the drawer the pencil that his Aunt Mary had given him for Christmas." The sequence he + past + find + in the drawer + a ruby must be changed, by T-VT, to he + _____ + _____ + _____ + _____ .

We find, then, that the complement that follows a Vt_3 can be a substantive, just a noun phrase, or an adverbial of place. All of these derive from insert sentences with *be*. Not all adverbials derive in this way, however. The adverbial *to Chicago* in "He sent the painting to Chicago" does not derive from *"The painting is to Chicago." This sentence is a single-base transform, whereas our other examples are double-base transforms.

985

We have not exhausted the varieties of Comp. What is the Vt_3 in "He regarded the question as stupid"? _____

986

The sentence "He regarded the question as stupid" has the base form he + past + regard + Comp + the question. If the object is *the question*, what must the Comp be? _____

987

The sentence "He regarded the question as stupid" is a transform of he + past + regard + as stupid + the question. The Vt_3 is *regard*. The object is *the question*. The Comp is *as stupid*. The VT is _____ .

988

He + past + regard + as stupid + the question derives from the matrix string he + past + regard + Comp + the question and the insert string the question + Aux + be + stupid. One word occurs in the result that doesn't occur in either of the base strings. What is it? ___

989

This transformation is slightly different from the ones we have been considering, because it adds something that is in neither of the base strings. The transformation inserts the substantive *stupid* preceded by the word *as* as the _____ of the matrix string.

990

After all transformations have been applied, we + past + reject + Comp + the plan and the plan + Aux + be + dangerous will yield as a result the sentence _____ .

991

In this transformation, was the matrix string (1) we + past + reject + Comp + the plan or (2) the plan + Aux + be + dangerous? ____

992

The sentence *"We rejected as dangerous the plan" is not wholly grammatical. To make it grammatical, we must apply to the underlying string T- ____ .

993

Apply **T-VT** to we + past + reject + as dangerous + the plan. _____ + _____ + _____ + _____ + _____

994

Apply **T-af** to we + past + reject + the plan + as dangerous. _____ + _____ + _____ + _____ + _____

995

The string we + reject + past + the plan + as dangerous is a T-terminal string. There are no more transformation rules to apply to it. This string represents the sentence _____ .

996

In "We rejected the plan as dangerous," what is the **Vt₃**? _____

997

In "We rejected the plan as dangerous," what NP functions as object?

_____

998

In "We rejected the plan as dangerous," what is the VT? _____

_____

999

Which of the following is not a possible **VT**: (1) *put away,* (2) *consider a friend,* (3) *elect president,* (4) *believe innocent,* (5) *see the dog,* (6) *regard as incompetent?* _____

1000

A **VT** is a structure in the verb phrase that takes an object. The **VT** may be a verb alone, a verb plus a particle, or a verb plus a complement. The complement may be a substantive, just a noun phrase, an adverbial, or *as* plus an adjective, depending on the kind of **Vt₃**. There are other possibilities also, but we shall not try to list them all.

MAIN POINTS OF LESSON TWENTY

$$VT \rightarrow \begin{Bmatrix} Vt_1 \\ Vt_2 + Prt \\ Vt_3 + Comp \end{Bmatrix}$$

A **VT** may be a simple transitive verb (like *see* or *buy*), a verb followed by a particle (*look up, put on*), or a verb followed by a complement.

Complement includes the various types of structures that follow the types of **Vt₃**'s. We may have a substantive (*consider a patriot/patriotic*), a noun phrase (*elect president*), an adjective preceded by *as* (*regard as incompetent*), an adverbial (*leave in the drawer*). A more complete grammar would subdivide the **Vt₃** class on the basis of these different kinds of complements: **Vt₃₋c** (*consider*), **Vt₃₋e** (*elect*), **Vt₃₋r** (*regard*), etc. Some of these subcategories would contain quite a few verbs, others very few.

By T-VT, **Vt₃** + Comp + NP ⟹ **Vt₃** + NP + Comp. This is obligatory except when the **NP** is long and complicated. *"He regarded as insolent John" is ungrammatical. However, "He regarded as insolent anyone who ventured to disagree with him" is grammatical. **T-VT** is obligatory for the first sentence, optional for the second.

OTHER VARIETIES OF Vt₃   177

Lesson Twenty-One
Vt_{to} and Vt_{ing}

The insert strings for the Vt_3 constructions we have been studying represent sentences with *be*.

RESULT SENTENCES	INSERT SENTENCES
We considered John foolish.	John was foolish.
We thought John a hero.	John was a hero.
We elected John president.	John was president.
We left John there.	John was there.
We regarded John as innocent.	John was innocent.

It is not true, however, that all sequences of **Comp + NP** derive from insert sentences with *be*. Some do not derive from insert sentences at all; these are single-base transforms, as in "He sent the painting to Chicago." Others derive from insert sentences with *be* or any kind of verbal.

1001

Consider the sentences "I persuaded John to come" and "John came." Both sentences contain the intransitive verb _____ .

1002

The sentence "I persuaded John to come" and "John came" both contain the noun phrase _____ .

1003

The sentence "I persuaded John to come" has embedded in it the insert sentence _____ .

---

178 ENGLISH SYNTAX

1004

The sentences "I asked John to close the door" and "John closed the door" both contain the verb _____ and the noun phrases _____ and _____ .

1005

The sentence "I asked John to close the door" has embedded in it the insert sentence _____ .

1006

The sentence "I wanted John to become my friend" has embedded in it the insert sentence _____ .

1007

The sentence "I wanted John to be a man" has embedded in it the insert sentence _____ .

1008

The sentence "I forced John to look cheerful" has embedded in it the insert sentence _____ .

1009

The sentence "I persuaded the class to elect me treasurer" has two insert sentences embedded in it. One is "I was treasurer." The other is _____ _____ .

1010

The verbs *persuade, want, force* belong to a class that we will designate as Vt_{to}. What is the Vt_{to} in "I urged John to study the matter carefully"?

_____

1011

What is the Vt_{to} in "He told me to pick up the pieces"? _____

1012

What is the Vt_{to} in "They notified us to come at once"? _____

1013

Say that the string I + Aux + persuade + to + go + John represents the sentence "I persuaded John to go." What string would then represent "He urged Sam to come"? _____ + _____ + ___ ___ + _____ + _____ + _____

1014

I + Aux + persuade + to + go + John is a VT construction. The VT is persuade + to + go. What is the VT of he + Aux + urge + to + come + Sam? _____ + _____ + _____

1015

The VT of I + Aux + persuade + to + go + John consists of Vt_{to} + Comp. The Vt_{to} is *persuade*. The complement is *to go*. What is the complement of he + Aux + urge + to + come + Sam? _____

1016

The Comp + NP of "I persuaded John to go" is to go + John. What is the Comp + NP of "He urged Sam to come"? _____ + _____

1017

The sentence "I persuaded John to go" has embedded in it the insert sentence "John went." "He urged Sam to come" has embedded in it the insert sentence _____ .

1018

The transformation that produces sentences with Vt_{to}'s is very similar to that for Vt_3's. Take "He urged Sam to come." This derives from two strings: he + Aux + urge + Comp + Sam and Sam + Aux + come. The first is the _____ string, and the second is the _____ string.

1019

Then the last element in the insert string, preceded by the word *to*, replaces the symbol ___ in the matrix string.

1020

Thus he + past + urge + Comp + Sam and Sam + Aux + come give
he + past + _____ + _____ + _____ + _____ .

1021

Is "He urged to come Sam" grammatical? _____

1022

To the string he + past + urge + to come + Sam, the transformation **T-VT** must be applied, to reverse the complement *to come* and the object *Sam*. This gives he + past + _____ + _____ + _____ .

1023

He + past + urge + Sam + to come contains a sequence of Af + v, so **T-af** must be applied. This gives _____ + _____ + _____ + _____ + _____ .

1024

The base strings I + past + tell + Comp + Alice and Alice + Aux + cut the lawn will give the result string I + past + _____ + _____ + _____ + _____ .

1025

What is the VT in I + past + tell + to + cut the lawn + Alice?

_____

1026

After **T-VT** and **T-af**, I + past + tell + to + cut the lawn + Alice will give the finished sentence _____ .

1027

Now consider the sentence "I found John studying." This has embedded in it the insert sentence "John studied." What insert sentence is embedded in "I caught Sam smoking"? _____

Vt$_{to}$ AND Vt$_{ing}$

1028

What insert sentence is embedded in "I heard the boys arguing"?

_____

1029

In these sentences, *find, catch, hear* belong to a class of verbs that we designate as Vt_{ing}. What is the Vt_{ing} in "I noticed someone creating a commotion"? _____

1030

The sentence "I noticed someone creating a commotion" has embedded in it the insert sentence _____.

1031

The transformation that produces "I noticed someone creating a commotion" or "I caught Sam smoking" is just the same as the one for Vt_{to}'s except that ing is inserted in place of *to*. The matrix I + past + catch + Comp + Sam and the insert Sam + Aux + smoke become I + past + catch + ing + smoke + Sam. We might say that the element ing replaces the element _____ of the insert sentence.

1032

When I + past + catch + Comp + Sam and Sam + Aux + smoke become I + past + catch + ing + smoke + Sam, the Aux of the insert sentence has been replaced by _____ .

1033

Henry + past + find + Comp + John and John + Aux + study give the string Henry + past + find + _____ + _____ + _____ .

1034

The string Henry + past + find + ing + study + John is a case of NP + Aux + Vt_{ing} + Comp + NP. The Vt_{ing} is *find*, and the object is *John*. What is the Comp? _____ + _____

182 ENGLISH SYNTAX

1035

What is the **VT** of **Henry + past + find + ing + study + John?**
_____ + _____ + _____

1036

Except when the object is long and complicated, **T-VT** is obligatory for any construction containing a **Comp**. The **Comp** and the following **NP** must be reversed. **T-VT** applied to **Henry + past + find + ing + study + John** gives **Henry + past +** _____ + _____ + _____ + _____ .

1037

Now look at the string **Henry + past + find + John + ing + study**. How many sequences of **Af + v** does it contain? _____

1038

Apply **T-af** to **Henry + past + find + John + ing + study.** _____ + _____ + _____ + _____ + _____ + _____

1039

Notice that we don't need any special rule here to reverse **ing** and **study**. **T-af** is already in the grammar, and it applies automatically. **Henry + find + past + John + study + ing** is the T-terminal string of the actual sentence _____ .

1040

One might ask why **ing** is not more simply inserted after the last element of the insert string. That would work for **John + Aux + study**, but not for **John + Aux + wash the car**, where it would give *wash the car + ing. **John + past + persuade + Comp + Ralph** and **Ralph + Aux + comb his hair** give **John + past +** _____ + _____ + _____ .

1041

Apply **T-VT** to **John + past + persuade + to comb his hair + Ralph**. **John + past +** _____ + _____ + _____ .

1042

Apply **T-af** to John + past + persuade + Ralph + to comb his hair. John + _____ + _____ + _____ + _____ .

1043

The word *to* is not an **Af**, so **T-af** does not apply to the sequence *to comb*. In "John persuaded Ralph to comb his hair," the verb *persuade* is a **Vt**____ .

1044

The base strings **someone** + **past** + **notice** + **Comp** + **Alice** and **Alice** + **Aux** + **eat candy** give **someone** + **past** + _____ + _____ + _____ + _____ .

1045

Apply **T-VT** to someone + past + notice + ing + eat candy + Alice. Someone + past + _____ + _____ + _____ + _____

1046

Apply **T-af** to someone + past + notice + Alice + ing + eat + candy. _____ + _____ + _____ + _____ + _____ + _____ + _____

1047

In the string underlying "Someone noticed Alice eating candy," the **VT** is _____ + ing + _____ .

1048

In the string underlying "I begged him to stop," the **VT** is _____ .

1049

Try this. In the string underlying "I begged him to stop trying to force me to take steps," the **Comp** which makes up a **VT** with *beg* is _____ .

184 ENGLISH SYNTAX

1050

Again we should remind ourselves that no one consciously goes through these steps in making sentences. The point is rather that a certain regularity underlies the sentences we have been considering: the parallelism between *to* and *ing*, between transitive and intransitive verbs with particle and complement, between the various types of complements in relation to objects. Even rather complicated sentences, like that in 1049, can be generated correctly and automatically from the rules given. This regularity must have a good deal to do with how we are able to create and understand English sentences.

MAIN POINTS OF LESSON TWENTY-ONE

$$VT \rightarrow \left\{ \begin{array}{l} Vt_1 \\ Vt_2 \\ Vt_3 \\ Vt_{to} \\ Vt_{ing} \end{array} \right. \left. \begin{array}{l} + \text{Prt} \\ \\ + \text{Comp} \end{array} \right\}$$

The subclasses of verbs Vt_{to} and Vt_{ing} are additional features of the general structure **VT**. Like the Vt_3's, these verbs are followed by complements. The complements after Vt_{to}'s and Vt_{ing}'s may be any verb phrase, with *to* or *ing* replacing the **Aux** of the insert string. The subject of the insert string is identical with the object of the **VT**.

When **ing** is inserted by this transformation in place of the **Aux** of the insert string, it automatically becomes a part of a sequence **Af + v**, since it will always precede a *be* or a verb from the insert string. Then **T-af** automatically applies. **T-af** does not apply to sequences with *to*, since *to* is not an **Af**.

Lesson Twenty-Two
THE PASSIVE TRANSFORMATION

Just as there are various subdivisions of **Vt₃** (**Vt₃₋c**, **Vt₃₋e**, etc.), so there are subdivisions of **Vt**$_\text{to}$ and **Vt**$_\text{ing}$. We shall just note a little of the complexity without trying to formulate it exactly.

We have seen that a sentence like "I persuaded John to go" derives from the matrix **I + persuaded + Comp + John** and the insert **John + went**. Suppose that the matrix and insert strings have the same subject, so that the **NP** subject and **NP** object of the result sentence refer to the same person: **I + persuaded + Comp + me and I + went**. The rules we have given would then produce the ungrammatical sentence *"I persuaded me to go." In this case, where the base strings have the same subject, there is an additional rule which makes the **NP** object of **NP + Aux + VT + NP** a *reflexive pronoun*. A reflexive pronoun is a personal pronoun with the suffix *-self: myself, yourself, yourselves, himself, herself, itself, ourselves, themselves*. Thus, from **I persuaded + Comp + me and I went**, we get **I persuaded to go me → I persuaded me to go → I persuaded myself to go. John told to forget it John → John told John to forget it → John told himself to forget it.** This is a general rule for objects, accounting also for "He hurt himself," "I was boring myself," and so forth.

If we compare the verb *persuade* with the verb *expect* we find that they are similar but that they differ when the subject refers to the same person as the object. "I persuaded John to go" and "I expected John to go" are both grammatical, and so is "I persuaded myself to go." But *"I expected myself to go" is not grammatical. After **Vt**$_\text{to}$'s of the type *expect*, when the two base strings have the same subject, the object must be deleted before the sentence is finished. Thus, from **I expected + Comp + me and I went**, we get **I expected to go me → I expected me to go → I expected to go.**

Vt$_\text{to}$'s like *try* are again slightly different. For these, meaning requires the two base strings to have the same subject, which then must be deleted. Thus *"I tried John to go" and *"I tried myself to go" (where *myself* is an object) are both ungrammatical, and we have only "I tried to go." We have then **Vt**_to_'s of the three subclasses represented by *persuade, expect,* and *try,* and we could find these paralleled in subclasses of **Vt**_ing_. In this way sentences of apparently quite different construction, like "I expected to go," "I expected John to go," "I persuaded myself to go," "I persuaded John to go," "I tried to go," "I imagined myself going," "I imagined John going," "I avoided going," can be seen to be closely related. They are generated by the same high-level rules, though slightly different rules apply to them at lower levels.

The close relationship of the whole **VT** complex can be seen clearly in the effect of the passive transformation, which applies to any construction of the description **NP + Aux + VT + NP** and in exactly the same way.

1051

Let us review verbals. In addition to verbals with **VT** (transitive), we have identified those with **VI** (intransitive verbs), those with **Vb** (*become* type), those with **Vs** (*seem* type), and those with **Vh** (*have* type). In "Peter walked away," we have a **V** _____ .

1052

"The men ate the mush" contains a **V** _____ .

1053

"I thought Sally pretty" contains a **V** _____ .

1054

"Whittaker became a minister" contains a **V** _____ .

1055

"The dress cost ten dollars" contains a **V** _____ .

1056

"He looked up the reference" contains a **V** _____ .

1057

The passive transformation applies to all (and only) base strings with **VT**'s. In "The men ate the mush," the verb is a **VT** (**Vt**_1_). *The men* functions as the subject, and *the mush* functions as the _____ .

1058

Any string containing a **VT** can be transformed into what is called a *passive*. The passive of "John saw Samuel" is "Samuel was seen by John." What is the passive of "Samuel saw John"? _____

_____

1059

The passive of "The men ate the mush" is "The mush was eaten by the men." What is the passive of "The boys repaired the car"? _____

_____

1060

The passive of "Sue met Evelyn" is "Evelyn was met by Sue." *Evelyn* is the object in the kernel string. In the passive transformation it becomes the _____.

1061

"Steve met Merrill" becomes the passive "Merrill was met by Steve." The subject of the kernel sentence is expressed in the passive by a _____ phrase.

1062

Let us now look more closely at the machinery of the passive. We can write the formula of "John saw Samuel" in this way: **NP₁ + Aux + VT + NP₂**. In "John saw Samuel," the **VT** is the verb ____, and the **Aux** is ____ tense.

1063

Here is **T-passive: NP₁ + Aux + VT + NP₂ ⇒ NP₂ + Aux + be + part + VT + (by + NP₁)**. Part is the morpheme that forms the past _____ of verbs.

1064

In "John saw Samuel," **Aux** is *past,* and **VT** is *see.* So we can write the formula in this way: **John + past + see + Samuel**. If we apply **T-passive** (**NP₁ + Aux + VT + NP₂ ⇒ NP₂ + Aux + be + part + VT + by + NP₁**) to this, we get **Samuel +** _____ **+** _____ **+** _____ **+** _____ **+ by John.**

188 ENGLISH SYNTAX

1065

Samuel + past + be + part + see + by John contains two sequences of Af + v. What are they? _____ + _____, _____ + _____

1066

If we apply T-af to Samuel + past + be + part + see + by John, we get Samuel + _____ + _____ + _____ + _____ + by John.

1067

What actual sentence is represented by Samuel + be + past + see + part + by John? _____

1068

T-passive works in exactly the same way whether the Aux consists of just tense or of tense plus other elements. Take the kernel string John + past + shall + have + part + see + Samuel. What actual sentence would this be if T-af were applied immediately? _____

1069

What elements constitute the Aux in John + past + shall + have + part + see + Samuel? _____ + _____ + _____ + _____

1070

In John + past + shall + have + part + see + Samuel, the auxiliary consists of past + shall + have + part. If we apply T-passive (NP$_1$ + Aux + VT + NP$_2$ $\Rightarrow$ NP$_2$ + Aux + be + part + VT + by + NP$_1$) to this string, we get _____ + _____ + _____ + _____ + _____ + _____ + _____ + _____ + _____.

1071

Samuel + past + shall + have + part + be + part + see + by John contains three sequences of Af + v. Therefore T-af must apply three times. Applying it, we get _____ + _____ + _____ + _____ + _____ + _____ + _____ + _____ + _____.

THE PASSIVE TRANSFORMATION   189

1072

Samuel + shall + past + have + be + part + see + part + by John represents the actual sentence _____

_____ .

1073

Here is T-passive again: NP₁ + Aux + VT + NP₂ ⇒ NP₂ + Aux + be + part + VT + (by + NP₁). Here, as always, the parentheses mean that the item may occur but need not. If we apply T-passive to "Evelyn wrote the letter," we get "The letter was written by Evelyn," or _____

_____ .

1074

Take the formula **Mrs. Alva + past + be + ing + hold + the baby.** If we apply **T-af** immediately, we get the sentence _____

_____ .

1075

Now apply **T-passive** (NP₁ + Aux + VT + NP₂ ⇒ NP₂ + Aux + be + part + VT + (by + NP₁) to Mrs. Alva + past + be + ing + hold + the baby. the baby + ____ + ____ + ____ + ____ + ____ + ____ + by Mrs. Alva

1076

After we apply **T-af** to **the baby + past + be + ing + be + part + hold + by Mrs. Alva,** we get the sentence _____

_____ .

1077

We have seen that **T-passive** can be applied to structures that contain VT's. Can it be applied to the string underlying the sentence "John became a teacher"? ____

1078

If we apply **T-passive** to "John became a teacher," we get the ungrammatical sentence *"A teacher was become by John." This is one way of

190 ENGLISH SYNTAX

proving that *become* belongs to a different subclass than such verbs as *see, meet, hold*. In "John became a teacher," *become* is not a **VT** but a **V** ____ .

1079

All kernel strings with **VT**'s can be made passive. Does "The climate suits his health" contain a **VT**? ____

1080

If it did, *"His health was suited by the climate" would be a grammatical sentence, and it is not. Does "Charles put away the books" contain a **VT**? ____

1081

What is the **VT** in "Charles put away the books"? ____

1082

"Charles put away the books" is **Charles + Aux + put away + the books**, where *put away* is the **VT**. T-passive is **NP₁ + Aux + VT + NP₂ ⇒ NP₂ + Aux + be + part + VT + (by + NP₁)**. Leaving out the **by + NP₁**, apply this to **Charles + past + put away + the books**.

____ + ____ + ____ + ____ + ____

1083

The books + past + be + part + put away represents the sentence ____ .

1084

What is the **VT** of "He tried it on"? ____

1085

"He tried it on" has the underlying string **he + past + try on + it**. If this is to be carried into a sentence, the particle *on* and the object *it* must reverse obligatorily by **T-VT**, since the object is a pronoun. However, before **T-VT** is applied, **T-passive** can be applied. Applied to this string, **NP₁ + Aux + VT + NP₂ ⇒ NP₂ + Aux + be + part + VT** gives ____ + ____ + ____ + ____ + ____ .

THE PASSIVE TRANSFORMATION

1086

It + past + be + part + try on represents the sentence _____ _____ .

1087

What is the **VT** of "He considered Sally pretty"? _____

1088

T-passive (NP$_1$ + Aux + VT + NP$_2$ $\Rightarrow$ NP$_2$ + Aux + be + part + VT) applied to he + past + consider pretty + Sally gives _____ + _____ + _____ + _____ + _____ .

1089

Sally + past + be + part + consider pretty represents the sentence _____ .

1090

What is the **VT** of "The class elected Spencer president"? _____ _____

1091

What is the passive sentence corresponding to "The class elected Spencer president"? _____

1092

T-passive gives an additional justification for the description of **VT**. In "They elected Spencer president," the real unit in the verb phrase is not *elect Spencer* but *elect president*. These words are separated by **T-VT,** but they appear together again if **T-passive** is applied instead. What is the passive sentence corresponding to "They regarded Tom as innocent"?

_____

_____

1093

What is the **VT** of "They regarded Tom as innocent"? _____ _____

1094

What is the **VT** of "We rejected the plan as impractical"? _____

1095

What is the passive sentence corresponding to "We expected John to come"? _____

1096

What is the **VT** of "We expected John to come"? _____

1097

What is the passive sentence corresponding to "We found John studying in the library? _____

1098

What is the passive sentence corresponding to "We caught Sam smoking"? _____

1099

What is the passive sentence corresponding to "Mary begged him to stop trying to force us to take steps"? _____

1100

The passive transformation works on (i.e., produces grammatical sentences from) any string containing a **VT**. It doesn't matter what the **Aux** is, and it doesn't matter what kind of **VT** it is—whether Vt_1; Vt_2 + **Prt**; or Vt_3, Vt_{to}, Vt_{ing} + **Comp**. Again we have an example of the regular and orderly nature of the language at this level.

MAIN POINTS OF LESSON TWENTY-TWO

T-passive: NP_1 + Aux + VT + NP_2 $\Rightarrow$ NP_2 + Aux + be + part + VT + (by + NP_1)

This transformation can be applied to any string having a **VT**. The object of the base string becomes the subject of the transform. The subject of the base string may or may not be expressed in a prepositional phrase with *by*. The morpheme **part,** added with *be*, will be attached to the verb of the **VT,** by **T-af,** forming the past participle.

The transformation applies for any **VT,** whether it be a **Vt₁,** a **Vt₂ + Prt,** or a **Vt₃, Vt_to, Vt_ing + Comp.** Any structure to which the transformation cannot be applied—i.e., any sentence which cannot be made passive—does not contain a transitive verb.

For any string containing a **Comp, T-passive** is applied before and instead of **T-VT.** Thus "Sally was elected chairman" is derived naturally from "The class elected-chairman Sally," not from "The class elected Sally chairman."

Lesson Twenty-Three
REVIEW OF DETERMINERS, T-there

In formulating double-base transformations, we have confined ourselves to indicating in a general way what happens. It may be of interest, however, to know how this can be done precisely. Actually there are several notations in use. The following is possibly the simplest.

Suppose we want to show how "My father found John teasing the cat" derives from the strings I + Pos + father + past + find + Comp + John and John + Aux + tease + the + cat. First we separate by hyphens those sequences of morphemes that form units for the purposes of the transformation. Morphemes within these units are separated as usual by plus signs.

$$I + Pos + father - past - find - Comp - John$$
$$John - Aux - tease + the + cat$$

Now we assign numbers to each segment: 1 to the first, 2 to the second, and so forth, for as many as there are, in this case 8. Then

$$\underset{1}{I + Pos + father} - \underset{2}{past} - \underset{3}{find} - \underset{4}{Comp} - \underset{5}{John}$$
$$\underset{6}{John} - \underset{7}{Aux} - \underset{8}{tease + the + cat}$$
$$\Rightarrow 1 + 2 + 3 + ing + 8 + 5$$

The transformation can be generalized in this way:

$$NP - Aux - Vt_{ing} - Comp - NP$$
$$NP - Aux - X$$
$$\Rightarrow 1 + 2 + 3 + ing + 8 + 5$$

The eighth segment—X—means anything that follows Aux in the insert sentence and permits the transformation to apply to any verb phrase.

Sometimes this notation is useful for single-base transformations too, particularly those that are long and involved. For example, we could use it for **T-passive: NP — Aux — VT — NP** $\Rightarrow$ **4 + 2 + be + part + 3 + (by + 1)**. Notice that here it is not necessary to number the two NP's as **NP₁** and **NP₂**.

There is one important variety of **VT** that we have not yet noticed and that we shall not describe in great detail. It is quite complicated, and grammarians are not certain how it is best related to its underlying structures. This is the construction with verbs of the *give* type, as in "John gave Mary the book" or "I sent him a postcard."

Verbs of the *give* type are probably best taken as a subclass of **Vt₃**— that is, as verbs that are followed by a complement. Then from two base strings we would derive a structure like the following:

Subject	VT	Object
John	gave-to-Mary	the book

Here *give* is the **Vt₃**, and *to Mary* is the complement. The sentence *"John gave to Mary the book" is of course ungrammatical. To this string, one of two transformations must be applied. Either we apply **T-VT**, reversing the complement and the object, and get "John gave the book to Mary"; or we apply **T-del**, deleting the *to*, and get "John gave Mary the book."

The sentence "John gave Mary the book" is traditionally described as containing two objects. The first, *Mary*, is called an *indirect object;* the second, *the book,* is called a *direct object*. These terms are used only for constructions with verbs of the *give* type.

These constructions have several passive possibilities. To the string "John gave-to-Mary the book" we can apply **T-passive** in the ordinary way and get "The book was given to Mary." Then we can delete the *to* and get "The book was given Mary." This last transformation is not very commonly applied in modern English. That is, "The book was given to Mary" is a much more common form than "The book was given Mary."

Still another transformation produces a structure in which the indirect object appears as subject of the passive transform: "Mary was given the book." This transformation might be formulated in several ways, none of which seems obviously the correct one at the present time.

1101

Before considering the *there* transformation, we will review determiners, which are related to it. The rewrite rule for noun phrase gives a choice:

proper noun, indefinite pronoun, _____ + _____ .

1102

Det stands for the word _____ .

1103

The rewrite of **Det** is this: **Det** → (pre-article) + **Art** + (Demon) + (number). Every determiner must contain _____ .

1104

Art is rewritten as a choice between _____ and _____ .

1105

The definite article is *the*. The nondefinite articles are Ø, _____ , and _____ .

1106

Pre-articles are structures like *several of, many of, few of, a few of, lots of*. All pre-articles contain the word _____ .

1107

In the phrase *several of the books*, the determiner is _____ .

1108

In *most of the spinach*, the pre-article is _____ .

1109

In *a lot of those girls*, the pre-article is _____ .

1110

In *a few of these newspapers*, the pre-article is _____ .

1111

Determiners in which pre-articles occur with **Nondef** are a little more complicated. **Several of** + **Nondef** + **books** is a possible product of the rewrite rules. **Nondef** cannot be *a* or *some* here. It must be _____ .

1112

Several of books is ungrammatical. In the construction **several of** + Ø + **books**, the word _____ must be dropped.

REVIEW OF DETERMINERS, T-there   **197**

1113

The structure many + of + Nondef + children will emerge as the noun phrase _____ .

1114

The structure six + of + Nondef + cats will emerge as _____ .

1115

Suppose, however, we have six + of + Def + cats. Def has no Ø form. Six + of + Def + cats must emerge as the noun phrase _____ .

1116

Now compare the noun phrases *both cats* and *several cats*. These look to be identical. However, there is a clear difference in essential meaning: one is definite and the other is nondefinite. Which one is definite? _____

1117

Since *both cats* is definite, it must have Def, and not Nondef, somewhere in the history of its generation. *Several cats* derives from several + of + Nondef + cats, in which Nondef is automatically Ø, and the general rule that *of* is dropped before Nondef applies. However, *both cats* must derive from both + of + the + cats. The deletion transformation, T-del, then changes this into *both cats* by deleting ____ + ____ .

1118

Thus *several cats* is a kernel structure, arrived at by kernel rules. But *both cats* is a transform, arrived at by T-del. The meaning relationships support this analysis. A transform preserves the meaning of the base that underlies it. *Both of the cats* and *both cats* have the same essential meaning; both are definite. But *several of the cats* and *several cats* do not have the same essential meaning; the first is definite, and the second is nondefinite. Therefore *several cats* cannot be derived by T-del from *several of the cats*.

Rather it derives by kernel rules from several + ____ + _____ + cats.

1119

Does *a few men* derive from (1) a few + of + the + men by T-del or from (2) a few + of + Nondef + men by kernel rules? ____

198   ENGLISH SYNTAX

1120

Is *a few men* (1) a kernel structure, (2) a transform? _____

1121

There is another interesting grammatical fact about *both* and two other words which share its grammatical properties. *Both cats* is a transform of *both of the cats*, by **T-del**, which deletes **of** + **the**. A different transformation, however, can delete just one of these words. Which one? _____

1122

The two other words which work in this way are *half* and *all*, both of which are inherently definite. As **both** + **of** + **the** + **men** becomes **both the men** by **T-del**, **half** + **of** + **the** + **trees** becomes _____.

1123

In the same way, **all** + **of** + **the** + **pie** becomes _____.

1124

Half differs in one respect, however, from *both* and *all*. *Both men* and *all men* are both possible, but *half men is not, except in an entirely different meaning. Does *lots of men* contain **Def** or **Nondef** in the history of its generation? _____

1125

Lots of and *a lot of* are pre-articles. Like the pre-articles *several of*, *many of*, *a few of* (and unlike *both of*, *half of*, *all of*), they can be followed by either **Def** or **Nondef**. **Lots** + **of** + **Def** + **men** is *lots of the men*. **Lots** + **of** + **Nondef** + **men** is _____.

1126

Note a difference between *lots of* and *several of*, *many of*, etc. For the latter, *of* is dropped automatically before **Nondef**, but for *lots of* the *of* is retained. *Lots men is ungrammatical. Similarly, **a lot** + **of** + **Nondef** + **men** becomes _____.

1127

Now let's look at the rather special pre-article, *one of*. Like *both of*, *all of*, *half of*, the pre-article *one of* is usually followed by **Def** rather than **Nondef**. There is, however, an interesting exception. The rewrite rule for determiner is Det → (pre-article) + Art + (Demon) + (number). Demon stands for _____ .

1128

Demon is D_1 or D_2. By a phonological rule, Def + D_1 is *this* or *these*. Def + D_2 is _____ or _____ .

1129

We said that **Nondef** + D_1 is *a certain* and **Nondef** + D_2 is *some*. This *some* is pronounced with more stress than the definite article *some*. Which of these sentences contains **Demon**: (1) "Some men were in the room." (2) "Some man was in the room"? _____

1130

Suppose we have "One man was in the room." Here *one man* is clearly in some sense *nondefinite*. *One of the men* and *one man* differ in meaning as *both of the men* and *both men* do not. However, *one man* is not as simply nondefinite as *a man* is. We can account for our feeling by supposing that in *one man* the word *one* contains the meaning *nondefinite* plus the meaning *demonstrative* in addition to the singular meaning which is basic to the pre-article *one of*. We formulate this by saying that **one** + **of** + **Nondef** + **Demon** → **one** by a phonological rule. **One** + **of** + **Nondef** + **Demon** + **answer** becomes _____ .

1131

Notice that *one man* corresponds in stress pattern to *some man*, which it is now shown to correspond to also in structure. Which of the following is not a pre-article: (1) *most of*, (2) *many of*, (3) *every of*, (4) *both of*? _____

1132

We say *many of the boys, one of the boys, most of the boys*, etc., but not *every of the boys*. The words *every* and *each* appear in the grammar as optional choices before the pre-article *one of*. What is the determiner in "Every one of the boys was late"? _____

1133

In "Each one of the boys was late," the determiner is _____ .

1134

"Both of the boys were late" is to "Both boys were late" as "Each of the boys were late" is to ———————— .

1135

Each boy is like *both boys*, not like *several boys*. Both *each boy* and *both boys* are deletion transforms. Both contain **Def** in the history of the generation. *Several boys*, however, contains **Nondef** and is not a transform. What word could be deleted from "Each boy was late"? ———

1136

The **N** after *each* can be deleted by **T-del**, as it can after many determiner structures: "Several boys were here" → "Several were here"; "This dress is expensive" → "This is expensive." Can the **N** be deleted in "Every dress is expensive"? ———

1137

Every differs from *each* in that either an **N** or the word *one* can be deleted after *each* but not after *every*. *"Every of the boys was late" and *"Every was late" are both ungrammatical. Does the sentence "Each was late" contain **Def** in its history? ———

1138

"Each one of the boys was late" → "Each of the boys was late" → "Each boy was late" → "Each was late" by the deletion transformation. The meaning doesn't change. The meaning *definite* persists after the actual definite article *the* disappears. This persistence of **Def** and **Nondef** through transformations and phonological rules is important in the very common transformation that we take up now. In the development of **VP**, we must choose **Aux** and then either verbal or *be*. If we choose *be*, we must have after it either substantive or ——— .

1139

Thus, one of the possible sentence types is **NP + Aux + be + Adv-p**. "A man is in the house" fits this description. What is the **Adv-p** in this sentence? ————————

1140

This is the transformation: X + Nondef + Y + Aux + be + Adv-p ⇒ there + Aux + be + X + Nondef + Y + Adv-p. X + Nondef + Y is just a way of indicating an **NP** that contains **Nondef** in its determiner. X and Y mean whatever occurs before or after the **Nondef** or nothing, if nothing occurs there. In "A man is in the room," **Nondef** is the nondefinite article *a*. In this case **X** is nothing. **Y** is the noun _____.

1141

X + Nondef + Y + Aux + be + Adv-p ⇒ there + Aux + be + X + Nondef + Y + Adv-p. For this, *a man* is a case of **X + Nondef + Y**. Then a man + present + be + in the house becomes _____ + _____ + _____ + a man + in the house.

1142

After T-af, there + present + be + a man + in the house becomes "There is a man in the house." We will call this the *there* transformation or **T-there**. **T-there** can in general be applied to sentences in which the subject contains **Nondef** and the predicate contains **be + Adv-p**. The predicate of "Some men were in the house" contains **be + Adv-p**. Does the subject contain **Nondef**? _____

1143

What does "Some men were in the house" become by **T-there?**

_____

_____

There are some restrictions on this transformation. It will not work, for example, for the sequence Ø + he + present + be + in the room, for this would give the ungrammatical *"There is he in the room." The transformation will, however, apply to structures with personal pronouns when these are preceded by pre-articles. **T-there** applied to **several + of + Ø + we + m + present + be + in the room** gives "There were several of us in the room."

1144

Note that we have *were*, not *was*, in both "Some men were in the house" and "There were some men in the house." The **NP** *some men* is still the

202 ENGLISH SYNTAX

subject after the application of **T-there**. What is the subject of "There were several books on the table"? _____

1145

"There were several books on the table" derives from the sentence _____ .

1146

T-there can be applied to a sentence whose subject is *several books* because *several* contains **Nondef**. Several + of + Nondef → several. T-there cannot be applied to "This book was on the table," because the word _____ contains _____ .

1147

T-there cannot be applied to "Both books were on the table," because *both books* is a transform of _____ .

1148

By **T-there**, "One glove was here" becomes _____ .

1149

One glove—like *a certain glove* and *some glove*—contains **Nondef** and therefore meets the condition of the *there* transformation. You remember that in the possessive transformation **NP + Pos** replaces not the article of the **NP** but the definite article. Can **T-there** be applied to "My father was in the bathtub"? _____

1150

The *there* of "There was a man here" does not belong to any word class. It is unique, in a class by itself, like *do* or *be* or *not*. It should not be confused with the adverb spelled the same way but pronounced differently, as in "He sat there" or "There goes my father."

MAIN POINTS OF LESSON TWENTY-THREE

Every noun phrase, unless it is a proper noun or an indefinite pronoun, contains a determiner, and every determiner contains, somewhere in the history of its generation, an article, either definite or nondefinite. **Def** may be present in the actual word *the*, **Nondef** in *a* and *some*. **Nondef** may be represented by Ø. Both **Def** and **Nondef** may be traced back through deletion transformations or through changes effected by phonological rules.

Transformations do not alter meanings; they only alter structures. *Both boys* is a transform of *both of the boys* and expresses the same meaning. However, *several boys* cannot be considered a transform of *several of the boys*, since the meaning is different, one being indefinite and one definite. *Several boys* develops from **several + of + Nondef + boys** by a phonological rule.

The pre-article *one of* always occurs with **Def** except in the combination **one of + Nondef + Demon,** which becomes *one* with added stress by a phonological rule. The words *each* and *every* enter the grammar as possible choices before *one of*. The structures may then be altered in various ways by deletion transformations.

T-there: X + Nondef + Y + Aux + be + Adv-p ⇒ there + Aux + be + X + Nondef + Y + Adv-p. This transformation applies to all structures with **be + Adv-p** in the predicate and **Nondef** in the subject. The regularity with which it works confirms the analysis of the determiner.

Lesson Twenty-Four
RELATIVE CLAUSES

The description of the determiner given in Lesson Twenty-Three is a rather careful one, but it is far from being complete. The English determiner is systematic, but the system is complex. People for whom English is a native language ordinarily aren't aware either of the system or of its complexity. They use such expressions as *some, many, any, a few of, much, a lot of, both of the, this* without knowing that there is anything complicated about them. For people learning English as a second language, however, the grammar in this area takes a good deal of study and practice, because there are many rules to learn, many more than we have given here.

For example, we use *much* in negative transforms like "The men didn't eat much mush." But we don't use it in the kernel sentence from which the transform derives. We don't ordinarily say, *"The men ate much mush." Instead we say, "The men ate a lot of mush." We say, "Few of them have ever been here" and "A few of them have never been here," but not *"A few of them have ever been here." *Few* means *not many*, and like *not many* it doesn't need an additional negative.

The word *some* alternates with *any* as *a lot of* alternates with *much:*

    He ate a lot of candy.
    Did he eat much candy?
    He didn't eat much candy.

    He ate some candy.
    Did he eat any candy?
    He didn't eat any candy.

These alternations carry over into the *there* transformation:

    There's some candy in the drawer.
    Is there any candy in the drawer?
    There isn't any candy in the drawer.

In the rewrite of **NP**, one choice is **Det + N** and another is indefinite pronoun. Indefinite pronouns—*everybody, nothing, someone, anyone,* etc.—cannot be preceded by determiners. They may be considered to have the determiner built into them, in the form *every-, no-, some-, any-*. This may be thought of as a fact of the history of the language, but in some ways these forms still have a live relationship with other determiners. For example, *every-* is definite, and indefinite pronouns with *every-* will not undergo the *there* transformation: *"There is everybody in the room" is ungrammatical, whereas "There is nobody in the room" and "There is somebody in the room" are grammatical. *Some* and *any* alternate in the indefinite pronoun as they do in other **NP**'s:

There is somebody in the room.
Is there anybody in the room?
There isn't anybody in the room.

The third choice in the rewrite of **NP** is proper noun. Proper nouns are not preceded by any determiner; therefore they cannot contain **Nondef** and do not undergo the *there* transformation.

We have seen several types of words functioning within the unit called determiner: articles, demonstratives, and words deriving from pre-articles. Taken all together, these determiners are one variety of what we call *noun modifiers*. Noun modifiers modify—or change or limit the meaning of—the nouns they go with. *Few people* doesn't mean the same thing as *many people*. *Few* changes the meaning of *people* in one way, and *many* changes it in another.

We have seen that determiners are a complicated kind of noun modifier, requiring many special rules to describe their behavior. By comparison the other kinds of noun modifiers are simple. Most of their behavior can be described by a few general rules. A foreign student learning English has much less trouble getting on to how they are used than he does with determiners.

The type that we will consider first is the *relative clause*. We shall see that most other types can be derived from the relative clause.

1151

In the sentence "The man who went away was Ellie's father," the structure *who went away* is a relative clause. What is the relative clause in "The man who helped us is the director"? _____

---

206   ENGLISH SYNTAX

1152

What is the relative clause in "The girl who was serving dropped the tray"? _____

1153

What is the relative clause in "The boy who borrowed the book didn't return it"? _____

1154

What is the relative clause in "Anybody who believes that is silly"?
_____

1155

Some relative clauses begin with *who* and some with *that*. What is the relative clause in "The girls that were helping us went on home leave"?
_____

1156

What is the relative clause in "I know the fellow that borrowed the book"? _____

1157

Now compare "The fellow borrowed the book" and "I know the fellow that borrowed the book." Where the kernel sentence begins with the noun phrase *the fellow,* the relative clause begins with the word _____ .

1158

Some relative clauses begin with the word *which*. What is the relative clause in "The house which burned down belonged to Mr. Caspar"?
_____

1159

Compare "The house burned down" and "The house which burned down belonged to Mr. Caspar." The subject of the kernel sentence is replaced in the relative clause by the word _____ .

RELATIVE CLAUSES 207

1160

The words *who (whom), which,* and *that,* when they are used in relative clauses, are called *relative pronouns.* What is the relative pronoun in the sentence "He brought in the book which was overdue"? _____

1161

What is the relative pronoun in "Who knows the fellow that borrowed the book?" _____

1162

What is the relative pronoun in "This is the child that I was telling you about"? _____

1163

The transformation that produces, from an insert sentence, a relative clause that modifies a noun phrase is a fairly simple one. We will call it **T-rel**:

$$X + NP + Y \Rightarrow NP + \begin{Bmatrix} who \\ which \\ that \end{Bmatrix} + X + Y$$

You may note that this is very similar to **T-wh**, the transformation that produces *wh* questions. **T-rel**, however, does not apply to strings which result from **T-yes/no**. As usual, **X** and **Y** stand for anything that occurs in these positions or for _____ .

1164

T-rel:

$$X + NP + Y \Rightarrow NP + \begin{Bmatrix} who \\ which \\ that \end{Bmatrix} + X + Y$$

Let us apply this to the base string **the + boy + past + go + away**. For this, the **NP** of the formula is **the + boy**. The **X** is nothing. The **Y** is ____ + ____ + ____ .

1165

T-rel:

$$X + NP + Y \Rightarrow NP + \begin{Bmatrix} who \\ which \\ that \end{Bmatrix} + X + Y$$

208 ENGLISH SYNTAX

Applied to **the + boy + past + go + away,** this will give _____ + _____ + **who** + _____ + _____ + _____ .

1166
If we apply **T-af** to **the + boy + who + past + go + away,** we get *the boy who went away.* Is this a sentence? _____

1167
The structure *the boy who went away* is not a sentence but a noun phrase. It can occur in any function open to the original noun phrase *the boy.* In the sentence "The boy who went away was Samuel," the noun phrase *the boy who went away* functions as _____ .

1168
In "Everybody liked the boy who went away," the noun phrase *the boy who went away* functions as _____ .

1169
In "No one had spoken to the boy who went away," the noun phrase *the boy who went away* functions as object of a _____ .

1170
T-rel:

$$X + NP + Y \Rightarrow NP + \begin{Bmatrix} who \\ which \\ that \end{Bmatrix} + X + Y$$

The choice among the relative pronouns *who, that,* and *which* depends upon the **NP**. *The boy who went away* and *the boy that went away* are both grammatical noun phrases. Is *the boy which went away* grammatical? _____

1171
Which of these noun phrases is *not* grammatical: (1) *the house who burned down,* (2) *the house that burned down,* (3) *the house which burned down?* _____

1172
When the **NP** of the formula refers to a person, like *the boy, the teacher, somebody,* we use the relative pronouns _____ or _____ .

1173

When the **NP** of **T-rel** refers to anything other than a person *(the cow, the house, the idea, something)*, we use the relative pronouns ____ or ____ .

1174

If we apply

$$X + NP + Y \Rightarrow NP + \begin{Bmatrix} who \\ which \\ that \end{Bmatrix} + X + Y$$

to "The house burned down," we get _____ .
(Use either appropriate relative pronoun.)

1175

If we apply **T-rel** to "The doctor cured the child," taking *the doctor* as the **NP** of the formula **X + NP + Y**, we get the noun phrase _____
_____ .

1176

"The doctor cured the child" is the + doctor + past + cure + the + child. Suppose we apply **T-rel** to this but take *the child* as the **NP** of **X + NP + Y**. Then **X** is what comes before the + child in the base string: the + doctor + past + cure. **Y** is _____ .

1177

Applying

$$X + NP + Y \Rightarrow NP + \begin{Bmatrix} who \\ which \\ that \end{Bmatrix} + X + Y$$

to the + doctor + past + cure + the + child, with the + child as the **NP**, we get _____ + _____ + that + _____ + _____ + _____ + _____ .

1178

After **T-af**, the + child + that + the + doctor + past + cure will give the noun phrase _____ .

---

210   ENGLISH SYNTAX

1179

Apply

$$X + NP + Y \Rightarrow NP + \begin{Bmatrix} \text{who} \\ \text{which} \\ \text{that} \end{Bmatrix} + X + Y$$

to **Henry + past + sell + the + cow**, taking **the + cow** as the **NP** and using the relative pronoun *which*. _____ + _____ + _____ + _____ + _____ + _____

1180

When the **NP** of **X + NP + Y** is an object in the base string, a special phonological rule applies if the relative pronoun is *who*. An object in a string is accompanied by the symbol **m**, which does not affect nouns but does affect some pronouns. The string **I + past + see + he + m** stands for the sentence _____.

1181

I + m is *me,* and **he + m** is *him*. What is **who + m**? _____

1182

When the **NP** of **X + NP + Y** is an object in the base string, the transform will include **m** after the relative pronoun. If the relative pronoun is *who,* it will then automatically become *whom*. The string **the + man + who + m + John + past + have + part + befriend** stands for the noun phrase _____.

1183

For many speakers of English, the rule **who + m → whom** is either optional or doesn't exist at all. That is, people do sometimes say *the man who John had befriended*. However, the more formal expression is *the man whom John had befriended*. The string **the + people + who + m + Al + present + will + see** stands for the **NP** _____.

1184

Another rule that applies when the **NP** of **X + NP + Y** is an object in the base string is the optional deletion of the relative pronoun in the transform. If we delete the relative pronoun in *the people whom Al will see*, we get _____.

RELATIVE CLAUSES 211

1185

T-del, deleting the relative pronoun, applied to *the house that he had bought the year before*, gives _____ .

1186

Take the string **John + past + speak + to + the + girl + last + week**. If **the + girl** is the **NP** of **X + NP + Y**, the **X** is **John + past + speak + to** and the **Y** is _____ + _____ .

1187

$$X + NP + Y \Rightarrow NP + \begin{Bmatrix} who \\ which \\ that \end{Bmatrix} + X + Y$$

applied to **John + past + speak + to + the + girl + last + week**, with *the girl* as the **NP**, gives _____ + _____ + **that** + _____ + _____ + _____ + _____ + _____ + _____ .

1188

The string **the + girl + that + John + past + speak + to + last + week** represents the noun phrase _____ .

1189

In "John spoke to the girl last week," *the girl* is object of a _____ .

1190

The special rules that apply when the **NP** is object of a verb apply also when it is object of a preposition: **who + m → whom** (for some speakers), and **T-del** can delete the relative pronoun. **T-del** applied to *the girl whom John spoke to last week* will give _____ .

1191

T-del applied to *the message that we had been waiting for* gives _____ .

1192

T-rel applied to "He had been living with the people," with *the people* as the **NP** and *that* as the relative pronoun gives _____ .

212   ENGLISH SYNTAX

1193

As we have given it, **T-rel** will not account for such a noun phrase as *the people with whom he had been living*. For this a special rule is required:

$$X + \text{Prep} + NP + Y \Rightarrow NP + \text{Prep} + \begin{Bmatrix} \text{who} \\ \text{which} \end{Bmatrix} + X + Y$$

What relative pronoun does *not* occur in this construction? _____

1194

When the preposition precedes the relative pronoun, *who* must be used for people and *which* for other noun phrases. **The people with that he had been living* is ungrammatical. If *who* occurs, the rule **who + m → whom** is virtually obligatory. **The people with who he had been living* is hardly natural. Also **T-del** will not now apply: **the people with he had been living* is ungrammatical. It is probably because constructions like *the people with whom he had been living* are so irregular—i.e., contain so many rules not found in the regular relative clause transformation—that speakers tend to use the other form. **T-rel** applied to "The boy works here" gives the noun phrase _____ .

1195

We will notice one more possibility of **T-rel**. This is a type in which the relative pronoun *who* replaces an **NP** before a possessive morpheme. **Who + Pos** then becomes *whose*. In "The boy whose father works here is Charles," the relative clause is *whose father works here*. What is the relative clause in "The people whose house burned down bought another one"? _____

1196

"The boy's father works here" is **the + boy + Pos + father + present + work + here**. If we take the **NP** of **X + NP + Y** as **the + boy**, **X** is zero. **Y** is _____ + _____ + _____ + _____ + _____ .

1197

Applying **X + NP + Y ⇒ NP + who + X + Y** to **the + boy + Pos + father + present + work + here**, we get _____ + _____ + who + _____ + _____ + _____ + _____ + _____ .

1198

This includes the sequence **who** + **Pos** which automatically becomes
_____ .

1199

T-rel will work with **Pos** no matter what the function of the noun phrase. From "They are in the teacher's class," we can derive the expanded noun phrase *the teacher* _____ .

1200

Notice the similarity between **T-rel** and **T-wh-NP**. Both work on a string X + NP + Y and transform it in much the same way. One difference is that the relative pronouns are not quite the same as the interrogatives. *What* does not occur as a relative pronoun, or *that* as an interrogative. Another difference is that **T-wh** operates on a string deriving from **T-yes/no**, and **T-rel** does not.

MAIN POINTS OF LESSON TWENTY-FOUR

$$\text{T-rel:} \quad X + NP + Y \Rightarrow NP + \begin{Bmatrix} who \\ which \\ that \end{Bmatrix} + X + Y$$

This transformation will generate nearly all the English relative clauses, which are thus seen to have the same essential structure. The relative clause modifies the **NP** of the base string, forming with it an expanded noun phrase. This expanded noun phrase can then occur in any function in a matrix string in which the original **NP** could occur.

The words *who, which,* and *that* are called relative pronouns. *Who* is used when the **NP** refers to a person, *which* when it does not. *That* is used for all **NP**'s. If the **NP** in the base string is an object, it will be accompanied by the morpheme **m**, which will convert *who* into *whom*. If it is a possessive, it will be accompanied by **Pos**, which will convert *who* into *whose*.

The relative clause *that I spoke to* is generated by the rule given above, but *to whom I spoke* is not. For this form a special rule is required:

$$X + Prep + NP + Y \Rightarrow NP + Prep + NP + \begin{Bmatrix} whom \\ which \end{Bmatrix} + X + Y$$

When the noun phrase is constructed in this way, the relative pronoun cannot be deleted.

Lesson Twenty-Five
THE VERB PHRASE AS NOUN MODIFIER

Most of the transformations we shall be concerned with from now on, including **T-rel,** are double-base transformations having two underlying strings—a matrix string and an insert string. The insert string provides some kind of structure, which is then inserted as part of the matrix string.

For example, in the sentence "The man who was waiting for us had a car," the matrix string is "The man had a car" and the insert string is "The man was waiting for us." The insert string provides the structure of a relative clause, which is then used as a modifier of the subject of the matrix string.

The mechanism can be shown by the use of hyphens in the manner illustrated earlier:

$$\underset{1}{\text{the} + \text{man}} - \underset{2}{\text{past} + \text{have} + \text{a} + \text{car}} - \underset{3}{\text{the} + \text{man}} -$$
$$\underset{4}{\text{past} + \text{be} + \text{ing} + \text{wait} + \text{for} + \text{us}} \Rightarrow 1 + \text{who} + 4 + 2$$

This is the general nature of the double-base transformation. Ordinarily, we won't need to specify it.

1201

In the sentence "The man who was waiting for us had a car," what kind of structure is *who was waiting for us?* _____

1202

What is the relative clause in "The lady who is milking the goats is my mother"? _____

1203

The sentence "The lady who is milking the goats is my mother" and "The man who was waiting for us had a car" are both grammatical. Are the following sentences also grammatical: "The lady milking the goats is my mother," "The man waiting for us had a car"? ____

1204

Compare "The lady who is milking the goats is my mother" and "The lady milking the goats is my mother." The second is just like the first except that it omits the two words _____ .

1205

The sentence "The lady who is milking the goats is my mother" can be represented as **NP** + **relative pronoun** + **tense** + **be** + **X**. For this sentence, the **X** is *milking the goats is my mother*. The **NP** is _____ .

1206

It is generally true that whenever a sequence **NP** + **relative pronoun** + **tense** + **be** + **X** is grammatical, the corresponding sequence **NP** + **X** will also be grammatical. (There are one important exception and one important complication that we will notice later on.) This says that from **NP** + **relative pronoun** + **tense** + **be** + **X**, _____ + _____ + ____ can be deleted.

1207

What words make up the sequence **relative pronoun** + **tense** + **be** in the sentence "The fellow who is walking with Steve is Jeff"? _____

1208

If we delete **relative pronoun** + **tense** + **be** from "The fellow who is walking with Steve is Jeff," we get the sentence _____ .

1209

If we delete **relative pronoun** + **tense** + **be** from "The cats that are playing in the kitchen are Siamese," we get the sentence _____ .

1210

In these sentences the structures *milking the goats, walking with Steve, playing in the kitchen* are called *participial phrases*. They derive from *who is milking the goats, who is walking with Steve, that are playing in the kitchen*. Participial phrases derive from _____ clauses.

1211

Participial phrases derive from relative clauses by the deletion transformation **NP + relative pronoun + tense + be + X ⟹ NP + X**. If we apply this transformation to "I spoke to the man who was sweeping the stairs," we get the sentence _____.

1212

In "I spoke to the man sweeping the stairs," the structure *sweeping the stairs* is a _____ phrase.

1213

What is the participial phrase in "The lady sitting in the swing spoke to me"? _____

1214

The participial phrase in "The lady sitting in the swing spoke to me" derives from the relative clause _____.

1215

What kind of structure is *the lady who was sitting in the swing?* _____

1216

The noun phrase *the lady who was sitting in the swing* derives from the sentence _____.

1217

We began by describing various kinds of sentences—kernel sentences with various optional changes. Next we showed how these can all be transformed into relative clauses. Then we showed how all the relative clauses containing the sequence **relative pronoun + tense + be** can be transformed into other kinds of noun modifiers. Those noun modifiers containing **ing**—like *sitting in the swing, walking with Steve*—are called _____ .

1218

Take the base sentence "The man was calling Don a liar." This sentence is one of the **VT** type. The **Vt₃** is *call*. What is the **VT**? _____

1219

T-rel applied to "The man was calling Don a liar" gives the noun phrase _____ .

1220

Apply the deletion transformation **NP** + **relative pronoun** + **tense** + **be** + **X** ⟹ **NP** + **X** to *the man who was calling Don a liar.* _____

1221

What is the **VT** in *the man calling Don a liar?* _____

1222

The relationships of the kernel are preserved throughout the transformations of the kernel. The relationships among *call* and *a liar* and *Don* are precisely the same in the relative clause and the participial phrase as in the underlying sentence. In *the man calling Don a liar*, what is the object of the **VT**? ____

1223

In "The children were putting away their books," the **VP** is **Aux** + **verbal**. The verbal is of the type **Vt₂** + ____ + ____ .

1224

In "The children were putting away their books," the **NP** *their books* functions as the object of the **VT** _____ .

218 ENGLISH SYNTAX

1225

Apply **T-rel** to "The children were putting away their books," taking *the children* as the **NP** of **X + NP + Y**. _____

_____

1226

Apply the deletion transformation **NP + relative pronoun + tense + be + X ⟹ NP + X** to the noun phrase *the children who were putting away their books*. _____

1227

Let's do it once more carefully. "The children were putting away their books" can be written **the children + past + be + ing + put + away + their books**. Here *the children* functions as subject and *their books* as object. The sequence **put + away** is a **VT**, composed of the **Vt₂** *put* and the particle *away*. What term applies to the sequence **past + be + ing**?

_____

1228

T-rel is **X + NP + Y ⟹ NP +** $\begin{Bmatrix} \text{who} \\ \text{which} \\ \text{that} \end{Bmatrix}$ **+ X + Y**. If we apply this to **the children + past + be + ing + put + away + their books**, taking *the children* as the **NP** and choosing *who*, we get the string **the children + ___ + ___ + ___ + ___ + ___ + ___ + their books**.

1229

Does **NP + relative pronoun + tense + be + X** fit the string **the children + who + past + be + ing + put + away + their books**? ___

1230

If we apply **NP + relative pronoun + tense + be + X ⟹ NP + X** to **the children + who + past + be + ing + put + away + their books**, we get **the children + ___ + ___ + ___ + ___**.

1231

The string **the children + ing + put + away + their books** contains one sequence of **Af + v**. What is it? ___ + ___

THE VERB PHRASE AS NOUN MODIFIER   219

1232

Therefore T-af must be applied to **the children + ing + put + away + their books**. This gives us **the children + ____ + ____ + ____ + their books**.

1233

Now take the string **Sam + past + catch + the fish**. T-passive is NP_1 + Aux + VT + NP_2 ⇒ NP_2 + Aux + be + part + VT + (by + NP_1). This can be applied to **Sam + past + catch + the fish** because *catch* is a **VT**. If we apply it, we get **the fish + ____ + ____ + ____ + ____ + by Sam**.

1234

We now have **the fish + past + be + part + catch + by Sam**. If we apply T-rel to this, we get **the fish + that + ____ + ____ + ____ + ____ + by Sam**.

1235

The string **the fish + that + past + be + part + catch + by Sam** represents the noun phrase _____ .

1236

The string **the fish + that + past + be + part + catch + by Sam** contains the sequence **relative pronoun + tense + be**, so T-del can be applied. This gives us ____ + ____ + ____ + ____ .

1237

The string **the fish + part + catch + by Sam** must become **the fish + catch + part + by Sam** by T- ____ .

1238

In the sentence "The fish caught by Sam was a halibut," what words derive from the base sentence "Sam caught the fish"? _____

220 ENGLISH SYNTAX

1239

Thus "Sam caught the fish" → "The fish was caught by Sam" (by **T-passive**) → "the fish that was caught by Sam" (by **T-rel**) → "the fish caught by Sam" (by **T-del**). The process is perfectly orderly, and it applies to all kernels with **VT**'s. In "The fish was caught by Sam" and *the fish caught by Sam,* the word *caught* is a _____ participle.

1240

Forms like *catching, waiting, trying* are present participles. The noun phrases *the fish caught by Sam* and *the boy catching the fish* contain the participial phrases *caught by Sam* and *catching the fish.* The first is a _____ participial phrase, and the second is a _____ participial phrase.

1241

The participial phrase *caught by Sam* is not a sentence of course. Is *the fish caught by Sam* a sentence? _____

1242

The structure *the fish caught by Sam* is not a sentence but an expanded noun phrase. It may be used in a sentence in any function open to the original noun phrase *the fish.* In "The fish caught by Sam was a halibut," the noun phrase *the fish caught by Sam* functions as _____ .

1243

In "The men ate the fish caught by Sam," the noun phrase *the fish caught by Sam* functions as object. Can **T-passive** be applied to "The men ate the fish caught by Sam"? _____

1244

T-passive applied to "The men ate the fish caught by Sam" gives _____ .

1245

"The fish caught by Sam was eaten by the men" results from two passive transformations (and other transformations) and contains two past participles. They are the words _____ and _____ .

THE VERB PHRASE AS NOUN MODIFIER

1246

What is the participial phrase in "Children raised by wolves seldom learn to read"? _____

1247

The noun phrase *children raised by wolves* comes from *children that are raised by wolves* from the passive sentence "Children are raised by wolves" from the kernel sentence _____ .

1248

What is the participial phrase in "A student bitten by a cobra should report immediately to the school nurse"? _____

1249

The noun phrase *a student bitten by a cobra* goes back through a relative clause to a passive sentence and ultimately to the kernel sentence _____ .

1250

The general point to notice is how the complicated sentences of English derive from a small and easily described kernel through a set of closely linked transformational rules. If we did not see this to be so, we couldn't explain how anything so seemingly complicated as language can be learned.

MAIN POINTS OF LESSON TWENTY-FIVE

Participial phrases used as modifiers of nouns derive from relative clauses. When the relative clause contains the sequence **relative pronoun + tense + be**, this sequence can be deleted: **NP + relative pronoun + tense + be + X ⇒ NP + X**. So "the man who was burning the trash" → "the man burning the trash"; "the boy that was being a nuisance" → "the boy being a nuisance." When the **X** of this sequence derives from a verb phrase, the result of the transformation is a participial phrase. Thus *burning the trash, being a nuisance* are participial phrases, deriving from the verb phrases of the sentences **NP + was burning the trash, NP + was being a nuisance.**

When the string underlying the participial phrase has undergone the passive transformation, the result is a past participial phrase. In *the boy bitten by a cobra*, *bitten by a cobra* is a past participial phrase. This construction goes back, through the relative and the passive transformations, to the **K**-terminal string underlying "A cobra bit the boy."

Lesson Twenty-Six
ADVERBIALS OF PLACE AS NOUN MODIFIERS

All participial phrases (i.e., verb phrases used as modifiers of noun phrases) derive from relative clauses. However, not all of them derive through a simple deletion of **relative pronoun + tense + be**. Take the sentence "This will interest people owning property." Here we have the noun phrase *people owning property,* which contains the participial phrase *owning property*. However, we cannot derive this from the underlying structures **people who are owning property* and **"People are owning property,"* because these structures are hardly grammatical. We may say "People own property," but not **"People are owning property."*

For a verb phrase of this sort, we start again with the grammatical kernel string and apply **T-rel**, deriving the relative clause in *people who own property*. Now, however, instead of **NP + relative pronoun + tense + be + X ⟹ NP + X**, we apply the related transformation **NP + relative pronoun + Aux + X ⟹ NP + ing + X**. This will give us **people + ing + own + property**. The obligatory **T-af** will then turn this into *people owning property*.

1251

Let us review briefly. Take the base sentence "The woman was weeping by the brook." If we apply **T-rel** to this, we get the noun phrase _____ _____ .

1252

If we delete **relative pronoun + tense + be** from *the woman who was weeping by the brook,* we get the noun phrase _____ .

---

224 ENGLISH SYNTAX

1253

In *the woman weeping by the brook,* the noun phrase *the woman* is modified by a _____ .

1254

The noun phrase *the woman weeping by the brook* can be used in any position open to the original noun phrase *the woman*. Substituting it for the NP subject in **NP + reminded me of my aunt**, we get the sentence _____
_____ .

1255

Substituting it for the **NP** object in **I thought attractive + NP**, we get
_____ .

1256

We said that there were one important exception and one important complication to the statement that all modifiers of nouns except determiners come from relative clauses. We come now to the complication. Suppose we start with "The woman was weeping." **T-rel** gives us the noun phrase _____ .

1257

Deletion of **relative pronoun + tense + be** from *the woman who was weeping* gives us _____ .

1258

Is the sentence "The woman weeping reminded me of my aunt" grammatical? _____

1259

When the participial phrase developed in this way consists of a single word—a past or present participle—an obligatory transformation shifts it to the position in front of the noun. In this case **Det + N + ing + weep ⇒ Det + ing + weep + N.** So *the woman weeping* becomes
_____ .

ADVERBIALS OF PLACE AS NOUN MODIFIERS

1260

This transformation generally applies to all single words in this position except adverbs. To give it a name, we will call it **T-NM**, where **NM** stands for *noun modifier*. **T-NM** says that any single-word participle after a noun is obligatorily shifted to a position before the noun. *The car speeding* becomes _____ .

1261

Suppose we start with "The blow stunned the cat." If we apply **T-passive** and include the optional (**by** + **NP₁**), we get the sentence _____ .

1262

From "The cat was stunned by the blow," we derive *the cat that was stunned by the blow* by **T-rel**. Deletion of **relative pronoun** + **tense** + **be** will give us _____ .

1263

This noun phrase could then occur in any **NP** position open to the noun phrase *the cat,* as in the sentence "The cat stunned by the blow lay on the floor." If we had omitted the optional (**by** + **NP₁**) in applying **T-passive** to "The blow stunned the cat," we would have got the passive sentence _____ .

1264

From this we could derive *the cat that was stunned* and then *the cat stunned*. We now have a structure for which **T-NM** is obligatory. **T-NM** applied to *the cat stunned* gives _____ .

1265

Then we can have sentences like "The stunned cat lay on the floor." Notice that neither *"The cat stunned lay on the floor" nor *"The stunned by the blow cat lay on the floor" is grammatical. **T-NM** must apply for the first structure and may not apply for the second. There are, however, cases in which a variation of **T-NM** is optional. **T-rel** applied to "The ranchers raise cattle" gives the noun phrase _____ .

226   ENGLISH SYNTAX

1266

By the transformation explained in the introduction to this lesson, in which **relative pronoun + Aux** is replaced by **ing,** we derive *the ranchers raising cattle* from *the ranchers who raise cattle.* "The ranchers raising cattle objected to the plan" is a grammatical sentence. Is "The cattle-raising ranchers objected to the plan" grammatical? ____

1267

We say *the ranchers raising cattle* or *the cattle-raising ranchers.* Note the hyphen. We say *a team breaking records* or _____ .

1268

We say *a committee finding facts* or _____ .

1269

Note the differences, however. When a participial phrase consisting of **VT + NP** occurs after the noun it modifies, the object occurs in its normal position, after the **VT.** However, when the participial phrase is shifted by **T-NM,** the object comes before the **VT:** *cattle-raising, record-breaking.* In writing, object and **VT** are then joined by a _____ .

1270

Another difference is that a plural object of a **VT** becomes singular when the participial phrase is shifted by **T-NM.** *A team breaking records* becomes *a record-breaking team.* What does *a man chasing butterflies* become?

_____

1271

Notice that the meaning relationships established in the kernel persist through the transformations. *Butterfly* is the object of *chase* in *a butterfly-chasing man* just as *butterflies* is in "A man chases butterflies." In the sentence "The river was flowing swiftly," the word *swiftly* is an adverbial of _____ .

1272

From "The river was flowing swiftly," we can derive, through **T-rel** and **T-del,** the noun phrase _____ .

ADVERBIALS OF PLACE AS NOUN MODIFIERS

1273

The noun phrase *the river flowing swiftly* is grammatical. Is *the swiftly flowing river* grammatical? ____ (The hyphen is not generally used to connect adverb and verb, as it is for object and verb.)

1274

Participles followed by adverbs of manner can also be shifted, optionally, by **T-NM**. *The river flowing swiftly* becomes *the swiftly flowing river*. *A singer crooning sweetly* becomes _____ .

1275

A rock balanced delicately becomes _____ .

1276

A cat stunned thoroughly becomes _____ .

1277

Now take the sentence "The man was in the house." Here the prepositional phrase *in the house* is an adverbial of _____ .

1278

"The man was in the house" is a kernel sentence with the general structure **NP + Aux + be + Adv-p**. If we apply **T-rel** to this sentence, we get the noun phrase _____ .

1279

Does the noun phrase *the man who was in the house* contain the sequence **relative pronoun + tense + be**? ____

1280

If we delete **relative pronoun + tense + be** from *the man who was in the house*, we get _____ .

1281

The noun phrase *the man in the house* can be used in any **NP** position open to the original noun phrase *the man*. If we use it as **NP** object in **I thought a burglar + NP**, we get the sentence _____ .

1282

From "The people were upstairs," we can derive, by **T-rel,** *the people who were upstairs,* and then, by **T-del,** _____ .

1283

In "We were very fond of the people upstairs," the word *upstairs* modifies _____ .

1284

In "We were very fond of the people upstairs," *upstairs* is an _____ of place.

1285

What is the adverbial of place in "I was told about it by the women there"? _____

1286

The noun phrase *the women there* goes back to the kernel sentence _____ .

1287

Notice that **T-NM,** in which a single-word modifier after a noun is obligatorily switched to the position before the noun, does not apply when the modifier is an adverb. *"I was told about it by the there women" is ungrammatical. The noun phrase *the paragraph above* derives from the noun phrase _____ *that is* _____ .

1288

The noun phrase *the paragraph that is above* derives from the kernel sentence _____ .

1289

T-NM is such a general rule that there is a tendency to extend it to adverbs that modify nouns. Along with "This is explained in the paragraph above," we have sentences like "This is explained in the above paragraph." Some people object to this usage, however. **T-NM** applied to *the man inside* would give _____ .

1290

Similarly, we have *the then president, the downstairs entrance, the outside door,* all deriving from an extension of **T-NM**. Could **T-NM** apply to *the girl in the car?* _____

1291

T-NM applied to *the girl in the car* would give the ungrammatical **the in the car girl*. **T-NM** applies sometimes when the **Adv-p** modifying a noun is an adverb, but almost never when it is a prepositional phrase. What is the kernel sentence from which *the girl in the car* derives? _____
_____

1292

What is the kernel sentence from which *the downstairs entrance* derives?
_____

1293

There are often several transformations between these noun phrases and the underlying kernel sentence. "The entrance is downstairs" → "the entrance which is downstairs" → "the entrance downstairs" → "the downstairs entrance." What is the kernel sentence from which *the tree lying across the creek* derives? _____

1294

What is the kernel sentence from which *the stunned cat* derives? "Something _____ ."

1295

What is the kernel sentence from which *the festering wound* derives?
_____

1296

What is the kernel sentence from which *the policeman directing traffic* derives? _____
_____

230 ENGLISH SYNTAX

1297

What is the kernel sentence from which *people owning property* derives?

_____

1298

What is the kernel sentence from which *trouble-making students* derives?

_____ .

1299

What is the kernel sentence from which *the carefully worked-out plans* derives? "Somebody _____ ."

1300

All the grammatical relationships of the language are established in the kernel. These relationships persist through the transformations that produce the various syntactic complexities of English.

MAIN POINTS OF LESSON TWENTY-SIX

Adverbials of place used as modifiers of nouns derive, like participial phrases, from kernel sentences through the relative clause construction. The adverbials of place derive from the kernel structure **NP + Aux + be + Adv-p**. The noun phrase with relative clause derived from this will contain the sequence **relative pronoun + tense + be**. This is deleted to form the simple noun modifier: "The man is in the house" → "the man who is in the house" → "the man in the house."

T-NM is a transformation which shifts a noun modifier from the position after the noun to the position before the noun. This is obligatory when the noun modifier is a single-word participle: "the woman sleeping" → "the sleeping woman"; "the cat stunned" → "the stunned cat." It is optional for certain multiple-word verb phrases like **VT + NP** and **VI + Adv-m**. *Ranchers raising cattle* can become *cattle-raising ranchers*. *The river flowing swiftly* can become *the swiftly flowing river*.

Lesson Twenty-Seven
ADJECTIVES

The noun-modifier constructions are a good example of the essential simplicity of the grammar. Such constructions as *the men who were helping us, the men in the yard, the men fighting in the street, the inside men, the men wounded in battle, the laughing men, the rejected men* seem highly various. Yet given the kernel and three transformations (**T-rel**, delete **relative pronoun + tense + be, T-NM**), we can construct all of these and, of course, countless others.

The operation of the **T-del** rule that deletes **relative pronoun + tense + be** discloses a further simplicity in the language. Our examples have contained relative clauses with the *be* coming from three different parts of the grammar: from the original rewrite of **VP** (*the men who were in the yard*); from the **be + ing** of **Aux** (*the men who were fighting in the street*); from the **be + part** inserted by the passive transformation (*the men who were wounded by the explosion*). However, it doesn't matter where the *be* came from. The sequence **relative pronoun + tense + be** deletes in the same way to give *the men in the yard, the men fighting in the street, the men wounded by the explosion*.

This machinery works in much the same way to produce another common kind of noun modifier, the adjective.

1301

In "The boy looked sad," *sad* is an adjective. *Look* is a **V**_____ .

1302

What kind of word is *foolish* in "The boy was foolish"? _____

1303

What is *outside* in "The boy was outside"? _____

1304

What is *a student* in "The boy was a student"? _____

---

232   ENGLISH SYNTAX

1305

In kernel sentences, *be* is followed by a noun phrase or an _____ or an _____ .

1306

In a kernel sentence, a **Vs** is always followed by an _____ .

1307

Will it be true that any single word that occurs in isolation in the position after *seem* in the kernel string **NP + Aux + seem +** ____ will be an adjective? ____

1308

It is further true that anything that will not occur after *seem*—any single word, that is, occuring in isolation—in the kernel sentence **NP + Aux + seem +** ____ is *not* an adjective. Adjectives occur in other positions also. In place of "The sink seems dirty," we can say *the dirty sink*. But the single-word position after *seem* is a convenient test for adjectives. What is the adjective in "The child was sad"? ____

1309

What is the adjective in "I met a child happy about attending school"?

_____

1310

The second noun phrase in "I met a child happy about attending school" derives from the base sentence "The child was happy about attending school." (The determiners need not be identical.) We could represent this as **NP + Aux + be + Adj +** about attending school. Here **Aux** is ____ , and **Adj** is the word _____ .

1311

T-rel applied to "The child was happy about attending school" gives *a child* _____ .

1312

Deletion of **relative pronoun + tense + be** from *a child who was happy about attending school* gives _____ .

ADJECTIVES 233

1313

Thus we see that an adjective construction in a noun phrase like *a child happy about attending school* derives exactly like the other noun modifiers that we have been discussing—through **T-rel** and **T-del**. No new rules are needed. What is the adjective in "The sink was dirty"? _____

1314

T-rel applied to "The sink was dirty" gives _____ .

1315

T-del applied to *the sink that was dirty* gives _____ .

1316

Obviously *the sink dirty is not a grammatical noun phrase. We do not have sentences like *"He left it in the sink dirty." Here *the sink dirty* must become _____ .

1317

Again we do not need a new rule. *The sink dirty* → *the dirty sink* by another operation of **T-NM**. When a noun is followed by a single-word adjective, **T-NM** is obligatory. The positions of the noun and adjective must be reversed. *A man old* must become _____ .

1318

A man old comes from the relative clause _____ .

1319

A man who is (or *was*) *old* comes from the kernel sentence _____ .

1320

Thus, adjectives appear in the kernel after *be* and become noun modifiers through **T-rel, T-del,** and **T-NM**, exactly like participial phrases and adverbials of place, except that **T-NM** is obligatory for single-word adjectives and participles and not for adverbs of place. The noun phrase *the reluctant witness* derives from the kernel sentence _____ .

1321

The fertile land derives from the kernel sentence _____ .

1322

What is the adjective in "He lived in a dreary neighborhood"?

_____

1323

What is the adjective in "A young girl came in"? _____

1324

The noun phrase *a young girl* derives from the kernel sentence "A (*or* the) _____."

1325

Is there an adjective in the sentence "A servant girl came in"? _____

1326

We cannot derive *servant* in *a servant girl* from *"The girl is servant" or *"The girl seems servant," because these are not grammatical sentences. Therefore *servant* is not an adjective, although it is a noun modifier. (*Servant girl* can also be said to be a compound noun—a single word made up, in this case, of two nouns.) *Servant* in *a servant girl* derives from a sentence like "The girl is a servant." Here *a servant* is a noun phrase, and *servant* is a _____.

1327

Since *servant* is a noun in "The girl is a servant," it is also a noun in *the servant girl*, which derives from "The girl is a servant." What kind of word is *witty* in "The witty principal made a speech"? _____

1328

Witty in "The witty principal made a speech" derives from a sentence like "The principal is witty." It is therefore an adjective. Is there an adjective in the sentence "The school principal made a speech"? _____

1329

The phrase *the school principal* cannot come from *"The principal is school." It comes from something like "He is principal of the school" or "The principal runs the school." It is therefore not an adjective but a _____.

ADJECTIVES   235

1330

Thus we see that nouns, along with verbs, adverbs, and adjectives, can be modifiers of nouns. The transformations that make nouns modifiers of other nouns are more complex than those for other word classes. This is the exception to the statement that all noun modifiers other than determiners derive through **T-rel, T-del,** and (for some) **T-NM**. We will not formulize the transformations that make nouns modifiers of other nouns but will just indicate the results and suggest the kernels. What kind of word is *table* in "He bought a table lamp"? _____

1331

What kind of word is *new* in "He bought a new lamp"? _____

1332

Notice that there is often a different stress—that is, a different pattern in loudness of pronunciation—in the combination noun-noun than in the combination adjective-noun. In *a new lamp,* the word *lamp* normally receives the loudest stress. What word normally receives the loudest stress in *a table lamp?* _____

1333

Sometimes, however, the noun-noun stress pattern is the same as the adjective-noun stress pattern. The word *comfortable* in "They have a comfortable sofa" comes from the kernel "The sofa is comfortable." It is an adjective. Is *living room* in "They have a living-room sofa" a noun or an adjective? _____

1334

The noun phrase *the living-room sofa* cannot be derived from *"The sofa is living room." It is related instead to a sentence like "The sofa is in the living room," where *living room* is obviously a noun. In "Weeping children annoy him," is the noun modifier *weeping* a noun, an adjective, or a verb? _____

1335

The noun phrase *the weeping children* comes, through **T-rel, T-del,** and **T-NM,** from the kernel sentence _____ .

1336

The sentence "The children are weeping" looks very much like the sentence "The children are sad." However, there is a difference in the structure. The K-terminal string underlying "The children are sad" is **the children + present + be + sad.** The K-terminal string underlying "The children are weeping" is **the children + present + ___ + ___ + weep.**

1337

"The children are weeping" is just "The children weep" with **be + ing** added from the auxiliary. *Weep* is a verb in "The children weep," and it is the same verb plus **ing** in "The children are weeping" and in *the weeping children*. In "They sat before the roaring fire," is *roaring* a noun, a verb, or an adjective? _____

1338

Roaring in *the roaring fire* comes from the kernel "The fire was roaring," which is a variation of "The fire roared." Therefore it is a verb. In "They sat before a wood fire," is *wood* a noun, a verb, or an adjective?

_____

1339

A *wood fire* goes back to some such kernel as "They burned wood in the fire," where it is clearly a noun. What kind of word is *immense* in "They sat before an immense fire"? _____

1340

Immense derives from the kernel "The fire was immense" → "the fire that was immense" → "the fire immense" → "the immense fire." It cannot be related to *"The fire was immensing" or *"They burned immense in the fire." What kind of word is *greedy* in "She ate like a greedy pig"?

_____

1341

What kind of word is *squealing* in "She sounded like a squealing pig"?

_____

ADJECTIVES   237

1342

What kind of word is *dinner* in "He ate at a dinner table"? _____

1343

What kind of word is *sagging* in "He wrote on a sagging table"?
_____

1344

What kind of word is *juvenile* in "His behavior was juvenile"?
_____

1345

The word *juvenile* occurs in the kernel as both adjective ("It was juvenile") and noun ("He was a juvenile"). But *juvenile behavior* can be derived only from an adjective, as in "His behavior was juvenile." We don't say *"His behavior was a juvenile." What kind of word is *Juvenile* in "He appeared in Juvenile Court"? _____

1346

Juvenile Court cannot come from "The court was juvenile," but only from something like "The court was for juveniles," where it is clearly a noun.

In the noun phrase *a blazing coal fire, blazing* is a _____ and *coal* is a _____ .

1347

In *a snowy winter day, snowy* is an _____ , and *winter* is a _____ .

1348

In *a wintry November day, wintry* is an _____ , and *November* is a _____ .

1349

When an adjective and a noun are used together as noun modifiers, the _____ comes first and the _____ second.

238　ENGLISH SYNTAX

1350

In addition to relative clauses and participial phrases, we have found verbs (participles), adverbs, adjectives, and nouns all occurring as noun modifiers. All of these become noun modifiers by transformation. They preserve in the transform the same meaning relationship to the word they modify that they had in the kernel.

MAIN POINTS OF LESSON TWENTY-SEVEN

Like verb phrases and adverbials of place, adjectives can be transformed into modifiers of nouns. The set of transformations is exactly the same for all of these structures. A kernel sentence with *be* is transformed into a relative clause, and then **relative pronoun + tense + be** is deleted. If the adjective is simple, **T-NM** is then obligatory: **a man angry** ⇒ **an angry man**. If the adjective is complex, **T-NM** is not applicable: *a man angry about something* does not become **an angry about something man*.

Nouns become modifiers of other nouns by more complicated transformations. These have not been formulized here. However, *a wood fire* is clearly related to "They burn wood in the fire," *a table lamp* to "The lamp is for tables," and so forth.

ADJECTIVES 239

Lesson Twenty-Eight

AMBIGUITY IN NOUN MODIFICATION

Noun modification in English includes many interesting complications. One of them is the word *interesting*. What is it in the first sentence of this paragraph? Is it an adjective or a verb? It looks rather like a verb: **interest** + **ing**. Yet it has more the feel of an adjective. If we compare *an interesting girl* with (1) *an attractive girl* and (2) *a smiling girl*, we might very well argue that *an interesting girl* is more like (1) than (2). We might point out, for instance, that we say both "The girl seemed attractive" and "The girl seemed interesting" but not *"The girl seemed smiling." We say *a very attractive girl* and *a very interesting girl*, but not *a very smiling girl*.

The machinery of English transformation throws some light on this problem. There is a particular set of transitive verbs that will occur in sentences like "It _____ John." These verbs can take nouns referring to human beings as objects but do not have to have nouns referring to human beings as subjects. We say, for example, "It interested John," "It pleased John," "It frightened John," "It terrified John," etc. This set of verbs can, in general, add the morpheme **ing** and then substitute for adjectives following **Vs** and *be*. We might indicate the transformation in this way:

$$NP + Aux + VT + NP \text{(person)} \Rightarrow NP + Aux + \begin{Bmatrix} Vs \\ be \end{Bmatrix} + VT + ing$$

So we can have relationships like these:

KERNEL	TRANSFORM
The story interested John.	The story seemed interesting (to John).
The idea terrified John.	The idea seemed terrifying.
The prospect frightened John.	The prospect was frightening.
The party amused John.	The party was amusing.

240 ENGLISH SYNTAX

Words like *terrifying, interesting, amusing* become adjectives by adoption, as it were. After they are put into the **Vs** and *be* sentences by this transformation, they behave just as regular adjectives do. In *an interesting girl*, we might say that *interesting* is an adjective derived by transformation from the transitive verb *interest*. But *smiling* in *a smiling girl* is just a verb. It is not an adjective, because there is no such sentence as *"The girl seemed smiling." The reason there isn't is that there is no such sentence as *"The girl smiled John." There are some exceptions to the transformation—for example, it doesn't hold for *impress, scare, bother, offend* and some other transitive verbs—but it has quite a lot of generality.

This is one of many complications in noun modification. We shall notice just a few more.

1351

Adjectives (but not nouns and verbs) can be modified by *intensifiers*. Intensifiers are words like *very, quite, rather*. In "The girl was very attractive," *attractive* is an adjective, and *very* is an _____ .

1352

"It was good," "It was mush," and "It was raining" are all alike except for the last word. They all consist of **it + past + be + X**. In these sentences, *good* is an adjective, *mush* is a _____ , and *raining* is a _____ .

1353

We say "It was very good" but not *"It was very mush" or *"It was very raining." In "It was very good," *very* is an _____ .

1354

In "It was quite hot," *hot* is an _____ , and *quite* is an _____ .

1355

We can state the following optional rule for English: **Adj → intensifier + Adj**. This is a kernel rule, not a transformation rule. It means that any adjective can be modified by an _____ .

1356

Any adjective can be modified by an intensifier, and intensifiers do not modify verbs and nouns. A word modified by a word of the *very, rather, quite* class is not a _____ or a _____ .

1357

In "John was rather insolent," *rather* is an _____ , and *insolent* is an _____ .

1358

Note that we say *a very interesting girl* but not **a very smiling girl*. In *a very interesting girl*, the intensifier is the word _____ , and the adjective is the word _____ .

1359

In "Sally is very pretty," *pretty* is an _____ , and *very* is an _____ .

1360

But in "Sally is pretty young," *pretty* is an _____ , and *young* is an _____ .

1361

In "We thought the idea rather silly," the adjective is the word _____ , and the intensifier is the word _____ .

1362

Any adjective can be modified by an intensifier. In "It's in the kitchen sink," is *kitchen* an adjective? _____

1363

In "He repaired the leaking sink," is *leaking* a noun, a verb, or an adjective? _____

242 ENGLISH SYNTAX

1364

Leaking sink is a transformation of "The sink was leaking," a variation of "The sink leaked." Is *scrubbing sink* related to "The sink scrubbed"? _____

1365

Scrubbing sink cannot be related to *"The sink scrubbed," because this sentence is ungrammatical. Sinks don't scrub. The transformation goes something like this: "She scrubs in the sink" → "The sink is for scrubbing" → "It's a scrubbing sink." In the last sentence, is *scrubbing* a noun, a verb, or an adjective? _____

1366

In "It's a scrubbing sink," *scrubbing* is a verb, because it relates to a verb in the base sentence "She scrubs in the sink." In "It's a reading room," is *reading* a noun, a verb, or an adjective? _____

1367

Is *reading room* more like (1) *leaking sink* or (2) *scrubbing sink*? _____

1368

If the derivation of *scrubbing sink* is "She scrubs in the sink" → "The sink is for scrubbing" → "It's a scrubbing sink," the derivation of *reading room* is "They read in the room" → _____ → _____ _____ .

1369

Is *smiling girl* more like (1) *leaking sink* or (2) *scrubbing sink*? _____

1370

If *leaking sink* is related to "The sink leaked," what is *smiling girl* related to? _____

1371

The meaning relationships of words in transforms are always the same as in the kernel. *Leaking sink* and "The sink leaked" express the same

AMBIGUITY IN NOUN MODIFICATION   243

meaning, though they express it in different ways. *Writing table* is related to a kernel like "They _____ on the table."

1372

Some structures can be derived from more than one kernel sentence. *Writing teacher* can have the meaning "The teacher is writing" or "The students write" (and the teacher instructs them). In both meanings, however, *writing* is a _____ .

1373

A structure which can be derived from two kernel sentences has two different meanings. A structure with two different meanings is said to be ambiguous. Is *writing table* ambiguous? _____

1374

Writing table can only come from "They write on the table," not from *"The table writes." It is not ambiguous. Is *burning place* ambiguous?

_____

1375

Burning place can come from either "They burn in the place" or "The place is burning," so it is ambiguous. In speech, however, the two meanings are distinguished by stress: *BURNing place* ("They burn in the place"), *burning PLACE* ("The place is burning"). In *leaking sink* and "The sink is leaking," *leak* is a _____ .

1376

Constructions like *leaking sink* (but not constructions like *writing table*) derive from base sentences through **T-rel**, **T-del**, and **T-NM**. If we apply **T-rel** to "The student is making trouble," taking *the student* as the **NP**, we get _____ .

1377

If we delete **relative pronoun** + **tense** + **be** from *the student who is making trouble*, we get _____ .

---

244   ENGLISH SYNTAX

1378

For the construction *a sink leaking,* **T-NM** is obligatory. *A sink leaking* must become *a leaking sink.* For *the student making trouble,* however, **T-NM** is optional. If we apply it, we get _____ .

1379

In *the trouble-making student,* is *trouble* a noun, verb, or adjective?

_____

1380

In *a fun-loving bunch,* is *loving* a noun, verb, or adjective? _____

1381

In *a record-smashing team,* is *record* a noun, verb, or adjective? _____

1382

In *a happy, fun-loving bunch,* is *happy* a noun, verb, or adjective? _____

1383

What is *very* in *a very happy, fun-loving bunch?* _____

1384

In *a rather industrious fact-finding committee,* the intensifier is the word _____ , and the adjective is the word _____ .

1385

The noun phrase *a rather industrious fact-finding committee* contains transformations from two kernel sentences. One is "The committee is finding facts." The other is "The committee is _____ ."

1386

The more transformations a noun phrase contains, the more chances there are that it will be ambiguous—that is, have more than one meaning. *An important fact-finding committee* would presumably mean that the committee found facts and that the _____ was/were important.

1387

An important-fact finding committee would presumably mean that the _____ was/were important.

1388

If we were to write this phrase without hyphens—*important fact finding committee*—it would be ambiguous. Is *old record smashing team* ambiguous? _____

1389

Old record-smashing team means that the team smashed records and the _____ was/were old.

1390

In "John's a car salesman," is *car* a noun, verb, or adjective? _____

1391

Notice the hyphen in "John's a new-car salesman." Does this sentence mean (1) that John is new at the job or (2) that he sells new cars? _____

1392

The hyphen in "John's a new-car salesman" shows that *new* derives from "The cars are new," not "The salesman is new." *New* modifies *car*. What does *new-car* modify? _____

1393

In "John's a good car salesman," *good* modifies *car salesman*. What does *splendid* modify in "Tom's a splendid basketball player"? _____

1394

In "Tom's a splendid basketball player," *splendid* modifies *basketball player*, not just *player*. What does *old* modify in "Lou's an old-coin collector"? _____

246   ENGLISH SYNTAX

1395

What does *old* modify in "Randy's an old coin collector"? _____

_____

1396

What does *American* modify in "Randy's an American Roman-coin collector"? _____

1397

In "Spencer is a very fine watch repairman," *very* is an _____, and *fine* is an _____.

1398

In "There were some young boys outside," *young* is an _____, and *outside* is an _____.

1399

In "They lived in a sleepy country town," *sleepy* is an _____, and *country* is a _____.

1400

In expanded noun phrases words belong to the same word classes that they belong to in the kernel sentences from which they are derived. They have the same meaning relationship to the noun they modify as they did in the kernel. If a noun modifier can come from two or more kernel sentences (like *writing* in *a writing teacher*), it will always be ambiguous.

MAIN POINTS OF LESSON TWENTY-EIGHT

Intensifiers are words like *very, rather, quite, pretty*. Intensifiers modify adjectives. They do not modify nouns and verbs.

Words have the same meaning relationships in transforms that they do in the structures that underlie the transforms. For example, the relationships among *committee, fact,* and *find* are the same in *the fact-finding committee* and in "The committee finds facts." Words belong to the same word class in transforms that they belong to in the structures that underlie the transforms. In this example, *find* is a verb and *fact* a noun in both structures.

It sometimes happens that a structure can be derived from two different underlying structures. Such a structure is said to be ambiguous. It has two meanings—those of both structures that underlie it. Thus *an English teacher* can be related to both "He teaches English" and "He is English."

Lesson Twenty-Nine
SENTENCES TRANSFORMED INTO NP's

The question of ambiguity is an important and interesting one in language. It is important for the writer, who must make sure that his sentence can be understood in just one way and not two or more. But it is also important for what it shows us about the nature of language itself.

There are several kinds of ambiguity. It is possible for a kernel sentence to be ambiguous. This may happen when one or more of the words belong to two different word classes or subclasses and there is no signal to show which is which. An example of this kind of ambiguity is the sentence "The detective looked hard." This could be either **NP + Aux + VI + Adv-m** ("The detective made a careful search") or **NP + Aux + Vs + Adj** ("The detective seemed tough").

Ambiguity is much more common, however, in transforms, when the transform can be derived from either of two underlying structures. It is particularly likely when the structure is the result of multiple transformations, as in *new car salesman* or *old coin collector*. In such structures, stress in speech or hyphenation in writing will often make clear which meaning is intended. The problem here is that modifiers can themselves be modified, so that one may not know, for example, whether the structure is **old + coin collector** or **old coin + collector**.

We can have similar complications in the positions after the noun that is being modified. Suppose we have the structure *the girl in the car* in which a prepositional phrase *in the car* modifies *the girl*. But the prepositional phrase itself contains the noun phrase *the car*, and this noun phrase can also be modified. We might have *the girl in the old car, the girl in the car nearby, the girl in the car in the garage.* The last example puts in another noun phrase, *the garage,* to which all of the modification structures are again applicable: *the girl in the car in the old garage, the girl in the car in the garage near the house,* etc.

When transformation is multiplied in this way, ambiguity becomes increasingly likely. In the noun phrase *the girl in the car that needed water,* there is no way of telling whether the structure underlying this is "The girl needed water" or "The car needed water," since both of these sentences are entirely grammatical.

This is not intended as an admonition to avoid complicated sentences. However, it is obvious that the more complex a sentence becomes—i.e., the more transforms it contains—the more care one must use to be sure that the underlying grammatical relations remain clear.

1401

The sentence "It was easy for John to milk the goats" is derived from two base sentences. The matrix sentence is **it was easy** + **Comp**. Here **Comp**, for complement, stands for whatever is going to turn out to be easy. The other base sentence is "John milked the goats." The sentence "It was necessary for someone to milk the goats" derives from the base sentences **it was necessary** + **Comp** and "Someone _____ _____."

1402

The sentence "It was hard for David to do it" derives from **it was hard** + **Comp** and _____.

1403

"It was hard for me to do it" derives from _____ + **Comp** and _____.

1404

"It was hard for him to do it" derives from _____ and _____.

1405

The **Comp** simply represents an unspecified part of the matrix sentence to be filled in by material from the insert sentence, like the **Comp** of **NP** + **Aux** + **Vt₃** + **Comp** + **NP** in the **VT** transformations. Let us return now to the structures in "It was easy for John to milk the goats." If "John milked the goats" consists of **John** + **past** + **X**, what does "I did it" consist of? _____ + _____ + _____

250   ENGLISH SYNTAX

1406

Say that "John milked the goats" consists of **John** + **past** + **X** and **for John to milk the goats** consists of **for** + **John** + **to** + **X**. For both structures, **X** stands for _____ .

1407

The structures **John** + **past** + **X** and **for** + **John** + **to** + **X** are exactly alike, except that *for* is added at the beginning of the second, and _____ replaces _____ .

1408

"John milked the goats" is to *for John to milk the goats* as "David did it" is to _____ .

1409

In both cases we add *for* at the beginning and replace tense with *to*. The same transformation applied to "Henry considered Mary beautiful" produces _____ .

1410

The same transformation applied to "The boys were good" produces _____ .

1411

If the subject of the base sentence is one of the personal pronouns that have special object forms—*I, he, she, we, they*—the pronoun takes the object form—*me, him, her, us, them*—after the word *for*, by a phonological rule. Thus "I did it" becomes *for me to do it*. "We inspected the car" becomes _____ .

1412

We will call this transformation **T-for-to** because it puts the word *for* at the beginning of the insert sentence and replaces tense with *to*. By **T-for-to**, "She wanted to help us" becomes _____ .

SENTENCES TRANSFORMED INTO NP's   251

1413

"It was easy for John to milk the goats" is produced by a double-base transformation; that is, there are two underlying sentences. The matrix sentence is **it was easy + Comp**. The insert sentence is "John milked the goats," which becomes *for John to milk the goats* by **T-for-to** and then replaces the **Comp** of the matrix sentence. What is the matrix sentence in "It was hard for David to do it"? _____

1414

In this transformation the matrix sentence has the general form **it + Aux + be + substantive + Comp**. The insert sentence can have any form at all. What is the insert sentence underlying "It was hard for me to persuade him to go"? _____

1415

What is the insert sentence underlying "It was time for us to pack up the dishes"? _____

1416

What is the insert sentence of "It was pleasant for them to have a new house"? _____

1417

Take the sentence "It was easy to milk the goats." This is just like "It was easy for John to milk the goats" except that the words _____ have been deleted.

1418

The sentence "It was pleasant to have a new house" is just like "It was pleasant for them to have a new house" except that the words _____ have been deleted.

1419

In general, the sequence **for + NP** in the structure **for + NP + to + X** can be deleted and the structure will still be grammatical. If we make this deletion in "It was time for us to pack up the dishes," we get _____

_____ .

252   ENGLISH SYNTAX

1420

By the deletion transformation, "It was natural for everybody to consider Mary beautiful" becomes _____ _____ .

1421

Thus any sequence **NP** + **tense** + **X** becomes **for** + **NP** + **to** + **X** by **T-for-to**, and then **for** + **NP** + **to** + **X** becomes **to** + **X** by deletion. The X can be any verb phrase minus the auxiliary. Both transformations applied to "The soldiers tried to do something about it" will give _____ .

1422

In "It was easy for John to milk the goats," the **NP** subject of the matrix sentence is the word _____ .

1423

Another transformation permits us to replace the subject of the matrix sentence with the verb phrase structure derived by **T-for-to**. Thus "It was easy for John to milk the goats" becomes "For John to milk the goats was easy." Similarly "It was hard for him to do it" becomes _____ _____ .

1424

This last transformation is applied rather infrequently. "It was hard for him to do it" is much more common than "For him to do it was hard." Still, both are grammatical. This transformation applied to "It was natural for the boys to think Edna foolish" gives _____ _____ .

1425

Structures from which **for** + **NP** have been deleted can replace the *it* subject of the matrix sentence in exactly the same way. "It was easy to milk the goats" becomes "To milk the goats was easy." Other, closely related, transformations give "To milk the goats was easy for John," "The goats were easy for John to milk." "It was easy for John to milk

SENTENCES TRANSFORMED INTO NP's 253

the goats" is to "To milk the goats was easy" as "It was natural for the boys to think Edna foolish" is to _____.

1426

Structures which take **NP** positions by transformations of this sort become **NP**'s themselves. In "To milk the goats was easy," the structure *to milk the goats,* though it derives from a verb phrase, has become a noun phrase by taking the subject position. Of course, it is not a noun phrase of the kernel type **Det + N**. In "To shuck oysters is tiresome," the noun phrase that functions as subject is the group of words _____ _____.

1427

The structure *to milk the goats* derives, through **T-for-to** and deletion, from a kernel sentence like "They _____."

1428

So far our examples have shown structures derived by **T-for-to** and deletion replacing first the complement in matrix sentences of the type it + **Aux + be + substantive + Comp** and then replacing the *it*. However, such structures can replace other **NP**'s in other functions. What group of words has replaced the substantive in "The idea was for John to milk the goats"? _____

1429

What group of words takes the role of substantive in "His real mistake was to consider Edna foolish"? _____

1430

What group of words is subject in "John's playing the piano annoyed the neighbors"? _____

1431

In "John's playing the piano annoyed the neighbors," the subject *John's playing the piano* derives from the base sentence "John played the piano." In "Henry's packing up the dishes helped a lot," the subject derives from the base sentence _____.

1432

In "Henry's packing up the dishes helped a lot," *Henry's* consists of the noun phrase *Henry* plus the _____ morpheme.

1433

Henry's packing up the dishes consists of **Henry + Pos + ing + X**. And "Henry packed up the dishes" consists of **Henry + tense + X**. In both structures **X** represents the words _____.

1434

Compare **Henry + tense + pack up the dishes** and **Henry + Pos + ing + pack up the dishes**. The second is just like the first except that ____ + ____ has replaced _____.

1435

We will call this transformation **T-Pos-ing**. The sequence **Pos + ing** replaces the tense of the base sentence. By this, **John + past + play + the piano** becomes _____ + ____ + ____ + **play the piano**.

1436

The string **John + Pos + ing + play + the piano** contains a sequence of **Af + v**. **T-af** therefore must apply to give _____ + ____ + _____ + ____ + _____.

1437

The string **John + Pos + play + ing + the piano** represents the actual structure _____.

1438

By **T-for-to** the sequence **NP + tense + X** becomes **for + NP + to + X**. By **T-Pos-ing** the sequence **NP + tense + X** becomes **NP + ____ + ____ + ____**.

1439

By **T-for-to**, "John milked the goats" becomes _____ _____.

1440

By T-Pos-ing, "John milked the goats" becomes _____
_____ .

1441

We say that by deletion *for John to milk the goats* can become *to milk the goats*. In the same way *John's milking the goats* becomes *milking the goats*. In the first structure we deleted for + John. In the second we deleted John + ____ .

1442

What is the subject of the sentence "Milking the goats took a lot of mother's time"? _____

1443

What is the object of the preposition in "Mother helped by milking the goats"? _____

1444

What is the object of the preposition in "The family survived through mother's milking the goats"? _____

1445

What is the substantive in "Mother's job was milking the goats"?
_____

1446

Does *milking the goats* have the same function in "Mother's job was milking the goats" that it does in "The hired man was milking the goats"? ____

1447

We might write "Mother's job was milking the goats" in this way: Mother's job + be + past + milk + ing + the goats. Is this *be* part of Aux—that is, does it come from be + ing? ____

256   ENGLISH SYNTAX

1448

It can't be part of **Aux**, because if it were, it and **ing** could be omitted. We must choose tense from **Aux**, but we don't have to choose **be** + **ing**. If we omit **be** + **ing** from "Mother's job was milking the goats," we get **mother's job** + **past** + **milk** + **the goats**. This would give the sentence _____ .

1449

What is the substantive of the sentence "John's suggestion was for mother to keep on milking the goats"? _____

1450

The parallelism between structures in *to* and structures in **ing** runs through the grammar with striking regularity. We encountered it earlier in the **VT**'s containing **Vt**$_{to}$ and **Vt**$_{ing}$: "I asked John to speak," "I heard John speaking," etc. We see much the same sort of mechanism in the transformations **T-for-to** and **T-Pos-ing**, which transform sentences into structures that can be used in **NP** positions.

MAIN POINTS OF LESSON TWENTY-NINE

T-for-to: NP + tense + X ⟹ for + NP + to + X
T-Pos-ing: NP + tense + X ⟹ NP + Pos + ing + X

These transformations produce, from underlying sentences, structures that can fill **NP** positions in matrix sentences. That is, they produce structures like *for John to milk the cows* and *John's milking the cows*, which can be used as subject, object, substantive, and object of prepositions.

The structure **for** + **NP** + **to** + **X** becomes **to** + **X**, and **NP** + **Pos** + **ing** + **X** becomes **ing** + **X** by deletion. *For John to milk the cows* becomes *to milk the cows*. *John's milking the cows* becomes *milking the cows*. These shortened structures can also become **NP**'s in matrix sentences, in which they can function as any **NP** does.

Structures formed by **T-for-to** can replace the unspecified **Comp** of matrix sentences of the type **it** + **Aux** + **be** + **substantive** + **Comp**—e.g., **it was easy** + **Comp**, **it was unusual** + **Comp**, as in "It was easy for John to milk the goats," "It was unusual to see William in school." Such structures can become **NP** subjects by replacing the *it:* "For John to milk the cows was easy," "To see William in school was unusual." We have also related structures like "To milk the cows was easy for John" and "The cows were easy for John to milk."

Lesson Thirty
SUBORDINATE CLAUSES

In the preliminary description of **Aux**, we rewrote it as **tense + (M) + (have + part) + (be + ing)**. Then we changed this slightly as follows:

> Aux → tense + (M) + (aspect)
> aspect → (have + part) + (be + ing)

We can now see one of the reasons for this seeming complication. There are some structures which can have aspect—that is, either **have + part** or **be + ing** or both, but which cannot have tense or **M**.

Take the sentence "It was natural for John to have replied in that way." This contains the structure *for John to have replied in that way*, from "John had replied in that way." This last could be written **John + tense + have + part + reply in that way**. In making this into *for John to have replied in that way*, we take out the tense but not the **have + part** and get **for + John + to + have + part + reply in that way**. After **T-af**, this gives us *for John to have replied in that way*.

Similarly, the sentence "It was explained by John's having been waiting for the bus" contains, as object of the preposition *by*, the structure *John's having been waiting for the bus*, from the kernel "John had been waiting for the bus." This kernel has the form **John + past + have + part + be + ing + wait for the bus**. T-Pos-ing replaces *past* with **Pos + ing**, giving **John + Pos + ing + have + part + be + ing + wait for the bus**. **T-af** will then convert this automatically, and we get *John's having been waiting for the bus*. Thus we see that machinery already described for the kernel works in the same way in transforms of the kernel.

There are some restrictions on these transformations. We can't have two **ing**'s in a row. For example, **T-Pos-ing** cannot apply to "John was waiting here," because this would give *"John's being waiting here." **T-for-to** can apply, however. The structure *for John to be waiting here* is grammatical.

1451

A clause is any structure that contains tense—present or past. Is "John replied angrily" a clause? ____

1452

"John replied angrily" has the form **John + reply + past + angrily**, and *past* is a tense. Therefore "John replied angrily" is a clause. Is "What does he want to do?" a clause? ____

1453

"What does he want to do?" is **what + do + present + he + want + to + do**. *Present* is a tense, so the structure is a clause. "John replied angrily" and "What does he want to do?" are sentences as well as being clauses. Not all clauses are sentences, however. Is *whom he saw* a clause?

____

1454

The structure *whom he saw* is a clause because it contains the tense *past*. It is derived from the sentence "He saw someone," but it is not itself a sentence. It is what we have called a _____ clause.

1455

Relative clauses are made by transformations in which a relative replaces some structure in the base sentence. In *whom he saw,* the relative pronoun *whom* has replaced an object. In *that came with us,* the relative pronoun *that* has replaced a _____ .

1456

In *where he was going,* the relative *where* has replaced an adverbial of _____ .

1457

In *when he arrived,* the relative *when* has replaced an _____ of _____ .

1458

There are some clauses which are not sentences and which are not relative clauses either. That is, they are not formed by the replacement of some structure by a relative. Is *that he was arriving tonight* a clause? ____

1459

The structure *that he was arriving tonight* has the form **that** + **he** + **be** + **past** + **arrive** + **ing** + **tonight**. *Past* is a tense, and so the structure is a clause. It is not a relative clause, however, and neither is it a sentence. It is what we will call a *subordinate* clause. The structure "He left yesterday" is a clause. Is it a sentence? ____

1460

"He left yesterday" and *that he left yesterday* are both clauses, but only the first is a sentence. What makes the second *not* a sentence is the addition of the word ____ .

1461

The word *that* in subordinate clauses like *that he left yesterday* and *that he was arriving tonight* is what we call a *subordinator*. It doesn't replace anything in a base sentence. It just subordinates the base sentence to something else. What is the subordinate clause in "I knew that John had seen them"? ____

1462

"John had seen them" is subordinated by the addition of the subordinator *that* and can then be used in a matrix sentence. Any sentence at all can be subordinated in this way. That is, any **S** can become **Sub** + **S** and thus a subordinate clause. The sentence "He thought that Mary was here" contains a sequence **Sub** + **S**. The **Sub** is the word ____ .

1463

The sentence "He thought that Mary was here" is a double-base transformation. That is, there are two underlying sentences. One is the insert sentence "Mary was here." The other is the matrix sentence **he thought** + **NP**. The insert sentence adds the word *that*, which makes it a subordinate clause, and then replaces the item ____ in the matrix sentence.

SUBORDINATE CLAUSES

1464

In he thought + **NP,** the element **NP** is an object. So in "He thought that Mary was here," the subordinate clause *that Mary was here* is also an **NP** and also functions as an object. In "We knew that she liked fish," the subordinate clause functions as an _____ .

1465

In "That she liked fish wasn't very generally known," what words constitute the subordinate clause? _____

1466

In "That she liked fish wasn't very generally known," the subordinate clause functions as _____ .

1467

Is the structure *for David to have done such a thing* a clause? ____

1468

A clause must contain _____ .

1469

The structure *for David to have done such a thing* contains *have* and *part*, but it doesn't contain *present* or *past*, so it is not a clause. Is the structure *his wanting to see me* a clause? ____

1470

The structure *whom he saw* is a _____ clause.

1471

The structure *that he saw them* is a _____ clause.

1472

Any sentence can be made into a subordinate clause by the prefixing of a subordinator. That is, any **S** can become **Sub + S. Sub** is an abbreviation of the word _____ .

1473

A subordinator shows that a following sentence pattern is subordinated to, or made part of, a matrix sentence. Usually the subordinate clause replaces an **NP** in the matrix sentence and functions as subject, object, and so forth. The sentence "I wonder whether he had heard about it" contains a subordinate clause. What is the subordinator? _____

1474

In "Whether he had heard about it isn't very important," the subordinate clause functions as _____ .

1475

In "Whether he had heard about it isn't very important," the matrix sentence is **NP + isn't very important**. What is the insert sentence?

1476

In transformations of this sort, the insert sentence is fully specified, but the matrix sentence is not. **NP + isn't very important** leaves the subject unspecified, since this will be filled by the insert sentence. We have seen this sort of thing before, as in **Jerry + considers + Comp + Mary**, where the **Comp** will be filled from an insert sentence like "Mary is pretty." What is the matrix sentence in "That he could have done it is absurd"?

NP + _____

1477

What is the insert sentence in "That he could have done it is absurd"?

1478

When a subordinate clause introduced by the subordinator *that* functions as an object, the *that* can be optionally deleted. Both "We knew that she liked fish" and "We knew she liked fish" are grammatical sentences. In "I suppose he knows the answer," what words are the subordinate clause? _____

1479

In "I suppose he knows the answer," the subordinate clause functions as _____ .

SUBORDINATE CLAUSES 263

1480

In "I suppose he knows the answer," the subordinator _____ has been deleted.

1481

That can be deleted only when the subordinate clause functions as object, not when it functions as subject. "We know she liked fish" is grammatical, but *"She liked fish was well known" is not. To make the last sentence grammatical, we must add the subordinator _____ .

1482

We have seen subordinate clauses taking **NP** positions—that is, functioning as subject, object, etc. So far we have seen relative clauses used only as modifiers of **NP**'s, as in *the man who was here*. In "The man who was here was Uncle Rudolph," the relative clause functions as a _____ .

1483

However, relative clauses may also take **NP** positions and function as subjects and objects. In "I knew who was here," the relative clause functions as _____ .

1484

The subject of "Whoever did it must have gone away" is a relative clause. It is the group of words _____ .

1485

The transformations that produce relative clauses used as **NP**'s are the same as those that produce relative clauses used as noun modifiers, except that there is some difference in the relative pronouns. When a relative pronoun replaces the subject of a kernel sentence and the relative clause is a noun modifier, the relative will be *who*, _____ , or _____ .

1486

Who and *which* are used in relative clauses that occur as **NP**'s, but *that* is not. What is the subject of the sentence "Who killed Cock Robin isn't known"? _____

264   ENGLISH SYNTAX

1487

It is more common for this meaning to be expressed in the form "It isn't known who killed Cock Robin," in which the relative clause replaces a **Comp** in a matrix sentence with the subject *it,* as in "It was easy for John to milk the goats." The structure of the relative clause is the same in any case. In "This is the man that killed Cock Robin," the relative clause functions as _____ .

1488

The relative *that* never occurs in relative clauses that take **NP** positions. We say, "This is the man that killed Cock Robin," where the relative clause functions as a modifier. But we do not say *"That killed Cock Robin isn't known" or *"It isn't known that killed Cock Robin." The word *what,* however, occurs in relative clauses used as **NP**'s. What words are the relative clause in "I wonder what happened"? _____

1489

In "I wonder what happened," the relative clause functions as _____ .

1490

Whoever, whatever, whichever, whomever also occur in relative clauses used as **NP**'s. What is the relative clause in "Whoever did it must have gone away"? _____

1491

What is the relative clause in "Give it to whomever you like"? _____

1492

In "Give it to whomever you like," we choose *whomever* and not *whoever* because the relative pronoun replaces the object of the kernel sentence "You like someone." What is the relative clause in "Give it to whoever wants it"? _____

1493

In "Give it to whomever you like" and "Give it to whoever wants it," the relative clauses are objects of a _____ .

1494

In "Give it to whoever wants it," we choose *whoever* and not *whomever* because the relative pronoun replaces the subject of the kernel sentence "Someone wants it." Which would we use, *whomever* or *whoever*, in the sentence "Give it to _____ admires John"? _____

1495

Which would we use, *whoever* or *whomever*, in the sentence "Give it to _____ John admires"? _____

1496

What is the relative clause in "I was surprised by what he said"?
_____

1497

What is the relative pronoun in "I was surprised by what he said"?
_____

1498

Does the relative pronoun in "I was surprised by what he said" replace the subject or the object of the kernel sentence? _____

1499

In the sentence "Whichever you like will be all right with me," the relative pronoun replaces the _____ of the kernel sentence that underlies the clause. The clause functions as _____ .

1500

Relative and subordinate clauses are similar to sentences in their internal structure. They must have a subject or a relative pronoun that replaces a subject. They must have an **Aux,** which must include at least tense, and a predicate with *be* or a verbal. These clauses differ from sentences in that they are themselves parts of sentences, functioning as modifier, subject, object, or in some other way.

MAIN POINTS OF LESSON THIRTY

A clause is defined as a structure that contains tense. A clause may also be a sentence. A clause that is not a sentence is either a relative clause or a subordinate clause.

In a relative clause a relative—like *who, which, whatever, where, when,* etc.—has replaced something in the base sentence. For example, it might replace a subject, an object, an adverbial of place or time. The relative then has the function of whatever it replaces.

A subordinate clause is introduced by a subordinator. The most common subordinator is the word *that,* which should not be confused with the relative pronoun *that.* The only function of the subordinator is to show that the clause is part of a sentence and not itself a sentence. Except for the addition of the subordinator, the subordinate clause has exactly the same structure as the base sentence underlying it.

When the subordinate clause functions as object, the subordinator *that* can be optionally deleted.

Lesson Thirty-One
INNER AND OUTER STRUCTURE

In order to unravel the structure of a sentence that contains a clause, we must keep two things clearly separate: (1) the structure of the clause itself; (2) the relation of the clause to the sentence of which it has become a part. We can call (1) the *inner* structure of the clause and (2) its *outer* structure.

Let us take the sentence "We'll give whoever needs it the money." This sentence contains the clause *whoever needs it*. This is a clause because it contains tense. We can show its structure as follows: **relative pronoun + present + VT + NP**. This clause has exactly the same structure as the base sentence "Someone needs it," except that a relative pronoun has replaced the subject *someone*. The rest is just the same: tense, transitive verb, object. All of this is the *inner* structure of the clause. It is the structure of the base sentence except for the change required by the transformation—the substitution of a relative pronoun for the original subject.

The *outer* structure is the relation of the clause to the sentence of which it has become a part. The general structure of the sentence "We'll give whoever needs it the money" can be shown thus: **NP + Aux + Vt$_{3-9}$ + NP + NP**. This is a sentence with a verb of the *give* type. The first **NP** after the verb is the indirect object, and the second is the direct object. It has the same general form as the simpler sentence "We'll give someone the money," in which *someone* is the indirect object. The transformation produces the relative clause *whoever needs it* from the insert sentence "Someone needs it" and puts this clause in as indirect object in the matrix sentence represented by "We'll give someone the money."

The relative clause *whoever needs it* has the inner structure required by the insert sentence and the outer structure required by the matrix sentence. It has the relative pronoun *whoever* instead of *whomever* because the inner structure requires it. *"Whomever needs it" is ungrammatical. It has *whoever* instead of *who* because the outer structure requires it. "Who needs it" is grammatical, but *"We'll give who needs it the money" is not.

1501

What is the participial phrase in "The man teasing the cat is Uncle Rudolph"? _____

1502

The participial phrase *teasing the cat* derives through a relative clause from the base sentence "The man _____ ."

1503

"The man teasing the cat is Uncle Rudolph" derives from two base sentences—a matrix sentence and an insert sentence. The insert sentence is "The man is teasing the cat." The matrix sentence is _____ _____ .

1504

The insert sentence "The man is teasing the cat" produces the participial phrase _____ .

1505

The insert sentence "The man is teasing the cat" determines the inner structure of the participial phrase *teasing the cat.* In both structures *tease* is a transitive verb and *the cat* functions as _____ .

1506

The matrix sentence determines the outer structure of the participial phrase. In "The man teasing the cat is Uncle Rudolph," the participial phrase functions as a noun _____ .

1507

What is the relative clause in "The boy who visited us wouldn't eat broccoli"? _____

1508

In "The boy who visited us wouldn't eat broccoli," the relative clause derives from the insert sentence "The boy visited us." What is the matrix sentence? _____

INNER AND OUTER STRUCTURE

1509

In the relative clause *who visited us,* we have *who* and not *whom* because the relative pronoun replaces a _____ in the insert sentence.

1510

In "The boy who helps us doesn't like spinach," is the choice of *who* instead of *whom* determined by the inner or the outer structure of the relative clause? _____

1511

Would it be grammatical to substitute the word *what* for *who* in "The boy who helps us doesn't like spinach"? _____

1512

*"The boy what helps us doesn't like spinach" isn't grammatical, at least in standard English. Could the relative clause *what helps us* be grammatical in any sentence? _____

1513

We have in English such grammatical sentences as "What helps us is our youth" and "I don't know what helps us." In these sentences the relative clause is used not as a modifier but as a noun _____ .

1514

The relative pronoun *what* occurs when the relative clause is used as a noun phrase but not when it is used as a _____ .

1515

Is it the inner or the outer structure of the clause that rules out *what* in a sentence like "The boy who helps us doesn't like spinach"? _____

1516

What is the relative clause in "Whoever wants it can have it"? _____

1517

What is the function of the relative clause in "Whoever wants it can have it"? _____

1518

"Whoever wants it can have it" is made from the insert sentence "Someone wants it" and the matrix sentence "Someone _____ _____ ."

1519

In "Whoever wants it can have it," we have *whoever* and not *whomever* because the relative pronoun replaces the _____ of the insert sentence.

1520

In "Whoever wants it can have it," the relative clause functions as the _____ of the matrix sentence.

1521

In "Whoever wants it can have it," the fact that *whoever* has replaced the subject of the insert sentence is a statement about the _____ structure of the clause. The fact that the clause functions as the subject of the matrix sentence is a statement about its _____ structure.

1522

"Who wants it" can be a grammatical clause, as in "Anybody who wants it can have it." But it is not grammatical in *"Who wants it can have it." In "Whoever wants it can have it," the choice of *whoever* instead of *who* is determined by the _____ structure of the clause.

1523

The sentence "I knew that Merrill would come" contains a subordinate clause. What is it? _____

1524

"I knew that Merrill would come" derives from two base sentences. The matrix sentence is **I knew + NP**. What is the insert sentence? _____

_____

1525

In "I knew that Merrill would come," the word *that* is a subordinator. It is added by the transformation **S** ⇒ ____ + ____ .

1526

In "I knew that Merrill would come," the subordinate clause *that Merrill would come* has exactly the same inner structure as the insert sentence "Merrill would come," except that the subordinator *that* has been added. As for its outer structure, the clause functions as the _____ in the matrix sentence.

1527

In "That Sue knew about it was obvious," the subordinate clause functions as _____ in the matrix sentence.

1528

The rule that produces subordinate clauses is **S** ⇒ **Sub + S**. We have seen that **Sub** may be such a word as *that* or *whether*. The subordinator *that* can be deleted in some sentences. Can it be deleted in "We knew that Merrill would come"? ____

1529

Can *that* be deleted in "That Sue knew about it was obvious"? ____

1530

That cannot be deleted when the subordinate clause is subject of the matrix sentence. *"Sue knew about it was obvious" is ungrammatical. Whether *that* can be deleted or not depends on whether the clause is used as subject or object in the matrix sentence. In other words, it depends on its _____ structure.

272   ENGLISH SYNTAX

1531

Recall the difference between relative clauses and subordinate clauses. In a relative clause, a relative replaces some structure in the insert sentence. Is any part of the insert sentence replaced in the clause *that Sue knew about it?* _____

1532

When the base sentence "Sue knew about it" is made into the subordinate clause *that Sue knew about it,* the structure remains exactly the same except that the _____ *that* is added.

1533

When the base sentence "Albert liked something" is made into the relative clause *what Albert liked,* the _____ of the insert sentence has been replaced by the relative pronoun _____ .

1534

Relative clauses beginning with the word *when, where, how* can also be used as NP's—that is, as subjects and objects. The transformations which produce them are similar to those that produce *wh* questions. If we substitute the interrogative *when* for the adverb of time *yesterday* in "Steve went yesterday," we get the *wh* question "When did _____ ?"

1535

If we substitute the interrogative *where* for the adverbial of place *to Boston* in "Jeff went to Boston," we get the *wh* question _____ .

1536

If we substitute the interrogative *how* for the adverb of manner *this way* in "Steve did it this way," we get the *wh* question _____ _____ .

1537

When, where, and *how* may also introduce relative clauses, but the word order is different. The reason is that T-wh works only on strings resulting from T-yes/no, whereas T-rel does not. In "I know where Jeff went," *where Jeff went* is a relative clause. What is the relative clause in "I know when Jeff left"? _____

1538

What is the relative clause in "I know how Jeff did it"? _____

1539

What is the relative clause in "I know why Steve complained about it"?
_____

1540

These relative clauses are like those with *who, what, whomever,* etc., in that a relative replaces something in the insert sentence. Since the relatives *when, where, how* (along with *how many,* etc.) replace adverbials, they are called *relative adverbs*. When the insert sentence "Bill left this morning" is made into the relative clause *when Bill left,* the relative adverb *when* replaces an adverbial of _____ .

1541

In the sentence "I know where Bill put it," the relative adverb has replaced an adverbial of _____ .

1542

In the sentence "I know what Bill put in the drawer," the relative pronoun *what* has replaced an **NP** functioning as _____ in the insert sentence.

1543

In the sentence "I have forgotten where they live," the relative clause is an **NP** functioning as _____ .

1544

In the sentence "When they shucked the oysters isn't very important," the relative adverb *when* has replaced an _____ in the insert sentence.

1545

In the sentence "When they shucked the oysters isn't very important," the relative clause is the group of words _____ _____ .

1546

In "When they shucked the oysters isn't very important," the relative clause functions as _____ .

1547

In "When they shucked the oysters isn't very important," *shuck* is a Vt_1, and the **NP** *the oysters* functions as _____ . These are matters of _____ structure.

1548

In "When they shucked the oysters isn't very important," could we just as well have the relative clause in the form *when did they shuck the oysters?* _____

1549

*"When did they shuck the oysters isn't very important," is not grammatical. The clause must have the form *when they shucked the oysters* because it is not a *wh* question but the _____ of the matrix sentence.

1550

The inner structure of a clause or phrase is determined by the insert sentence from which it comes. The outer structure is determined by the matrix sentence in which it is used.

MAIN POINTS OF LESSON THIRTY-ONE

Inner structure is the set of relationships within a clause. Outer structure is the relationship of the clause to the matrix sentence in which it is used. The choice of relatives and subordinators is determined by both inner and outer structure. For example, the choice of *who* or *whom* is a matter of inner structure. The choice of *who* or *whoever* is a matter of outer structure.

Relatives which replace **NP**'s of the insert sentence—*who, what, which, that, whoever,* etc.—are called relative pronouns. Relatives which replace adverbials—*where, when, how,* etc.—are called relative adverbs.

The transformation which produces relative clauses is generally the same as the one which produces *wh* questions. However, **T-wh** operates on a string which is the result of **T-yes/no,** and **T-rel** does not. So the *wh* question has the question form ("When did John go?") and the relative clause does not have this form (*when John went*).

Lesson Thirty-Two
CONJUNCTIONS

In describing the relative and interrogative pronouns, we have restricted ourselves to a rather formal—not to say stuffy—use of *who/whom, whoever/whomever*. The usage we have described is more suitable to writing than to speech, and is more often found in formal than in informal writing. These rules would bar such sentences as "Who are you going with?," "Who did you see?," "Give it to whoever you like." We don't mean to say that these expressions are not used in English or that they are ungrammatical. They are just generated by a somewhat different grammar than the one we have chosen to describe.

There is a strong tendency in English speech to eliminate the words *whom* and *whomever* altogether. Many speakers of English, including many educated people, never use these words in conversation. They use *who* or *whoever* even when it is an object that is replaced in the base sentence. Some facts about the grammar make it easy for this process to go on. For example, when the relative clause is a noun modifier and the relative pronoun replaces an object in the base sentence, the relative pronoun can be deleted. That is, we can say *a man I met* instead of *a man whom I met*. This enables us to avoid the choice between the ungrammatical **a man who I met* and the awkward-sounding *a man whom I met*.

It is probably safer to use *who* against the rule than to use *whom* against the rule. If you use *who* when the grammar calls for *whom*, people may think you ignorant. But if you use *whom* when the grammar calls for *who*, they may think you ignorant and pretentious to boot. *Whom* and *whomever* used ungrammatically suggest that the user wants to be elegant but doesn't know how. There are several places in the grammar where one is easily trapped into an ungrammatical *whom* or *whomever*. For example, *"Give it to whomever needs it" is ungrammatical. The relative clause goes back to the base "Someone needs it"; the relative pronoun replaces a subject, not an object, and so it ought to be *whoever,* not *whomever*. People who say *"Give it to whomever needs it" probably do so because the relative pronoun follows the preposition *to*. But it is the relative clause, not the relative pronoun, which is the object of the preposition. It is a case of choosing the relative pronoun according to the outer structure, when it is the inner structure that decides.

Another well-known trap is a sentence like "Whoever/whomever you think should have it will get it." The grammar calls for *whoever* here, but people not infrequently say (or, more likely, write) *whomever*. They do so because they take the sentence as including a clause *whomever you think*, from a base "You think somebody." But actually there is no such base underlying this clause. The relative pronoun substitutes for the subject of the insert sentence "Somebody should have it," and therefore it is *whoever* instead of *whomever*.

We turn now to another transformation, whose misuse often produces ungrammaticality in written work. This is the transformation that generates compound constructions—that is, constructions that are joined by conjunctions.

1551

The most common conjunction in English is the word *and*. Conjunctions are used to connect or join sentences or parts of sentences. In the sentence "John and Edna quarreled," the conjunction *and* connects two _____ phrases.

1552

In "John howled and screamed," *and* connects two _____ .

1553

Verbs would not be quite a correct answer for 1552. In "John howled and screamed," *howled* is not just a verb but a verb plus its auxiliary, and so is *screamed*. In this sentence, the auxiliary for both *howled* and *screamed* consists of _____ .

1554

In "Felicity slammed the door and walked away," *and* connects two _____ .

1555

In "John bought a book and a necktie," *and* connects two noun phrases that function as _____ .

---

278   ENGLISH SYNTAX

1556

In "Edna gave John and Samuel some canned salmon," *and* connects two noun phrases that function as _____ objects.

1557

In "Edna seemed young and wholesome," *and* connects two _____ _____.

1558

In "John whistled loudly and beautifully," *and* joins two _____.

1559

In "People who eat fish and who like it irritate me," *and* joins two _____.

1560

In "People who eat fish and like it irritate me," *and* joins two _____ _____.

1561

In "I knew that Samuel was leaving and that he didn't intend to return," *and* joins two subordinate clauses that function as _____.

1562

In "I knew that Samuel should and would leave," *and* joins two _____.

1563

We see that *and* can connect sentence structures of all sorts. The general rule is that *and* (and other conjunctions) must join similar structures. More precisely, they must join structures generated similarly by the grammatical rules. The sentence "John and Edna talked" derives from two kernel sentences. One is "John talked." What is the other? _____

CONJUNCTIONS 279

1564

We will call the conjunction transformation **T-conj**. T-conj applied to "John talked" plus "Edna talked" gives "John and Edna talked." We could write this as follows: **NP + VP, NP + VP ⇒ NP + and + ____ + ____ .**

1565

In "John and Edna talked," the structures *John* and *Edna* both go back to **NP** subjects of kernel sentences, so the rule that conjunctions join structures generated similarly by the grammatical rule is observed, and the sentence is grammatical. In "John howled and screamed," the *and* joins two _____ .

1566

"John howled and screamed" is a combination of the two base sentences "John howled" and "John screamed." Both are cases of **NP + VP**. Applying **T-conj** to **NP + VP, NP + VP,** we get for this sentence **NP + ____ + ____ + ____ .**

1567

"John bought a book and a necktie" comes from the two base sentences "John bought a book," "John bought a necktie." Each is a case of **NP + Aux + VT + NP**. The transformation produces **NP + Aux + ____ + ____ + ____ + ____ .**

1568

The kernel sentences "John is sober" and "John is serious" are both cases of **NP + ____ + ____ + Adj**.

1569

T-conj applied to "John is sober" and "John is serious" gives **NP + Aux + be + Adj + and + Adj**. This will represent the actual sentence _____ .

1570

All of our examples so far have observed the rule that conjunctions should join structures generated similarly by the grammatical rules—

that is, which have similar structures in the base sentences underlying the transform. Let us take an example that breaks the rule: *"John is serious and a student." Here the *and* joins an adjective and a _____ _____.

1571

"John is serious" is a case of **NP + Aux + be + Adj**. "John is a student" is a case of **NP + Aux + be + NP**. The structures differ, and therefore **T-conj** cannot be grammatically applied. The kernel sentences underlying "John should and will go" are "John should go" and _____ _____.

1572

"John should go" and "John will go" are both cases of **NP + tense + M + VI**. The elements **tense + M** occur in both sentences and can be grammatically joined by a conjunction. Is the sentence "John should and has gone" grammatical? _____

1573

"John should go" is **NP + tense + M + VI**. "John has gone" is **NP + tense + have + part + VI**. Tense + M and tense + have cannot be combined because they are different structures. (We can't say that they are both **Aux**; the **Aux** of the second sentence is **tense + have + part**.) Is "John should go and has gone" grammatical? _____

1574

"John should go" and "John has gone" are like structures on one level. They are both cases of **NP + VP**. On this level **T-conj** can be applied. That is, the verb phrases can be joined as verb phrases. But their parts cannot be joined, because their parts are not alike. In "John likes to fish and hunt," the conjunction joins two _____.

1575

Can **T-conj** be applied to "John likes to fish" and "John likes sunshine"?

CONJUNCTIONS   281

1576

If we applied it, we would get the ungrammatical sentence *"John likes to fish and sunshine." "John likes to fish" and "John likes sunshine" look rather alike, but in the first sentence the object derives from an underlying base sentence "John fishes," whereas in the second the object is a simple **NP**. Can "John hopes to fish" and "John intends to fish" be joined by **T-conj**? _____

1577

Hope and *intend* in these sentences are both **Vt**$_{to}$'s, so **T-conj** can be applied. Is the sentence "John dislikes and refuses to fish" grammatical? _____

1578

Refuse is a **Vt**$_{to}$, but *dislike* is a **Vt**$_{ing}$. *"John dislikes and refuses to fish" is ungrammatical, because its generation would include the ungrammatical base sentence *"John dislikes to fish." Is "John is a good fisherman and who enjoys the sport" grammatical? _____

1579

*"John is a good fisherman and who enjoys the sport" is ungrammatical because the *and* connects two unlike structures—a _____ and a _____ .

1580

"John is a good fisherman and enjoys the sport" is grammatical because the *and* joins two _____ .

1581

The term for structures joined by a conjunction is *conjuncts*. In "John is a good fisherman and enjoys the sport," the conjuncts are verb phrases. In "John and his brother are good fishermen," the conjuncts are _____ phrases.

1582

There are only three conjunctions that join parts of sentences in a simple way. They are *and, or,* and *but*. In the sentence "John or Edna should know," the conjuncts are two _____ phrases.

1583

In "John usually eats here or in a restaurant," the conjuncts are two _____ .

1584

In "We always chose oysters that were very large or that had easily detached shells," the conjuncts are two _____ .

1585

In "John was young but wise," the conjunction *but* joins two conjuncts. The conjuncts are _____ .

1586

"John was young but wise" derives from the two base sentences _____ and _____ .

1587

The rule about the conjuncts having like structure applies to *but* and *or* as well as *and*. Is "John was young but a philosopher" grammatical? ____

1588

"John was young" is a case of **NP + Aux + be + Adj**. However, "John was a philosopher" is a case of ___ + ___ + ___ + ___ .

1589

The conjunction *but* has the special value that the conjunct that follows it is unexpected, given the conjunct that precedes. Given that John is young, it is not expected that he will be wise. For this reason, *but* will not ordinarily join simple noun phrases. "John and Edna laughed" and

CONJUNCTIONS 283

"John or Edna laughed" are both grammatical, but *"John but Edna laughed" is not. Could **T-conj** be applied to "John frowned," "John agreed" with the conjunction *but?* ____

1590

*"John howled but screamed" is ungrammatical, but "John frowned but agreed," in which the second conjunct is unexpected, is grammatical. In "John or Edna is going to help us," the conjunction ____ joins two noun phrases functioning as _____ .

1591

In "John and Edna are going to help us," the conjunction ____ joins two noun phrases functioning as _____ .

1592

When *and* joins two singular noun phrases, it makes them plural, but when *or* joins two singular noun phrases, it leaves them singular. Should *is* or *are* be used in the sentence "Roger Danby and his uncle Fred ____ coming later"? ____

1593

Should *was* or *were* be used in "Roger Danby or his uncle Fred ____ supposed to meet us"? ____

1594

When parts of a sentence are joined by a conjunction, they are said to be *compound*. In "George and Mabel are going steady," we have a compound subject. In "I have always liked George and Mabel," we have a compound _____ .

1595

In "He was sober and serious," we have a compound adjective. In "He spoke soberly and seriously," we have a compound _____ .

---

284 ENGLISH SYNTAX

1596

In "Mrs. Alva picked up and left," we have a compound predicate. In "The delegates who complained and left the hall were from Nigeria," there is a compound predicate in the relative clause. It is the group of words _____ .

1597

In "The delegates making trouble and refusing to cooperate are from Lower Orpington," there is a compound _____ phrase.

1598

In "Give George or Felicity the information," the compound indirect object is _____ .

1599

The term for two sentence parts joined by a conjunction is _____ .

1600

The general rule is that conjunctions must combine only like structures from base sentences. Writers sometimes break this rule intentionally in minor ways, but in general it obtains.

MAIN POINTS OF LESSON THIRTY-TWO

Conjunctions are words that join sentences or parts of sentences. The only English conjunctions that join parts of sentences in a simple way are *and, or,* and *but.*

The elements joined by a conjunction are called conjuncts.

The construction formed by a conjunction and two conjuncts is called a compound construction. The term compound is traditionally used with both structures and functions. That is, one might speak of both a compound noun phrase and a compound subject.

The general rule is that the conjuncts of a compound construction must have like structures—i.e., be generated similarly in their respective base sentences. In other words, it is grammatical that the conjuncts be two verb phrases, two Vt_{to}'s, two adjectives, and so on; it is ordinarily not grammatical that one be a noun phrase and the other a relative clause, one an auxiliary and the other part of an auxiliary, etc.

Lesson Thirty-Three

CORRELATIVES AND CONJUNCTIONS THAT JOIN SENTENCES

We have stated the general rule that conjunctions join like structures. That is, they join two **NP**'s, two **VP**'s, two verbals, two relative clauses, and so on. Sometimes this rule is broken intentionally by writers of English, but it is in general observed.

The rule is satisfied if two conjuncts are identical at the highest level. They don't have to be identical at lower levels. If, for example, a conjunction joins two **VP**'s, the rule is satisfied, even if the two **VP**'s differ markedly in their inner structure. Sentences which follow this rule are said to be parallel; sentences which do not are not parallel.

Suppose, for example, we have the sentence "John smiled and paid me the money." The conjunction *and* joins two **VP**'s, and so the sentence is parallel, even though the **VP**'s differ in their inner structure:

NP	VP
John	smiled.
John	paid me the money.

→
NP	VP	and	VP
John	smiled	and	paid me the money.

If the two conjuncts are alike not only on the highest level but also on lower levels, the sentence is not only parallel but balanced:

John gave me a smile.
John paid me the money.

→ John gave me a smile and paid me the money.

Similarly, the sentence "John was a fellow who helped other people when he could and who was always friendly" is parallel. The conjuncts are both relative clauses. The sentence "John was a fellow who went where he pleased and who did what he wanted" is not only parallel but also balanced. The conjunction joins two relative clauses which are much alike in their inner structure.

Parallelism is a matter of grammaticality; in general, sentences which are not parallel are not grammatical. Balance is a matter of style; one may balance a sentence to gain stylistic effects.

1601

Conjunctions are sometimes used in pairs. When they are, they are called *correlative conjunctions*. In the sentence, "Either George or Ellie will want to go," the correlative conjunctions are *either* and *or*. In "Neither George nor Ellie will want to go," the correlatives are _____ and _____ .

1602

In "Neither George nor Ellie will want to go," the correlatives join two _____ phrases.

1603

In "DeWitt decided to buy either a necktie or a scarf," the correlatives join two noun phrases used as _____ .

1604

In "George either enjoyed the party or was being very polite," the correlatives join two _____ .

1605

In "Mr. Rumbold neither will nor should help us in this matter," the conjuncts are two _____ plus tense.

1606

In "DeWitt will probably either come early or stay late," the conjuncts are two verb phrases minus the auxiliary. A verb phrase, other than those with *be*, minus the auxiliary is called a _____ .

1607

The sentence "Both George and Ellie will want to go" also contains two correlatives. What are they? _____ , _____

1608

In "DeWitt was both pleased and suspicious," the correlatives join two _____ .

CORRELATIVES AND CONJUNCTIONS THAT JOIN SENTENCES

1609

In "George has lived both in Leeds and in Manchester," the conjuncts are adverbials of _____ .

1610

In "DeWitt has lived in both Arroyo Grande and Pismo Beach," the conjuncts are _____ .

1611

Is the sentence "John has lived both in Pismo Beach and Arroyo Grande" grammatical? _____

1612

At least, it is not altogether grammatical, although of course it is not a very obvious mistake. The general rule that the conjuncts should be like structures holds for correlative conjunctions as well as for plain conjunctions. In "John has lived both in Pismo Beach and Arroyo Grande," *both* is followed by an **Adv-p**, but *and* is followed by a _____ .

1613

The sentence "DeWitt lived not in Arroyo Grande but in Pismo Beach" also contains a pair of correlative conjunctions. What are they? _____ , _____

1614

The correlatives *not/but* will join certain conjuncts that *but* cannot join alone. In "Not John but Edna was the culprit," *not/but* join two noun phrases functioning as _____ .

1615

Sometimes the correlatives *not/but* are expanded to *not only/but also*. In "John not only insulted the old lady but also kicked her," the correlatives join two _____ .

1616

In "DeWitt bought not only a tie but also a scarf," the conjuncts are noun phrases functioning as _____ .

1617

In "John was always either wildly happy or hopelessly sad," what are the correlative conjunctions? _____ , ____

1618

In "John was a man who neither feared nor understood the consequences," the correlative conjunctions are _____ and ____ .

1619

In "John disliked both salmon and mackerel," the correlative conjunctions are ____ and ____ .

1620

In "John was not only capable but also industrious," the correlative conjunctions are _____ and _____ .

1621

The conjuncts joined by conjunctions may be whole sentences. In "John arrived, and Samuel went away," two sentences are joined by the conjunction ____ .

1622

In "John knew what he wanted, but he didn't want to pay for it," two sentences are joined by the conjunction ____ .

1623

When two sentences are joined by a conjunction, the result is called a *compound sentence*. Is "John and Ellie quarreled" a compound sentence? ____

1624

"John and Ellie quarreled" has a compound subject, but it isn't a compound sentence. What are the two base sentences from which it derives? _____ , _____

CORRELATIVES AND CONJUNCTIONS THAT JOIN SENTENCES

1625

Is "Chris laughed and said that he had known it all the time" a compound sentence? ____

1626

"Chris laughed and said that he had known it all the time" contains a compound predicate. It derives from the sentences "Chris laughed" and _____.

1627

Is "Chris laughed, and Ellie asked him what was funny" a compound sentence? ____

1628

"Chris laughed, and Ellie asked him what was funny" is composed of the two base sentences "Ellie asked him what was funny" and _____ _____ .

1629

Is "John was gay, but Samuel seemed worried about something" a compound sentence? ____

1630

If you have been watching the punctuation, you will have noticed that we have used a comma before the conjunction when the conjunction joins two sentences but not when it joins parts of sentences. This is a general rule. Should we have a comma before *and* in "DeWitt examined the necktie and decided that he didn't want it"? ____

1631

Should we have a comma before the conjunction in the sentence "The house was old but we found it very comfortable"? ____

1632

We have seen that parts of sentences are connected by three simple conjunctions: ____ , ____ , ____ .

ENGLISH SYNTAX

1633

And, or, and *but* are also used to connect whole sentences. In addition, *for, yet, so,* and *nor* are used as conjunctions to connect whole sentences. What is the conjunction in "We quickly forgave him, for we were sure that he had meant no harm"? ____

1634

What is the conjunction in "We asked to see his slides, so he showed them to us"? ____

1635

What is the conjunction in "I wanted to believe him, yet I had my doubts"? ____

1636

What is the conjunction in "He didn't want to help us, nor were we willing to beg him"? ____

1637

Look again at "He didn't want to help us, nor were we willing to beg him." In the second half, after *nor,* the subject and **be + past** are reversed. Starting with **nor + NP + past + be + X** we get **nor + _____ + _____ + _____ + X.**

1638

The transformation after the conjunction *nor* is the same as **T-yes/no:**
    NP + tense-M   + X ⟹ tense-M   + NP + X
    NP + tense-have + X ⟹ tense-have + NP + X
    NP + tense-be   + X ⟹ tense-be   + NP + X
    NP + tense + verbal ⟹ tense   + NP + verbal

This is obligatory after the conjunction ____ .

1639

Suppose we have **John wouldn't help us, nor + we + past + will + help him.** The *nor* transformation is obligatory. This produces **John wouldn't help us + nor + _____ + _____ + _____ + help him.**

CORRELATIVES AND CONJUNCTIONS THAT JOIN SENTENCES

1640

Nor + past + will + we + help him contains a sequence Af + v. It is therefore changed by T-af to nor + will + past + we + help him, and it appears finally as _____ .

1641

Suppose we start with John doesn't like me + nor + I + present + like + him. Does the part after *nor* contain (1) a tense-M, (2) a tense-have, (3) a tense-be, (4) a tense + verbal? ____

1642

By T-nor, John doesn't like me, nor + I + present + like + him becomes John doesn't like me + nor + _____ + ____ + ____ + him.

1643

John doesn't like me + nor + present + I + like + him contains a floating tense—that is, a tense which has nothing that it can be a tense for—so T-do is obligatory. This changes it to nor + ____ + _____ + ____ + ____ + him.

1644

John doesn't like me + nor + do + present + I + like + him finally appears as "John doesn't like me, _____."

1645

The same transformation is obligatory after *not only* when the following conjunct is a sentence. *"Not only I like John, but also he likes me" is ungrammatical. The first conjunct must be changed to *not only* _____ _____ .

1646

In "Bruce was either sick or lazy," *either* and *or* are _____ conjunctions.

1647

Correlative conjunctions connect whole sentences as well as parts of sentences. In which of the following do they connect whole sentences:

292   ENGLISH SYNTAX

(1) He either goes or stays. (2) Either John goes or Samuel stays. (3) Either John or Samuel goes? ____

1648

Correlative conjunctions, like other conjunctions, must in general follow the rule that the conjuncts must have the same general structure. Which of the following breaks the rule: (1) Either Martin pays his dues, or he will be expelled from the club. (2) Martin will either pay his dues or resign. (3) Martin either pays his dues or we will expel him? ____

1649

Which of these breaks the rule: (1) Not only was John willing to help us, but he couldn't wait to begin. (2) John was not only willing to help us, but he seemed actually eager. (3) John was not only willing but actually eager? ____

1650

The punctuation rule most generally observed is that conjunctions have a comma before (not after) them when they connect whole sentences. There is no comma when the conjunctions connect parts of sentences.

MAIN POINTS OF LESSON THIRTY-THREE

Conjunctions used in pairs—*either/or, neither/nor, both/and, not (only)/but (also)*—are called correlative conjunctions. The same general rule applies to them that applies to simple conjunctions: The conjuncts joined must have the same general structure.

The conjunctions *and, or,* and *but* join either parts of sentences or whole sentences. The conjunctions *for, nor, yet, so* join only whole sentences. After *nor* a transformation identical with **T-yes/no** is obligatory. **Tense-M, tense-have,** and **tense-be** reverse with the subject. If tense is followed by a verbal, only tense reverses, and then **T-do** is obligatory. The same transformation applies after the correlative *not only* when the following conjunct is a sentence.

When the two conjuncts joined by a conjunction are sentences, a comma is generally used before the conjunction. When the conjuncts are not sentences, a comma is not used.

Lesson Thirty-Four
SERIES

We should note that punctuation rules are not at all the same sort of thing as grammatical rules. When we state a grammatical rule, we are stating a fact about the language. When we state a punctuation rule, we are making an observation about the writing system. It is important to keep speech and writing separate in our thinking if we are to hope to understand either.

The essential difference between speech and writing is that speech is an organic development, whereas writing is a conscious invention. Speaking is as natural to mankind as walking is, and we have no power to change the fundamental features of speech—that is, the fundamental features of the grammar. It is true that we are often ungrammatical, sometimes intentionally and sometimes unintentionally. It is also true that the grammar changes slowly with the passage of time. But ungrammaticality, intentional or unintentional, is but a brief departure from a stable, continuing system, and changes in the grammar through the centuries are brought about by forces quite beyond the control of users of the language. In a real sense, the grammar has a life of its own. We learn its forms when we are little children, and after that it governs us more than we govern it.

The writing system, however, is different. It is an invention designed to represent and preserve on paper the forms of speech. Since it was invented by people, it can be controlled by people. For example, we could, if we wished, decide to abolish the comma altogether and to replace it with some other sign—like ∨ or * or →. Or if we wanted to, we could reform our spelling system, as some peoples have actually done, by government legislation. But no legislation could get rid of the *do* transformation or control other rules of the grammar. If the phonological rule who + m → whom is going out of the spoken language, so that "Who are you going with" and "Who did you see" become the regular forms, no amount of legislation can put it back in.

294   ENGLISH SYNTAX

It is because punctuation is, as it were, man-made and man-controlled, as the grammar is not, that we must be a little careful about statements we make on punctuation. When we say that conjunctions joining sentences have a comma before them and conjunctions not joining sentences do not, we are not stating a law of the universe or even a law of language. We are just making a very general observation about the practices of writers and publishers. Generally, writers punctuate this way, but they don't all do so all of the time. Some, in certain circumstances, don't use commas before conjunctions that connect sentences. Some, in certain circumstances, use commas before conjunctions not connecting sentences.

A punctuation rule is just a general guide for the young writer in doubt about what to do. If it is taken as just that, it can be very useful.

1651

Sentence parts can occur not only in pairs, as in "John and Edna talked," but also in groups of three or more, as in "John, Edna, and Samuel talked." Such a sequence of sentence parts is called a *series*.

In "John, Edna, and Samuel talked," we have a series of _____ phrases.

1652

In "John howled, screamed, and blustered," there is a series of _____.

1653

"We can, should, and must protest" contains a series of _____ plus tense.

1654

"The girl seemed quiet, gentle, and rather pretty" contains a series of _____.

1655

The sentence "Delaney was a man who knew what he wanted, who was capable of getting it, and who intended to have it" contains a series of _____.

SERIES   295

1656

The sentence "Delaney was a man who knew what he wanted, was capable of getting it, and intended to have it" contains a series of _____ .

1657

The sentence "Mulligan was not brilliant, but he did his work quickly, competently, and quietly" contains a series of _____ .

1658

The sentence "Mulligan was not brilliant, but he did his work quickly, competently, and quietly" contains the two conjunctions ____ , ____ .

1659

The sentence "Mulligan was not brilliant, but he did his work quickly, competently, and quietly" is a _____ sentence.

1660

Each of the series we have seen so far consists of three elements. The last two elements have been connected by a conjunction. We have used the punctuation pattern **A, B,** and **C**. If we punctuate "We painted the house the garage and the barn" on the same pattern, we will have commas after the words _____ and _____ .

1661

If we punctuate "John sat down opened the bag and ate his lunch" on the pattern **A, B,** and **C**, we will have commas after _____ and _____ .

1662

If we punctuate "Samuel was quick quiet and competent" on the same pattern, we will have commas after _____ and _____ .

296   ENGLISH SYNTAX

1663

If we punctuate "It was understood that we would meet at seven that everyone would bring a lunch and that we would go in Mr. Wheeler's car" on the same pattern, we will have commas after _____ and _____.

1664

If we punctuate "Anyone who wants to go who has his parents' permission and who needs a ride should see Mr. Caspar" on the same pattern, we will have commas after _____ and _____.

1665

The sentence "Mrs. Persky was not very dependable but she was interesting lively and attractive" needs commas, according to the rules so far given, after _____ and _____ and _____.

1666

According to the rule, we have a comma before the *but* in "Mrs. Persky was not very dependable, but she was interesting, lively, and attractive" because the sentence is _____.

1667

If we punctuate "They were people who liked to fish enjoyed the mountains and didn't mind being lonely" according to the pattern **A**, **B**, and **C**, we will have commas after _____ and _____.

1668

Series are produced by the same transformation process that produces compounds. The sentence "John and Edna talked" derives from the two base sentences _____ and _____.

1669

The sentence "John, Edna, and Samuel talked" derives from the three base sentences _____, _____, and _____.

SERIES 297

1670

The sentence "John fished, loafed, and sat in the sun" derives from the base sentences _____ , _____ , and _____ .

1671

The sentence "Ed worked quickly, quietly, and well" derives from the base sentences _____ , _____ , and _____ .

1672

The grammatical rule that applies to compounds also applies to series: the series must be composed of elements that are the same in the base sentences. Is the sentence "John liked to fish, hike, and sunshine" grammatical? ____

1673

*"John liked to fish, hike, and sunshine" is composed of the three base sentences "John liked to fish," "John liked to hike," and "John liked sunshine." The first two are the same, but the third is different. *Fish* and *hike* are verbs functioning as complements. *Sunshine* is a _____ functioning as _____ .

1674

Can the base sentences "John liked to fish," "John liked to hunt," "John liked to sit in the sun" produce a grammatical series? ____

1675

All are cases of **NP + Aux + VT**$_{to}$ **+ to + verbal,** so they can be combined. If we combine just the verbals after the *to* in "John liked to fish," "John liked to hike," and "John liked to sit in the sun," we get "John liked to fish, _____ ."

1676

"John liked to fish," "John liked to hike," and "John liked to sit in the sun" are all cases of **NP + Aux + VT**$_{to}$ **+ to + verbal.** Instead of combining just the verbals, we could combine the **to + verbal**'s. This would give us "John liked to fish, _____ ."

298   ENGLISH SYNTAX

1677

However, the sentence *"John liked to fish, hike, and to sit in the sun" is ungrammatical. Here we have combined two sequences of **to + verbal** with one _____ .

1678

Is the sentence "John liked to fish, liked to hike, and liked to sit in the sun" grammatical? ____

1679

"John liked to fish, liked to hike, and liked to sit in the sun" is grammatical, though not very economical. This sentence contains a series of _____ .

1680

The sentence "He knew that he had to decide, that he had to decide quickly, and that everything depended on his decision" contains a series of _____ clauses.

1681

We could write the series in "He knew that he had to decide, that he had to decide quickly, and that everything depended on his decision" as follows: **Sub + S, Sub + S, and Sub + S**. Is the sentence "He knew that he had to decide, he had to decide quickly, and that everything depended on his decision" grammatical? ____

1682

The series in *"He knew that he had to decide, he had to decide quickly, and that everything depended on his decision," instead of being composed of **Sub + S, Sub + S, and Sub + S**, is composed of _____ , ____ , and _____ .

1683

If we punctuate the sentence "John read the document picked up a pen and signed it" according to the pattern **A, B, and C**, we will have commas after _____ and _____ .

SERIES   299

1684

If we punctuate "Edna her brother Theobald and a cousin from White Plains who was visiting them decided to go to a movie" according to the same pattern, we will have commas after _____ and _____ .

1685

If we punctuate "Edna and Maybelle laughed and gossiped and Theobald watched television" according to the rule for punctuating compound structures, we will have a comma after _____ .

1686

If we punctuate "Edna and Maybelle were laughing and gossiping so Theobald went to the kitchen and made himself a salmon sandwich" according to the same rule, we will have a comma after _____ .

1687

If we punctuate "John knew that I was alone and that I needed help yet he didn't come around" according to the same pattern, we will have a comma after _____ .

1688

The sentence "Sally was quiet, attractive, and interesting" contains a series of _____ .

1689

In "Sally was a quiet, attractive, and interesting girl," a series of adjectives occur as noun _____ .

1690

When adjectives occur in series as modifiers of a noun, the conjunction is often omitted: *a quiet, attractive, interesting girl*. The noun phrase *a large empty dirty house* should have commas after _____ and _____ .

1691

A pair of adjectives may occur as modifiers of a noun. We say either *a large and empty room* or *a large, empty room*. In the second phrase, we might say that the comma takes the place of the _____ .

300   ENGLISH SYNTAX

1692

The noun phrase *an ugly squalid street* should have a comma after _____ .

1693

Some sequences of adjectives used as noun modifiers are written without commas separating the adjectives. We would write *a little old lady* without a comma after *little*. Should there be a comma after *nice* in *a nice young man?* _____

1694

The sentence "A nice young man came in" can be considered the result of a transformation combining "A young man came in" and "The young man was nice." "A little old lady went out" can be considered the result of a transformation combining "An old lady went out" and _____ .

1695

The sentence "He lived on a dreary, ugly street" results from a transformation combining "He lived on a street" and "The street was dreary and ugly." "He wrote an angry, hysterical letter" results from a transformation combining "He wrote a letter" and _____ _____ .

1696

We have a comma between adjectives used as noun modifiers when the series results from a compound adjective—two adjectives connected by *and* in the predicate of the base sentence. *A nice young man* does not come from "The man was nice and young" but from "The young man was nice." *A dreary, ugly street,* however, comes from _____ _____ .

1697

We have said that the comma in *a dreary, ugly street* in a way substitutes for the conjunction of *a dreary and ugly street.* You can tell whether you need a comma by determining whether you could grammatically have an *and*. Could you have an *and* between the adjectives in *a nice young man?* _____

SERIES 301

1698

Could you grammatically have an *and* between the adjectives in *a young interesting man?* _____

1699

Therefore, *a young interesting man* should be written with a comma after _____ .

1700

We might notice that the phrases *a nice young man* and *a young, interesting man* are not pronounced in the same way. There is a break after *young* in the second phrase that does not occur after *nice* in the first. They differ because they are produced by different transformations.

MAIN POINTS OF LESSON THIRTY-FOUR

A group of three or more structures joined by the conjunction transformation is called a series. A series usually has a conjunction (usually *and*) between the last two elements. The most common punctuation pattern is **A, B,** and **C**.

The rule that applies to compound structures applies also to series: the elements must derive from like structures in the underlying sentences.

The conjunction is frequently omitted when a pair or series of adjectives occur as noun modifiers. In writing, a comma then replaces the conjunction. This applies only to true compounds or series—groups of adjectives that come from compounds or series in the insert sentence: "The man was happy and talkative" → "a happy, talkative man." No punctuation is used when the adjectives are derived independently: "The French girl was pretty" → "a pretty French girl."

Lesson Thirty-Five
SENTENCE CONNECTORS

We need to add something to our rule that we generally have a comma before conjunctions that connect two sentences. It is more accurate to say that we generally have *at least* a comma. Instead of a comma, we may have a semicolon or a period. In other words, all of the following represent normal American punctuation:

> We stopped at Samuel's house late in the afternoon, but there was no one home.
>
> We stopped at Samuel's house late in the afternoon; but there was no one home.
>
> We stopped at Samuel's house late in the afternoon. But there was no one home.

We could put the matter in a formula, as follows:

> S, conjunction S.
> S; conjunction S.
> S. Conjunction S.

One sometimes hears it said that one must not begin a sentence with *and* or *but*. This prohibition does not reflect actual practice, however. Writers frequently use the punctuation pattern—S. And S.—as anyone can easily see by observing published writing. All of the "Samuel" sentences above are correctly punctuated, in the sense that all of these are ways in which good writers deliberately punctuate.

The three "Samuel" sentences differ from one another not in grammar or meaning but only in writing style. The effect of the comma between the sentence patterns is to tie the patterns closely together and to make the reader go on quickly to the second. The semicolon or period between the sentence patterns tends to emphasize the break between them. The effect is to make the reader pause at the end of the first pattern and to make the second more emphatic. Compare these:

> I did everything I could for Angela, and she didn't even thank me.
> I did everything I could for Angela. And she didn't even thank me.

The use of the period in place of the comma in the second sentence makes the fact that Angela didn't thank me stand out more prominently.

1701

Sentences can be joined by conjunctions. Can you remember the seven conjunctions that join sentences patterns? ____, ____, ____, ____, ____, ____, ____

1702

Only three of these conjunctions join parts of sentence patterns. What are they? ____, ____, ____

1703

When two sentences are joined by a conjunction, the result is a _____ sentence.

1704

A conjunction that joins two sentences is generally preceded in writing by a comma, a _____, or a _____.

1705

Another kind of word that joins sentence patterns is what we have called a subordinator. In "We knew that Donald was coming," the subordinator is the word _____.

1706

Subordinators do not, however, join sentences in the same way that conjunctions do. In "We knew that Donald was coming," the two base sentences are **we knew + NP** and _____.

1707

In "We knew that Donald was coming," **we knew + NP** is the matrix sentence, and "Donald was coming" is the insert sentence. With the subordinator *that* added, the insert sentence becomes the _____ of the verb of the matrix sentence.

---

304 ENGLISH SYNTAX

1708

In "Donald was coming, and we knew it," there is no insert sentence and no matrix sentence. Two base sentences, "Donald was coming" and "We knew it," are simply joined by the _____ *and*.

1709

Another class of words that join sentence patterns are what we will call *sentence connectors*. In the sentence "Donald was coming; therefore we had to get ready," the sentence connector is the word *therefore*. In "Donald was coming; moreover, everybody knew it," the sentence connector is _____ .

1710

In "Donald was feeling better; however, his sister Maybelle was still sick," the sentence connector is _____ .

1711

In "Donald didn't really want to come; nevertheless he finally agreed," the sentence connector is _____ .

1712

We have so far identified four sentence connectors: *therefore, moreover, however,* and *nevertheless*. In all the examples given, what punctuation mark has preceded the sentence connector? _____

1713

If a sentence connector between two sentence patterns is not preceded by a semicolon or a period, we have a kind of punctuation error called a *run-on sentence*. Is "Donald was feeling better, however, his sister was still sick" a run-on sentence? _____

1714

Is "It had begun to rain very hard. Nevertheless, the umpires refused to call the game" a run-on sentence? _____

SENTENCE CONNECTORS   305

1715

The general rule is that two sentence patterns must have between them at least a conjunction (with a comma before it), a semicolon, or a period. "It was raining very hard, but nobody wanted to stop playing" is not a run-on sentence, because there is a _____ between the sentence patterns.

1716

Is "It was raining harder than ever, moreover, everybody was tired and hungry" a run-on sentence? _____

1717

Is "Donald never behaved himself at parties; therefore we decided not to invite him" a run-on sentence? _____

1718

Conjunctions differ from sentence connectors in that conjunctions must come between the sentences they join, but sentence connectors may also appear inside or at the end of the second sentence. In "Donald never behaved himself at parties; we nevertheless decided to invite him," the sentence connector is the word _____.

1719

In "It was raining harder than ever. The umpires refused to call the game, however," the sentence connector is the word _____.

1720

What is the sentence connector in "Theobald hadn't done his homework regularly. Consequently he got a low grade"? _____

1721

What kind of word is *so* in "Theobald hadn't done his homework regularly. So he got a low grade"? _____

306   ENGLISH SYNTAX

1722

"Theobald hadn't done his homework regularly. He consequently got a low grade" is grammatical. Is "Theobald hadn't done his homework regularly. He so got a low grade" grammatical? ____

1723

Sentence connectors will move around in the second sentence pattern; conjunctions won't. The words *consequently* and *so* have similar meanings, but they differ in the sentence positions in which they can occur. What kind of word is *yet* in "Brad was usually a good correspondent. Yet we hadn't heard from him for months"? _____

1724

"Brad was usually a good correspondent; we hadn't heard from him for months, however" is grammatical. Is "Brad was usually a good correspondent; we hadn't heard from him for months yet" grammatical? ____

1725

Conjunctions between sentence patterns must be preceded by a comma, a semicolon, or a period. Sentence connectors between sentences must be preceded by a _____ or a _____ .

1726

If two sentence patterns have neither a conjunction, a semicolon, or a period between them, the punctuation error is called a _____ sentence.

1727

The seven words used as conjunctions in English are ____ , ____ , ____ , ____ , ____ , ____ , ____ .

1728

We have listed only a few of the sentence connectors. In "Our leading man got sick; hence we had to cancel the play," the sentence connector is the word _____ .

SENTENCE CONNECTORS

1729

In "Our leading man got sick. We were thus obliged to cancel the play," the sentence connector is the word _____ .

1730

In "Daniel and Michael were close friends. Furthermore, their fathers had been classmates in college," the sentence connector is _____ .

1731

Is "Daniel and Michael were close friends. Their fathers, furthermore, had been classmates in college" grammatical? _____

1732

Sentence connectors can occur at the end or in the middle of the second pattern, as well as at the beginning of it. This is what distinguishes them from _____ .

1733

The punctuation fault opposite to a run-on sentence is what is called a *fragment*. This is the writing of part of a sentence as if it were a whole sentence. Is "People who were there at Christmas" a sentence or a fragment? _____

1734

In a sense this whole text is a lesson in how to avoid fragments, because it is mainly concerned with explaining what English sentences are and what they are not. What is the first rule in the grammar? S → _____ + _____ .

1735

This rule means that every kernel English sentence consists of a noun phrase and a verb phrase. The noun phrase functions as the _____ of the sentence, and the verb phrase functions as the _____ .

308   ENGLISH SYNTAX

1736

Every kernel sentence has a subject and a predicate. Some sentences do not—replies, commands, etc. But these are transforms, not kernel sentences. We have seen what subjects and predicates consist of and how they can be expanded by transformation. What is the subject of "People who were there at Christmas said that it was very cold"? _____

_____

1737

In "People who were there at Christmas said that it was very cold," *people who were there at Christmas* is part of a sentence—its subject—and not a whole sentence. This noun phrase contains the relative clause _____ .

1738

The clause *who were there at Christmas* is made from a kernel sentence—"People were there at Christmas"—by the transformation **T-rel**. But the transformation changes the kernel sentence into a relative clause. The clause *who were there at Christmas* contains the predicate _____

_____ .

1739

Parts of sentences may contain subjects and predicates and still be just parts of sentences, not whole sentences. In "People who were there at Christmas said that it was very cold," what is the object of *said?*

_____

1740

"That it was very cold" and "It was very cold" both contain subjects and predicates. Are they both sentences? _____

1741

That it was very cold is not a sentence. The sentence "It was very cold" has been made into a subordinate clause by the transformation **S** $\Rightarrow$ **Sub** + **S,** where **Sub** stands for _____ .

SENTENCE CONNECTORS   **309**

1742

When "It was very cold" is transformed into *that it was very cold,* it can be part of a sentence—subject, object, etc.—but will no longer be a sentence by itself. If written with a capital letter and a period, it's a fragment. Could *whom did they see* be written as a sentence? _____

1743

"Whom did they see?" is a type of sentence, a *wh* question, transformed from a base sentence first by **T-yes/no** and then by **T-wh**. Could *whom you saw* be written as a sentence? _____

1744

Whom you saw has been transformed from the sentence **you saw + NP** by **T-rel**. It is not a sentence but a relative _____ .

1745

If *whom you saw* is punctuated as a sentence, the punctuation fault is called a _____ .

1746

If "He didn't call me back; consequently I supposed he didn't want to go" were written with a comma in place of the semicolon, we would have the punctuation fault called a _____ .

1747

In "He didn't call me back. I consequently supposed he didn't want to go," the word *consequently* is a _____ .

1748

Which of the following words is not a sentence connector: *therefore, thus, for, hence?* _____

1749

A conjunction between two sentences is preceded by a _____ , a _____ , or a _____ . A sentence connector between two sentences is preceded by a _____ or a _____ .

310 ENGLISH SYNTAX

1750

If you punctuate part of a sentence—a noun phrase, a relative clause, a prepositional phrase, for example—as a sentence, you commit the writing fault called a fragment. If you write two sentences without a conjunction, a semicolon, or a period between them, you commit the writing fault called a run-on sentence.

MAIN POINTS OF LESSON THIRTY-FIVE

Sentence connectors are such words as *therefore, consequently, thus, moreover, nevertheless*. They connect two sentences, indicating some meaning relationship between them. They differ from conjunctions in that they may come within or at the end of the second sentence as well as between the two sentences, whereas conjunctions joining sentences must occur between the sentences. Sentence connectors differ from subordinators (and relatives) in that subordinators make an insert sentence part of a matrix sentence, whereas sentence connectors just connect two base sentences.

The general rule of sentence punctuation is that two sentences must have at least a conjunction, a semicolon, or a period between them. If they do not, the result is the writing error called a run-on sentence.

The opposite, as it were, of a run-on sentence is what is called a fragment. This is the punctuation of a part of a sentence as if it were a complete sentence.

Lesson Thirty-Six
SENTENCE MODIFIERS

We have so far discussed the punctuation that comes *before* a sentence connector that stands between two sentence patterns, but we haven't said anything about the punctuation that comes after the sentence connector. One reason for the hesitation is that there isn't very much that can be definitely said.

Sentence connectors frequently appear with a comma after them:

> Samuel wasn't much interested in music. However, he decided to go to the concert.
>
> Samuel wasn't much interested in music; moreover, he couldn't afford to attend the concert.

There is no general rule, however. The following punctuation is common:

> Samuel liked to pretend that he was interested in music. Therefore he decided to attend the concert.

Something depends on the particular sentence connector used. *Moreover, however, consequently, otherwise* are perhaps more likely than not to have the comma after them. *Hence, thus, therefore* are perhaps less likely. Something depends on the individual writer too. Some writers use more commas than others.

When the sentence connector comes within a sentence pattern or at the end of it, it is usually set off by one comma (when it comes at the end) or by two (when it comes in the middle):

> He decided to attend the concert, however.
>
> He decided, however, to attend the concert.
>
> He couldn't afford, moreover, to attend the concert.

Commas are not always required, however. Compare these sentences:

> He nevertheless decided to attend the concert.
>
> He decided, nevertheless, to attend the concert.

It would probably be possible to state a set of rules explaining just when sentence connectors are set off by commas and when they are not. For example, we could say that *nevertheless, therefore,* and some others are not set off when they come between the subject and the verb phrase but are set off when they come within the verb phrase. The whole set of rules would be long and complicated, however. Probably the student can do just as well by reading such sentences as the last two aloud and listening to the difference. In "He decided, nevertheless, to attend the concert," there is a marked interruption in the speech flow before and after *nevertheless*. These breaks are what the commas mark. In "He nevertheless decided to attend the concert," there are no such interruptions. The voice passes smoothly from the subject through the sentence connector to the verb phrase.

1751

What kind of word is *fortunately* in "Fortunately, Todd had plenty of time"? _____

1752

Fortunately is composed of *fortunate* plus *-ly*. What kind of word is *fortunate?* _____

1753

The sentence "Fortunately, Todd had plenty of time" derives from two base sentences. The insert sentence is "It was fortunate." What is the matrix sentence? _____

1754

Given the insert sentence "It was fortunate" and the matrix "Todd had plenty of time," we take the adjective *fortunate* from the insert sentence, add *-ly,* and put it in front of the matrix sentence. The result is _____ _____ .

1755

In "Fortunately, Todd had plenty of time," the adverb *fortunately* functions as what we will call a *sentence modifier*. It was not Todd that was fortunate. It was not the verb phrase. It was the fact that _____ _____ .

SENTENCE MODIFIERS

1756

What is the sentence modifier in "Unluckily, Chris was not at home"?

_____

1757

The adverb *unluckily* is composed of the adjective _____ + _____ .

1758

"Unluckily, Chris was not at home" derives from an insert and a matrix sentence. The matrix is "Chris was not at home." What is the insert sentence? _____

1759

In "Unluckily, Chris was not at home," the adverb *unluckily* functions as a _____ .

1760

What is the sentence modifier in "Interestingly, Daniel decided to tell the story"? _____

1761

The base sentences underlying "Interestingly, Daniel decided to tell the story" are the matrix _____ and the insert _____ .

1762

Do the sentences "Interestingly, Daniel decided to tell the story" and "Daniel decided to tell the story interestingly" mean the same thing?

_____

1763

"Daniel decided to tell the story interestingly" means that he decided to tell the story in an interesting way. "Interestingly, Daniel decided to tell the story" means that it was interesting that _____
_____ .

314   ENGLISH SYNTAX

1764

In "Daniel decided to tell the story interestingly," the adverb does not result from a transformation. It is part of the kernel. The verb phrase here is **past + Vt**$_{to}$ **+ to + Vt**$_i$ **+ NP +** _____ .

1765

The rewrite of verbal provides for adverbials of manner. So the adverb in "Daniel decided to tell the story interestingly" is not a sentence modifier but part of the verbal. What is the sentence modifier in "Unhappily, no one was listening"? _____

1766

Sentence modifiers usually come at the beginning of the sentences they modify, but they can come elsewhere too. What is the sentence modifier in "No one was listening, unhappily"? _____

1767

Which of the following sentences contains a sentence modifier: (1) No one was listening unhappily. (2) No one was listening, unhappily?

_____

1768

"No one was listening unhappily" means that no one was listening who was unhappy about it. "No one was listening, unhappily" means that it was an unhappy thing that no one was listening. In the second sentence the adverb is a sentence modifier; in the first it is not. We distinguish these in writing by using a comma before the _____ .

1769

In this example, the comma *must* be used to distinguish the two meanings. Sentence modifiers are generally set off by commas, however, even when there is no danger of confusing two meanings. In "In the meantime, they played bridge," *in the meantime* is a _____ phrase.

1770

Adverbials in the form of prepositional phrases also occur as sentence modifiers. "In the meantime, they played bridge" comes from an insert

SENTENCE MODIFIERS 315

sentence like "It happened in the meantime" and the matrix sentence _____.

1771

What is the sentence modifier in "At that moment the house collapsed"? _____

1772

In "At the time of which we were speaking, no one was there," the sentence modifier is a _____ phrase.

1773

At the time of which we were speaking is a complicated prepositional phrase. It contains the preposition *at* and its object, the noun phrase *the time*. *The time* is modified by *of which we were speaking*, which is a _____ clause.

1774

Notice that we wrote "At that moment the house collapsed" with no comma but "At the time of which we were speaking, no one was there" with one. Prepositional phrases used as sentence modifiers are generally set off by commas when they are long and complicated. What is the sentence modifier in "In my opinion, he did it"? _____

1775

Some writers would write "In my opinion he did it," not using the comma. What is the sentence modifier in "By that time Stanley was sixteen years old"? _____

1776

In "When he was sixteen, Stanley got a job," the sentence modifier is a clause. A clause is a construction containing tense. In *when he was sixteen*, the tense is contained in the word _____.

1777

"When he was sixteen, Stanley got a job" comes from an insert sentence like "He was sixteen then" and the matrix sentence _____.

316   ENGLISH SYNTAX

1778

In the transformation that converts "He was sixteen then" into *when he was sixteen,* the word *when* replaces an _____ in the insert sentence.

1779

Because clauses of the type *when he was sixteen* are derived from base sentences in which adverbials are replaced, they are often called *adverbial clauses.* However, the process is simply that which produces relative clauses. In "I didn't know him when he was a little boy," the relative clause is _____ .

1780

The clause *when he did it* comes from an insert sentence like "He did it then," with the word *when* replacing the adverbial of time *then.* In "I know when he did it," the clause functions as the _____ of the verb.

1781

In "When he did it, he regretted it," the *when* clause functions as a _____ .

1782

Such a clause as *when he did it* is made by exactly the same process whether it functions as a modifier or as a noun phrase, so we will call it a relative clause, however it functions. Is *that he did it* in "I know that he did it" made by the same process? _____

1783

In *when he did it,* the word *when* has replaced something in the insert sentence. In *that he did it,* the subordinator *that* has not replaced anything. It has simply been prefixed to the insert sentence. We call clauses in which a subordinator is simply prefixed *subordinate clauses.* What is the subordinate clause in "I know he did it"? _____

1784

In "I know he did it," the subordinator _____ has been deleted.

SENTENCE MODIFIERS   317

1785

What is the subordinate clause in "I wonder whether he is going"?

_____

1786

What is the subordinator in "I wonder whether he is going"? _____

1787

Subordinate clauses often occur as sentence modifiers. What is the sentence modifier in "If he is going, he should tell us"? _____

1788

What is the subordinator in "If he is going, he should tell us"? _____

1789

"If he is going, he should tell us" is composed of the insert sentence _____ and the matrix sentence _____ .

1790

When clauses occur at the beginning of sentences as sentence modifiers, they are regularly set off by commas. In "If he really wants to belong to the club he should pay his dues," there should be a comma after the word _____ .

1791

In "When we arrived at school the fire had already been put out," there should be a comma after the word _____ .

1792

In "Since he was very fond of art he read a great many comic books," a clause is used as a sentence modifier at the beginning of the sentence. There should be a comma after the word _____ .

1793

What is the subordinator in "Unless you're in a hurry, we might play a few duets"? _____

1794

In "After he got work he paid his bills," there should be a comma after the word _____ .

1795

What kind of structure is the sentence modifier in "In the interests of everyone, we should find out all about it"? _____

1796

What is the function of the clause *whether he does it or not* in the sentence "Whether he does it or not is his own business"? _____

1797

Should there be a comma in the sentence "Whether he does it or not is his own business"? ____

1798

Ordinarily we don't separate a subject and a predicate with a comma. Should there be a comma in "Whether he does it or not he will be punished"? ____

1799

In "Until Theobald learns to behave himself no one is going to invite him to parties," there should be a comma after the word _____ .

1800

Clauses used as sentence modifiers are regularly set off by commas. Single-word adverbs are set off more often than not. Prepositional phrases are generally set off when they are long and complicated.

MAIN POINTS OF LESSON THIRTY-SIX

Structures may apply their meaning to a whole sentence pattern, not just to some part of it. Structures which do so are said to function as sentence modifiers.

Sentence modifiers may be adverbs, prepositional phrases, relative and subordinate clauses, in addition to some others to be discussed later.

Sentence modifiers most commonly occur at the beginning of the sentence pattern that they modify. They may also, however, occur at the end of the sentence pattern or within it.

Sentence modifiers which occur at the end of the matrix sentence or within it are always set off from the matrix sentence by commas. Sentence modifiers at the beginning of the matrix sentence are usually set off by commas but not always. Clauses regularly are, and so are long prepositional phrases. Short prepositional phrases and adverbs sometimes are and sometimes are not.

Lesson Thirty-Seven

SENTENCE MODIFIERS DERIVED FROM RELATIVE CLAUSES

You may have noticed that our terms for clause types refer to the way in which they are made from insert sentences, not to the way in which they are used in matrix sentences. There are, apart from sentences, two kinds of clauses: relative clauses and subordinate clauses. A relative clause is a clause in which a relative pronoun or relative adverb replaces something in the insert sentence. Thus *who, which, that, what, whoever,* etc., may replace **NP**'s. *Where, when, how,* etc., may replace adverbials.

In the subordinate clause, on the other hand, nothing in the insert sentence is replaced or changed. A subordinator—*that, whether, if, unless,* etc.—is simply placed in front of the insert sentence to indicate that it is a subordinate clause. The particular subordinator used indicates the meaning relationship of the subordinate clause to the matrix sentence.

Both relative clauses and subordinate clauses may have different functions in the matrix sentence. Both, for example, may be used as **NP**'s —that is, as subject or object. Both may be used as modifiers—either as noun modifiers or as sentence modifiers. For instance, in "The idea that John expressed was absurd," the noun phrase *the idea* is modified by the relative clause *that John expressed.* This is a relative clause because *that* has replaced the object of the insert sentence "John expressed the idea." The word *that* is a relative pronoun. However, in "The idea that John had taken the money was absurd," the modifier *that John had taken the money* is a subordinate clause. The insert sentence is "John had taken the money." The word *that* is here a subordinator, not a relative, because it doesn't replace anything in the insert sentence. It is just a signal that the insert sentence has been made a part of a matrix sentence.

Relative clauses can also function as sentence modifiers. Heretofore we have encountered them only as noun modifiers. What is the relative clause functioning as a noun modifier in "The children who teased the cat should be punished"? _____

1802

Relative clauses derive from insert sentences by **T-rel**:

$$X + NP + Y \Rightarrow NP + \begin{Bmatrix} who \\ which \\ that \end{Bmatrix} + X + Y$$

In variations of **T-rel**, other relatives appear, but this is the transformation that produces noun modifiers. In "The children teased the cat," the two noun phrases are _____ and _____ .

1803

Either can be the **NP** of **X + NP + Y**. Let the first **NP** of **the children + past + tease + the cat** be the **NP** of **X + NP + Y**. Then **Y** is **past + tease + the cat**. **X** is _____ .

1804

$$X + NP + Y \Rightarrow NP + \begin{Bmatrix} who \\ which \\ that \end{Bmatrix} + X + Y$$ applied to **the children + past + tease + the cat**, with *the children* as the **NP**, gives _____ **+ who +** _____ **+** _____ **+** _____ .

1805

The same transformation applied to **the children + past + be + ing + tease + the cat** gives **the children +** _____ **+** _____ **+** _____ **+** _____ **+** _____ **+** _____ .

1806

The children + who + past + be + ing + tease + the cat gives, after **T-af**, the noun phrase _____ .

1807

When a noun phrase contains the sequence **relative pronoun + tense + be**, this sequence can be deleted. Does **the children + who + past + be + ing + tease + the cat** contain this sequence? _____

1808

T-del applied to the children + who + past + be + ing + tease + the cat gives _____ + ___ + _____ + _____ .

1809

The children + ing + tease + the + cat represents the noun phrase _____ .

1810

In "The children teasing the cat should be punished," *teasing the cat* is called a _____ phrase.

1811

Some participial phrases derive from relative clauses in a slightly different way. If T-del is applied to people + present + own + property, we get people + _____ + _____ + _____ + _____ .

1812

People + who + present + own + property does not contain the sequence relative pronoun + present + be, because there is no *be*. However, in noun phrases of this type we can delete the relative pronoun and replace tense with ing. We will call this T-del-ing. This transformation applied to people + who + present + own + property gives _____ + _____ + _____ + _____ .

1813

T-del-ing applied to anybody + who + past + have + a cold gives _____ + _____ + _____ + _____ .

1814

The sequence anybody + ing + have + a cold represents the noun phrase _____ .

1815

In the *children teasing the cat, people owning property, anybody having a cold,* the participial phrases function as _____ .

SENTENCE MODIFIERS DERIVED FROM RELATIVE CLAUSES

1816

Participial phrases can also function as sentence modifiers, under certain conditions. In the sentence "John, teasing the cat, smiled wickedly," the participial phrase is _____ .

1817

In "John, teasing the cat, smiled wickedly," the matrix sentence is "John smiled wickedly." The insert sentence is "John _____ _____ ."

1818

If we apply **T-rel** to "John was teasing the cat," we get the noun phrase _____ .

1819

John who was teasing the cat contains the sequence **relative pronoun + tense + be,** so **T-del** can be applied to it. Application of **T-del** gives us _____ .

1820

"John, teasing the cat, smiled wickedly" is a grammatical sentence. Is "Teasing the cat, John smiled wickedly" also a grammatical sentence? _____

1821

The participial phrase deriving from "John was teasing the cat" can occur after the **NP,** as in "John, teasing the cat, smiled wickedly," or it can be shifted to the beginning of the sentence, as in "Teasing the cat, John smiled wickedly." We will call the transformation which shifts the modifier to the beginning of the sentence **T-SM,** where **SM** stands for sentence modifier. **T-SM** applied to "Ellie, reaching out her hand, grabbed an orange" gives _____ _____ .

1822

T-SM applied to "The dentist, looking into my mouth, gasped in surprise" gives _____ .

324 ENGLISH SYNTAX

1823

With "Mr. Caspar stayed home" as the matrix sentence, **T-rel** applied to "Mr. Caspar had a bad cold" gives the result sentence "Mr. Caspar, _____."

1824

Can **T-del** be applied to the relative clause in "Mr. Caspar, who had a bad cold, stayed home"? _____

1825

However, **T-del-ing,** in which the relative is deleted and **ing** replaces tense, can be applied in "Mr. Caspar, who had a bad cold, stayed home." This would give the sentence _____ _____.

1826

T-SM applied to "Mr. Caspar, having a bad cold, stayed home" gives _____.

1827

"Having a bad cold, Mr. Caspar stayed home" derives from the matrix sentence "Mr. Caspar stayed home" and the insert sentence "Mr. Caspar had a bad cold" through three transformations: **T-rel, T-_____,** and **T-_____**. (These are in addition to **T-af**.)

1828

The participial phrase in "John, teasing the cat, smiled wickedly" goes back to the insert sentence "John was teasing the cat" through the transformations **T-_____** and **T-_____**.

1829

"John, teasing the cat, smiled wickedly" becomes "Teasing the cat, John smiled wickedly" by **T-_____**.

1830

The abbreviation **SM** stands for _____.

1831

T-SM cannot be applied to all participial phrases. The sentence "Anybody waiting for Dr. Harrison may come in" is grammatical. Is "Waiting for Dr. Harrison, anybody may come in" also grammatical? ____

1832

The participial phrase in "Anybody waiting for Dr. Harrison may come in" is a noun modifier, and T-SM applies only when the participial phrase is a sentence modifier. It follows that one can determine whether a participial phrase is a noun modifier or a sentence modifier by noting whether T-SM will apply. Will it apply to the participial phrase in "Edwin, waiting for Dr. Harrison, read *The Beekeeper's Weekly*"? ____

1833

"Waiting for Dr. Harrison, Edwin read *The Beekeeper's Weekly*," the result of T-SM, is a grammatical sentence. The participial phrase in "Edwin, waiting for Dr. Harrison, read *The Beekeeper's Weekly*" is therefore not a noun modifier but a _____ .

1834

Is the participial phrase in "My father, seeing what had happened, called the police" a noun modifier or a sentence modifier? _____
_____

1835

Is the participial phrase in "The man chasing the cat is Uncle Rudolph" a noun modifier or a sentence modifier? _____

1836

Participial phrases to which T-SM can be applied are sentence modifiers, and the relative clauses from which they derive are sentence modifiers too. In "Uncle Rudolph, chasing the cat, broke an ankle," the participial phrase derives from the relative clause _____ .

1837

In "Uncle Rudolph, who was chasing the cat, broke an ankle," the relative clause is a _____ modifier.

1838

The participial phrase in "The man who is chasing the cat is Uncle Rudolph" is a _____ modifier.

1839

T-del applied to the relative clause in "The man who is chasing the cat is Uncle Rudolph" gives "The man chasing the cat is Uncle Rudolph." **T-SM** will not apply to this, however, because it would produce the ungrammatical sentence *"Chasing the cat, the man is Uncle Rudolph." Therefore both the participial phrase and the relative clause in these sentences are _____ .

1840

In "John, injured by the explosion, went to the hospital," *injured by the explosion* is a _____ participial phrase.

1841

The sentence "John was injured by the explosion" comes from "The explosion injured John" by T-_____ .

1842

T-rel applied to "John was injured by the explosion" gives _____ .

1843

T-del applied to *John, who was injured by the explosion* gives _____ .

1844

T-SM applied to "John, injured by the explosion, went to the hospital" gives _____ .

1845

The past participial phrase in "John, injured by the explosion, went to the hospital" is a _____ modifier.

SENTENCE MODIFIERS DERIVED FROM RELATIVE CLAUSES

1846

"Any child bitten by a cobra should see the nurse" is grammatical, but *"Bitten by a cobra, any child should see the nurse" is not. The past participial phrase is a _____ modifier.

Participial phrases and the relative clauses from which they derive are sentence modifiers only and always if **T-SM** can be applied to them.

1847

We shall see that a meaning distinction parallels this structural distinction. A noun modifier specifies or singles out the noun it modifies. A sentence modifier does not specify any noun but just adds another idea to the sentence. In "Anne, smiling quietly, shook her head," the participial phrase is a _____ modifier.

1848

T-SM applied to "Anne, smiling quietly, shook her head" gives _____ _____ .

1849

The participial phrase in "Smiling quietly, Anne shook her head" goes back to the insert sentence _____ .

1850

You have probably noticed that the sentence modifiers in these examples have been set off from the rest of the sentence by commas and the noun modifiers have not been. This is a general rule for participial phrases and relative clauses.

MAIN POINTS OF LESSON THIRTY-SEVEN

The transformations **T-rel** and **T-del** or **T-del-ing** produce relative clauses and participial phrases. **T-rel** puts in a relative pronoun or adverb and makes a noun phrase with a relative clause out of the insert sentence. **T-del** deletes the **relative pronoun + tense + be** to make a participial phrase from the relative clause. **T-del-ing**, a variation of **T-del**, deletes the relative and substitutes the morpheme *-ing* for the tense.

Some participial phrases can be shifted from their position after an **NP** to the position at the beginning of the sentence. The transformation that does this is called **T-SM**. **SM** stands for sentence modifier.

Participial phrases to which **T-SM** is applicable are sentence modifiers, both before and after the application of **T-SM**. So are the relative clauses from which such participial phrases derive. Participial phrases (and their relative clauses) to which **T-SM** is not applicable are noun modifiers.

Lesson Thirty-Eight
DANGLING MODIFIERS

The chief requirements of a grammar are to describe and explain the facts of the language and to do this in the simplest possible way. This first requirement makes the second more difficult. That is, it would not be difficult to set up a simple grammatical system if one were at liberty to ignore the facts of the language as they appear in people's actual use of the language. The grammarian must, however, take the language as it is, not as he might imagine it to be. In practice, he will have to omit a great deal. No grammar, no matter how large, contains all of the facts of the language it describes. But the grammarian cannot distort nor select only those facts which are convenient to his description.

When we say that the grammar must describe the facts in the simplest possible way, we mean, in effect, with the smallest possible number of rules. This requirement doesn't stem principally from love of neatness and economy or from concern for the learner. Rather it stems from the fact that the fewer the rules the more general their application must be and the more relationships within the language they will disclose. If it can be shown that two seemingly different structures need not be described by different rules but can be described by the same rule, it must be true that the structures are somehow related. Thus the search for simplicity often discloses relationships in the language that might not otherwise be perceived.

We have had a good example of very general and powerful rules in those that describe noun modifiers. Noun modifiers in English seem to have enormous variety; yet most (but not quite all) of them can be generated from the kernel by just three rules: **T-rel**, **T-del** (or **T-del-ing**), and **T-NM**. **T-rel** makes relative clauses from base sentences; **T-del** shortens these to participial phrases, adjectives, and the like; **T-NM** shifts some of these to the position before the noun.

Now we also see a great many sentence modifiers generated in almost exactly the same way. Again we have **T-rel** and **T-del** working in the same way, with **T-SM**, parallel to **T-NM**, shifting the modifier optionally to the beginning of the sentence. **T-rel** and **T-del** produce this whole set of modifiers, and **T-NM** and **T-SM** automatically divide them into noun modifiers and sentence modifiers. At this point, incidentally, a completely general statement can be made about punctuation: all sentence modifiers generated in this way are set off from the rest of the sentence by commas, no matter what position they occupy; noun modifiers are not set off.

Moreover, these rules—however remote and fictitious they may seem—must actually be in some sense very real, must go toward answering the fundamental question: how do human beings ever learn and manage their languages? Any language seems to be so enormously complicated as to be beyond the power of the human brain to encompass it. Yet all human beings, dull or bright, contrive to learn at least one language. There must be some kind of simplicity in language, therefore, and this simplicity can be none other than that represented by general rules in the grammar.

Obviously we do not consciously go through the steps **T-rel**, **T-del**, **T-SM** in making sentence modifiers. But as speakers of the language, we certainly know these rules, in some sense of knowing, and we know the relationships they represent.

1851

Relative clauses and participial phrases are not the only sentence modifiers produced by the rules we have given. The deletion transformation, **T-del**, applies to any relative clause containing the sequence **relative pronoun** + _____ + ____ .

1852

Can **T-del** be applied to the relative clause in "John, who was enthusiastic about the class, studied hard"? _____

1853

T-del applies to any relative clause with the sequence **relative pronoun + tense + be**. So it will apply to clauses made from sentences with **be + Adj** in the verb phrase, as well as those with **be + ing** (or **part**) + **verbal**. **T-del** applied to "John, who was enthusiastic about the class, studied hard" gives _____ .

DANGLING MODIFIERS

1854

T-SM shifts a sentence modifier to the position at the beginning of the sentence. Applied to "John, enthusiastic about the class, studied hard," it gives _____ .

1855

In "Enthusiastic about the class, John studied hard," the first word of the sentence modifier is an _____ .

1856

In "Mr. Caspar, who was a kindly man, gave the child ten dollars," what kind of structure is *a kindly man?* _____

1857

The relative clause in "Mr. Caspar, who was a kindly man, gave the child ten dollars" comes from the insert sentence "Mr. Caspar was a kindly man." This has the general structure **NP + Aux + ____ + ____** .

1858

T-del applied to "Mr. Caspar, who was a kindly man, gave the child ten dollars" gives _____ .

1859

The sentence modifier in "Mr. Caspar, a kindly man, gave the child ten dollars" is a _____ phrase.

1860

A noun phrase occurring as a sentence modifier is called an *appositive*. Notice, however, that appositives are generated in exactly the same way as the other sentence modifiers we have been studying—by **T-rel** and **T-del**. **T-SM** applied to "Mr. Caspar, a kindly man, gave the child ten dollars" gives _____ .

1861

In "The Williams house, an old brick mansion, was located on Holborn Street" the appositive is the noun phrase _____ .

1862

In "Alice, a little ball of fun, set fire to the draperies," the appositive is the noun phrase _____ .

1863

What words are the sentence modifier in "Thinking John a weakling, Samuel hit him"? _____

1864

The sentence modifier in "Thinking John a weakling, Samuel hit him" comes from the insert sentence "Samuel _____ ."

1865

The subject of both insert and matrix sentences in "Thinking John a weakling, Samuel hit him" is the word _____ .

1866

The subject of both the insert and matrix sentences in "Hearing the explosion, we investigated" is _____ .

1867

The subject of both insert and matrix sentences in "Winding through the valley, the stream flows by Jackson Hole" is _____ .

1868

The subject of both insert and matrix sentence in "Furiously angry about something or other, the dentist selected a drill" is _____ .

1869

It is an automatic consequence of the rules we have given that the insert and matrix sentences of the type we have been discussing will have the same subject. It is possible, however, to break the rules, and the result is ungrammaticality. In *"Being a nice day, we went to the beach," the matrix sentence is _____ .

DANGLING MODIFIERS

1870

*"Being a nice day, we went to the beach" would go back through the rules to *"We, being a nice day, went to the beach" from *"We, who were a nice day, went to the beach" to the ungrammatical insert sentence _____ .

1871

*"We were a nice day" is ungrammatical, so *"Being a nice day, we went to the beach" is ungrammatical also. It contains what is called a *dangling modifier*. Is the sentence "Seeing Samuel, her heart beat faster" grammatical? _____

1872

*"Seeing Samuel, her heart beat faster" is ungrammatical because it has the ungrammatical insert sentence *"Her heart _____ ."

1873

*"Looking out the window, the day seemed stormy" is ungrammatical because the ungrammatical insert sentence is _____ _____ .

1874

*"Opening the book, an idea occurred to Kawther" is ungrammatical because the insert sentence is _____ .

1875

*"Having invited us to dinner, we wanted to look our best" contains a dangling modifier. The insert sentence is _____ .

1876

Is "Having invited ourselves to dinner, we wanted to look our best" grammatical? _____

1877

"We had invited ourselves to dinner" is grammatical and so, therefore, is "Having invited ourselves to dinner, we wanted to look our best." A sentence modifier deriving from a relative clause for which the insert sentence cannot grammatically have the same subject as the matrix is called a _____ modifier.

1878
The insert sentence of the past participial phrase in "Stunned by the blow, the cat collapsed" is the passive sentence "The cat _____ _____."

1879
The insert sentence of "Fried in bacon grease, the oysters proved delicious" is the passive sentence _____.

1880
Is the sentence "Fried in bacon grease, our guests enjoyed the oysters" grammatical? ____

1881
At least, it's unlikely to be. To be grammatical, "Fried in bacon grease, our guests enjoyed the oysters" would require the unusual insert sentence _____.

1882
*"Destroyed by the explosion, the rescuers entered the building" is ungrammatical because the insert sentence is _____ _____.

If they were destroyed by the explosion, they couldn't have entered the building. We have here a case in which both the insert sentence ("The rescuers were destroyed by the explosion") and the matrix ("The rescuers entered the building") are grammatical, but the joining of them is ungrammatical. Clearly, the nature of the matrix puts some restriction on the sort of insert that can be added to it. For example, "Mary is a sweet little girl" and "Mary is an old lady" are both grammatical, but *"Being a sweet little girl, Mary is an old lady" is not grammatical.

1883
What kind of word is *by* in "Theobald improved his grades by studying hard"? _____

DANGLING MODIFIERS   335

1884

In "Theobald improved his grades by studying hard," *by studying hard* is a prepositional phrase in which the object of the preposition is part of a verb phrase. In this sentence, *studying hard* derives from the insert sentence "Theobald _____."

1885

Again, insert and matrix sentences have the same subject, in this case *Theobald*. In "The boy lost his mind through trying to improve his grades," the subject of both matrix and insert sentences is _____ .

1886

Prepositional phrases of this type can also be shifted to the beginning of the sentence. "The boy lost his mind through trying to improve his grades" becomes "Through trying to improve his grades, the boy lost his mind." "Theobald improved his grades by studying hard" becomes _____ .

1887

In this construction the insert and the matrix sentences have the same subject. Is "By working hard, better results were obtained" grammatical? _____

1888

*"By working hard, better results were obtained" has the insert sentence *"Better results worked hard." "By working hard, John obtained better results" is grammatical. The insert sentence is _____ .

1889

*"In trying to do too much, all was lost" is ungrammatical. The insert sentence is _____ .

1890

Verb phrases with *to* and *in order to* also occur as sentence modifiers. The structure *in order for John to understand the lesson* derives from the base sentence _____ .

336   ENGLISH SYNTAX

1891

The sentence *"In order for John to understand the lesson, John had to study very hard" is ungrammatical because of the repetition. To make this grammatical, we delete the two words _____ .

1892

Nevertheless, in the sentence "In order to understand the lesson, John studied very hard," the insert sentence has the subject _____ .

1893

A deleted subject in a sentence modifier of this sort is the same as the subject of the matrix sentence. In "In order to understand Ohio, one must understand Toledo," the subject of the insert sentence is _____ .

1894

*"In order to save room for dessert, no vegetables were eaten" is ungrammatical, because the insert sentence is _____
_____ .

1895

What words could be deleted from the sentence modifier in "In order to save room for dessert, I ate no vegetables"? _____

1896

Thus "I saved room for dessert" → "in order for me to save room for dessert" → "in order to save room for dessert" → "to save room for dessert," and all of these structures are shown to be related. What is the insert sentence for "To keep up with the events of the day, Rosemary used to hang around the poolhall"? _____
_____

1897

In a variation of this structure, the insert sentence has the same subject not as the subject of the matrix sentence but as the subject of another insert sentence that provides the complement of an adjective. In "It was necessary for John to understand Toledo," the subject of the insert sentence is _____ .

1898

From "In order for John to understand Ohio, it was necessary for John to understand Toledo," we must delete the words _____ in the sentence modifier.

1899

In the sentence "In order for one to understand Ohio, it is necessary for one to understand Toledo," we must delete the first *for one*. Optionally we can delete the second *for one* and the *in order*. This will give us the sentence _____.

1900

Thus from **it is necessary** + **Comp** and "One understands Toledo" we derive "It is necessary for one to understand Toledo." From this and "One understands Ohio" we derive "In order for one to understand Ohio, it is necessary for one to understand Toledo." The first *for one* is obligatorily deleted to eliminate the repetition. The second *for one* and the *in order* are optionally deleted. We then have "To understand Toledo, it is necessary to understand Ohio." The two insert sentences are shown in the history of the construction to be identical, and the sentence modifier does not dangle.

MAIN POINTS OF LESSON THIRTY-EIGHT

The transformations **T-rel** and **T-del** also produce adjective phrases and noun phrases as sentence modifiers, from base sentences with the form **be** + **Adj** and **be** + **NP**. Noun phrases occurring as sentence modifiers are called *appositives*. **T-SM** will apply to adjective phrases and noun phrases that are sentence modifiers, as it will to participial phrases.

Sentence modifiers produced through **T-rel** and **T-del** come from insert sentences with the same subject as the matrix sentence. When such an insert sentence is ungrammatical or nonsensical, as in *"Being a nice day, we went to the beach," for which the insert sentence is *"We were a nice day," the fault is called a *dangling modifier*.

Some sentence modifiers are produced by transformations other than **T-rel** or **T-del**. The prepositional phrase of a base sentence may become a sentence modifier by being shifted to the beginning of the sentence. When the object of the preposition is part of a verb phrase, as in "By working hard, John improved his grades," the subjects of the insert and matrix sentences must be identical.

Constructions of the type *in order for John to do it* may occur as sentence modifiers. When the subjects of the insert and matrix sentences are identical, the former is obligatorily deleted: "In order (for John) to do it, John had to work hard." The *in order* may be optionally deleted: "To do it, John had to work hard."

Lesson Thirty-Nine
PUNCTUATION OF SENTENCE MODIFIERS

The term *sentence modifier* is not an especially common one in grammars. All grammars of English distinguish between structures like "The man chasing the cat is Uncle Rudolph" and "Uncle Rudolph, chasing the cat, broke an ankle," but they distinguish them in various terms and explain the differences in various ways. It is probably most common to call *chasing the cat* a noun modifier in both sentences but to say that it is *restrictive* in the first and *nonrestrictive* in the second. The terms are pretty good ones because they give some clue to what happens. Restrictive modifiers restrict or identify or limit the meaning of something, and nonrestrictive modifiers do not.

However, there is some difficulty in saying that nonrestrictive modifiers are modifiers of nouns. Compare these sentences:

Having a slight headache, Mr. Caspar took an aspirin.
Because he had a slight headache, Mr. Caspar took an aspirin.

If the participial phrase in the first sentence is a noun modifier, then the subordinate clause in the second would seem to be a noun modifier too. Both structures have the same general relation to the main sentence and both convey the same information: that Mr. Caspar had a slight headache. No grammarian, however, would want to call the clause a noun modifier; and if the clause is not, then neither is the phrase.

Furthermore, if the phrase isn't a noun modifier here, neither is it a noun modifier in its position before the application of **T-SM**:

Mr. Caspar, having a slight headache, took an aspirin.

And if the phrase is not a noun modifier, the relative clause from which it derives can't be one either:

Mr. Caspar, who had a slight headache, took an aspirin.

Transformations change structure, but they don't change meaning relations. The essential relations of the various parts of the sentence persist through all the transformations.

Probably grammarians have wanted to call phrases like *having a slight headache,* as in the example, noun modifiers because they perceive the connection between the headache and Mr. Caspar: Mr. Caspar had the headache. The sentence *"Having a slight headache, an aspirin was taken" is ungrammatical. This point is taken care of, however, in the observation that, if the sentence is constructed grammatically, the insert sentence and the matrix sentence will have an identical subject as an automatic consequence of the transformations.

What we *call* a grammatical structure doesn't matter so much as identifying and understanding the structure and seeing its relationships to other structures. However, terminology may sometimes impede understanding. We may well use the terms restrictive and nonrestrictive, but it seems best to say that restrictive structures are noun modifiers and nonrestrictive structures are sentence modifiers.

1901

The general rule is that sentence modifiers are set off by a comma and noun modifiers are not. In "Smiling shyly Mimi greeted the guests," there should be a comma after the word _____ .

1902

We have seen some exceptions to this punctuation rule. When the sentence is a simple adverb or a simple prepositional phrase, the comma is not always used. But when the sentence modifier is a clause, a participial phrase, an adjective, a noun phrase, a preposition or *in order to* plus a verb phrase, the rule is usually followed. In "Because he had a slight headache Mr. Caspar took an aspirin," there should be a comma after the word _____ .

1903

In "In order to understand Italy it is necessary to understand Empoli," there should be a comma after _____ .

1904

In "A fast man on the draw Sanders got the drop on his opponent," there should be a comma after _____ .

1905

In "Visible for many miles Mount Holyoke was the greatest tourist attraction of the region," there should be a comma after _____ .

1906

In "By whipping the child frequently the parents succeeded in improving his manners," there should be a comma after _____ .

1907

In "Pleased at having been invited the girls began thinking about what they would wear," there should be a comma after the word _____ .

1908

What group of words is the sentence modifier in "Mr. Wheeler having gone home, we spoke to Mr. Caspar"? _____

1909

Mr. Wheeler having gone home is an example of a construction traditionally called a *nominative absolute*. What is its base sentence? _____

1910

Mr. Wheeler having gone home is a case of **NP** + **ing** + **have** + **part** + **Vl** + **Adv-p**. "Mr. Wheeler had gone home" is a case of **NP** + **tense** + **have** + **part** + **Vl** + **Adv-p**. Nominative absolutes are created by a transformation which replaces _____ with _____ .

1911

The nominative absolute construction **NP** + **ing** + **have** + **part** + **Vl** + **Adv-p** becomes, by **T-af**, **NP** + _____ + _____ + _____ + _____ + _____ .

1912

What is the nominative absolute in "The car being out of gas, we took the bus"? _____

1913

What is the insert sentence for "The car being out of gas, we took the bus"? _____

1914

In the nominative absolute construction, does the insert sentence have the same subject as the matrix sentence? _____

1915

The same punctuation rule applies, however. In "The work being finished we picked up the tools and went home," there should be a comma after the word _____ .

1916

In "The canned salmon having gone bad the children had to eat tuna," there should be a comma after the word _____ .

1917

When a clause or a nominative absolute modifies a matrix sentence, the insert sentence and the matrix do not have the same subject. In the other constructions we have examined as sentence modifiers, they do. The sentence *"Amused by his insolence, no action was taken" is ungrammatical. The insert sentence is _____ .

1918

Is the sentence "Amused by his insolence, nobody wanted to take action" grammatical? _____

1919

"Nobody was amused by his insolence" is a good sentence, but it is not a possible sentence here. Obviously, someone *was* amused by his insolence; that's why no action was taken. What is the insert sentence of "The door being locked, we climbed through a window"? _____

1920

The structure *the door being locked* is called a _____ .

PUNCTUATION OF SENTENCE MODIFIERS

1921

In "By accepting the enemy's terms the Gauls were able to keep the peace," there should be a comma after the word _____ .

1922

In "There being no more pitchers in the bullpen the Giants gave up baseball," there should be a comma after the word _____ .

1923

What words are the sentence modifier in "Smiling shyly, Mimi greeted the guests"? _____

1924

"Smiling shyly, Mimi greeted the guests" derives, by **T-SM**, from "Mimi, _____ , _____ ."

1925

"Mimi, smiling shyly, greeted the guests" derives by **T-del**, from "Mimi, _____ , _____ ."

1926

Structures to which **T-SM** can be applied are sentence modifiers, and so are the relative clauses that underlie them. Sentence modifiers are set off by commas. In "John who was leafing through the book found a fifty-dollar bill," there should be commas after _____ and _____ .

1927

Sentence modifiers are somewhat harder to recognize before **T-SM** than after it, because before **T-SM** they occupy a position also possible for noun modifiers. Consider (1) "Mimi, who was smiling shyly, greeted the guests" and (2) "The girl who was smiling shyly was Mimi." These sentences are very similar. They both contain the relative clause *who was smiling shyly,* and in both, the insert sentence and the matrix have the same subject: *Mimi* in (1) and *the girl* in (2). But in (1) the clause is a _____ modifier, and in (2) it's a _____ modifier.

344 ENGLISH SYNTAX

1928

T-rel is slightly different when it produces sentence modifiers from when it produces noun modifiers. In the production of a sentence modifier, **T-rel** requires a break in the voice between the relative clause and the matrix sentence. In "Mimi, who was smiling shyly, greeted the guests," the breaks are indicated by _____ .

1929

T-rel produces sentence modifiers and not noun modifiers under more or less statable circumstances. For example, it produces sentence modifiers, usually, when the subject of the insert sentence is a proper noun. Which of these has a proper noun as subject: (1) "The girl was smiling shyly," or (2) "Mimi was smiling shyly"? _____

1930

If we apply **T-rel** to "Mr. Wheeler laughed heartily," will the clause be (1) a sentence modifier or (2) a noun modifier? _____

1931

In the introduction to this lesson, we referred to the terms *restrictive* and *nonrestrictive*. Noun modifiers are restrictive. Sentence modifiers are nonrestrictive. In "Mr. Wheeler, who was laughing heartily, answered the question," the relative clause is _____ .

1932

T-del applied to "Mr. Wheeler, who was laughing heartily, answered the question" gives _____ .

1933

A sentence modifier is nonrestrictive in that it doesn't restrict or limit the meaning of anything but merely adds another idea to the sentence. In "Mr. Wheeler, laughing heartily, answered the question," one idea is that Mr. Wheeler answered the question. The other is that Mr. Wheeler _____ .

1934

A noun modifier, however, identifies or singles out a particular person or thing, thus restricting the meaning of the noun. "The man laughing heartily is Mr. Wheeler" means that not just any man is Mr. Wheeler but specifically the man who is _____ .

1935

In "Mr. Wheeler, laughing heartily, answered the question," the participial phrase does not identify Mr. Wheeler. He is already identified by the name. In "The papers lying on the desk blew off," the participial phrase is not a sentence modifier but a _____ modifier.

1936

Is the participial phrase in "Mrs. Alva dusting the desk scattered the papers" (1) a noun modifier or (2) a sentence modifier? ____

1937

In "Mrs. Alva dusting the desk scattered the papers," there should be commas after _____ and _____ .

1938

The participial phrase, or the relative clause from which it derives, is usually a sentence modifier, not a noun modifier, when the subject of the matrix and insert sentences is a _____ noun.

1939

A proper noun generally identifies a person completely, so of course a modifier can't identify it any more. Is the subject of "My mother scattered the papers" completely identified? ____

1940

The subject of "My mother scattered the papers" is completely identified by the possessive determiner *my*. *My mother* can mean only one person. Therefore the clause in "My mother who was dusting the desk scattered the papers" is a sentence modifier and nonrestrictive, and there should be commas after _____ and _____ .

1941

Is the subject of "Somebody scattered the papers" completely identified? ____

1942

Somebody in "Somebody scattered the papers" isn't identified at all. In "Somebody dusting the desk scattered the papers," the subject is identified by the participial phrase. This participial phrase should not be set off by commas because it is the modifier of a _____ phrase.

1943

In "The girl whistling a tune is Maybelle," the participial phrase serves to indicate which girl is Maybelle. In "The girl, whistling a tune, dusted the piano," does the participial phrase indicate which girl dusted the piano? _____

1944

In "The girl, whistling a tune, dusted the piano," the participial phrase is punctuated as a sentence modifier, so it doesn't identify *the girl*. She is identified in some other way; perhaps she is the only girl in the room. Does the participial phrase in "The girl dusting the piano suddenly screamed" identify *the girl?* _____

1945

There are two girls in the room. One is dusting the piano. One is fixing her hair. The participial phrase in "The girl dusting the piano suddenly screamed" indicates which girl _____ .

1946

There are three men in a clothing store. One is examining neckties. Use a relative clause from the insert sentence "The man was examining neckties" within the matrix sentence "The man turned white." _____

1947

There are three men in a clothing store. One, whose name is DeWitt, is examining neckties. Use a relative clause from the insert sentence "DeWitt was examining neckties" in the matrix "DeWitt turned white."

PUNCTUATION OF SENTENCE MODIFIERS

1948

There is one house in a region, and it overlooks a valley. Use a relative clause from the insert sentence "The house belonged to Felix Robinson" in the matrix "The house overlooked a valley." _____

_____

1949

There are two houses in a region. One overlooks a valley, and the other does not. Use a relative clause from the insert sentence "The house belonged to Felix Robinson" in the matrix "The house overlooked a valley." _____

1950

There is no particular difficulty in recognizing and punctuating sentence modifiers which occur at the beginning of the sentence, since they are identified by the position. Sentence modifiers within the sentence, however, occur where noun modifiers also occur. One must therefore decide whether the modifier is a noun modifier and restrictive or a sentence modifier and nonrestrictive, in order to punctuate properly.

MAIN POINTS OF LESSON THIRTY-NINE

Sentence modifiers are nonrestrictive and noun modifiers are restrictive. That is, noun modifiers restrict or identify or limit the meaning of some noun phrase. Sentence modifiers simply add some additional information to that contained in the matrix sentence.

Relative clauses and participial phrases used as noun modifiers can occur only after the noun they modify. Participial phrases used as sentence modifiers appear either after a noun or at the beginning of the sentence. In other words, **T-SM** applies to constructions that are sentence modifiers but not to those that are noun modifiers.

Adverbs and simple prepositional phrases occurring as sentence modifiers may or may not be set off by commas. Other sentence modifiers are regularly set off. Noun modifiers are not separated by commas from the nouns they modify.

The *nominative absolute* construction is one in which **ing** replaces the tense of an insert sentence: "The door was locked" → "the door being locked." This construction is always a sentence modifier.

Lesson Forty
PRACTICE WITH SENTENCE MODIFIERS

Nominative absolute is a good example of the arbitrariness of terminology. It *means,* as we have seen, a structure like *the door being locked* or *Mr. Wheeler having gone home.* Why these structures are so-called is another question. The term *absolute* suggests that the structure has no close grammatical connection with anything in the sentence modified. For example, the insert sentence from which the nominative absolute is made does not have to have the same subject as the matrix sentence with which it is used. The term *nominative* is suggested by the fact that if the NP is a personal pronoun, we use *he,* not *him; they,* not *them;* and so on: *he having gone home, they having gone home.*

The term *nominative absolute* was chosen in the first place because of the strong influence that Latin grammar had on the early grammarians of English. When English grammars began to appear in the seventeenth and eighteenth centuries, the grammar that everyone knew was Latin. Until that time, Latin (along with Greek) had been the grammar studied in the schools. We get our term *grammar school* from the fact that the chief study in those days was Latin grammar. Naturally, when people began making grammars of English, there was a strong tendency to use the terminology employed for Latin. Constructions like *Mr. Wheeler having gone home* were seen to resemble in meaning a Latin construction called an *ablative absolute,* in which two words in the ablative case were conjoined. English had no ablative case, but it did have, or at least it seemed to have, a nominative, and so the nominative absolute was devised.

Had the Latin influence in grammar-making been confined to terminology, it would have been harmless enough. So long as we agree on what to call some structure, it doesn't matter much what we agree on. We can call *Mr. Wheeler having gone home* a nominative absolute or an *X* or whatever we like. It is convenient to use the Latin terms just because they are familiar.

We must, however, be careful not to mix up English and Latin. The early grammarians of English did not always avoid this danger. They not only used the Latin terms but also tried to find in English the Latin categories, some of which existed in English and some of which did not. The nominative case, for example, scarcely exists in English. It is at any rate a ponderous term to use for the half-dozen words—*I, he, she, we, they, who*—that have separate subject and object forms. English nouns don't make any distinction at all, though Latin nouns did. Older English grammars often described six tenses of English verbs: present, past, future, present perfect, pluperfect, and future perfect. This was a direct result of the Latin influence, because Latin had such a system, in which the different tenses were distinguished by different endings on the verbs. English, as we have seen, has only a two-tense system. Tense is rewritten as either *present* or *past,* and all other modifications of verb meaning come from other parts of the auxiliary. It would never have occurred to grammarians to find six tenses in English if they had not been thinking of Latin.

1951

In "John, who knew all about it, smiled quietly," the relative clause is a _____ modifier.

1952

T-del-ing drops the relative pronoun and replaces tense with **ing**. Applied to "John, who knew all about it, smiled quietly," this would give

_____ .

1953

T-SM shifts structures derived from relative clauses by **T-del** or **T-del-ing** to the beginning of the sentence. It can be applied to sentence modifiers but not to noun modifiers. Applied to "John, knowing all about it, smiled quietly," it gives _____ .

1954

When the insert sentence of a relative clause has a proper noun as subject, the clause is generally a _____ modifier.

1955

A proper noun is completely identified, so a clause or phrase cannot identify it any further. In "Mr. Danby flattered by the letter smiled

350   ENGLISH SYNTAX

broadly," the participial phrase is a sentence modifier. Therefore, there should be commas after _____ and _____ .

1956
The passive insert sentence for "Mr. Danby, flattered by the letter, smiled broadly" is _____ .

1957
The transform "Mr. Danby was flattered by the letter" derives by **T-passive** from the kernel sentence _____ .

1958
In "The letter written by Mr. Payne was never received," the past participial phrase consists of the words _____ .

1959
In "The letter written by Mr. Payne was never received," the participial phrase identifies the letter. Out of all possible letters, it was the one written by Mr. Payne that was not received. The participial phrase is therefore a _____ modifier.

1960
Use a participial phrase from the insert sentence "David was stunned by the blow" in the matrix "David collapsed on the sofa." _____

1961
Use a relative clause from the insert sentence "Anyone may be embarrassed about speaking" in the matrix "Anyone will be excused."

1962
There are several men near John in the theater. Use a participial phrase from the insert sentence "The man was seated on John's right" in the matrix "The man cleared his throat." _____

PRACTICE WITH SENTENCE MODIFIERS

1963

There are several women and one man near John in the theater. Use a participial phrase from the insert sentence "The man was seated on John's right" in the matrix "The man cleared his throat." _____
_____

1964

There are several dogs in the yard. Use a relative clause from the insert sentence "The dog was chained to the tree" in the matrix "The dog kept howling." _____

1965

There are three cats, one dog, and a panther in a room. Use a participial phrase from the insert "The dog was soothed by my touch" in the matrix "The dog lay still." _____

1966

The sentence "Eager to help us, John fell into the fishpond" derives by **T-SM** from _____ .

1967

All phrases to which **T-SM** is applicable, and also the relative clauses that underlie them, are sentence modifiers and nonrestrictive. "John, eager to help us, fell into the fishpond" derives by **T-del** from _____
_____ .

1968

In "Mary tired of playing with the lamb roasted it" there should be commas after _____ and _____ .

1969

T-SM applied to "Mary, tired of playing with the lamb, roasted it" gives
_____ .

352   ENGLISH SYNTAX

1970

T-SM could be applied to "David, anxious about his mother, decided to telegraph," giving "Anxious about his mother, David decided to telegraph." Could **T-SM** also be applied to "Anybody anxious about his mother should telegraph"? _____

1971

*"Anxious about his mother, anybody should telegraph" is ungrammatical. The adjective phrase is restrictive, identifying the noun phrase *anybody,* and therefore it must come after it, not before. Assuming that the sentence "The fellows willing to help us came down to the lake" is properly punctuated, the adjective phrase is a _____ modifier.

1972

"The fellows willing to help us came down to the lake" means that there were other fellows, not willing to help us, who did not _____ _____ .

1973

Assuming that "The fellows, willing to help us, came down to the lake" is properly punctuated, the adjective phrase is a _____ modifier.

1974

"The fellows, willing to help us, came down to the lake" means that all the fellows were willing to help us and came down to the lake, while the girls, perhaps, stayed in camp. In the sentence "Anyone who wants to help us should come down to the lake," the indefinite pronoun *anyone* is restricted and specified by a _____ clause.

1975

In "Samuel who didn't want to help us stayed in camp," the clause is a sentence modifier, and there should be commas after _____ and _____ .

1976

The insert sentence for "Samuel, who didn't want to help us, stayed in camp" is _____ .

PRACTICE WITH SENTENCE MODIFIERS

1977

"Mr. Wheeler, knowing the whole story, couldn't help smiling" derives by **T-del-ing** from _____ .

1978

In "Mr. Wheeler who knew the whole story couldn't help smiling," there should be commas after _____ and _____ .

1979

In "The story didn't fool Mr. Wheeler who had already talked to Mr. Caspar," there should be a comma after _____ .

1980

Not all students cheat in examinations. Make a sentence with a relative clause from the insert sentence "Students cheat" and the matrix "Students will be failed." _____

1981

John has only one roommate. Make a sentence with a relative clause from the insert sentence "John's roommate had cheated on the examination" and the matrix "John's roommate was failed." _____

1982

There are several little girls in a room. Make a sentence with a relative clause from the insert sentence "The little girl was poking the fire" and the matrix "The little girl burned herself." _____

1983

Make a sentence with a relative clause from the insert sentence "John needed it badly" and the matrix "Samuel gave it to John." _____

1984

Make a sentence with a relative clause from the insert sentence "Children were hungry" and the matrix "The group gave food to children."

_____

1985

T-del applied to "Sally, who was a great reader, enjoyed the book" gives

_____ .

1986

A noun phrase resulting from deletion of **relative pronoun + tense + be** is called an appositive. In "Samuel, a friend of Theobald's, came too," the appositive is the group of words _____ .

1987

"Samuel, a friend of Theobald's, came too" derives by **T-del** from

_____ .

1988

"We visited their house, a twenty-room mansion" derives by **T-del** from

_____ .

1989

Make a sentence with an appositive deriving from the insert sentence "Morro Bay is a charming town near San Luis Obispo" and the matrix "We visited Morro Bay." _____

1990

Make a sentence with an appositive from the insert sentence "Mabel was a very beautiful girl" and the matrix "Mrs. Alva introduced John to Mabel." _____ .

1991

Make a sentence with an appositive from the insert sentence "Mabel was the little servant girl" and the matrix "Mabel served the cookies."

_____

PRACTICE WITH SENTENCE MODIFIERS 355

1992

Appositives are always nonrestrictive sentence modifiers. In "He wants to sell his car a 1954 Ford" there should be a comma after _____ .

1993

In "His mother an Indian wove beautiful blankets," there should be commas after _____ and _____ .

1994

In "They had to cross the river a boiling torrent to escape the Indians," there should be commas after _____ .

1995

In "They bought the old Morrison house which had been built in 1692," there should be a comma after _____ .

1996

Could the relative pronoun *that* be substituted for *which* in "They bought the old Morrison house, which had been built in 1692"? ____

1997

*"They bought the old Morrison house, that had been built in 1692" is ungrammatical. Could *that* grammatically replace *who* in "My mother, who was dusting the piano, fainted"? ____

1998

The relative pronoun *that* does not occur in relative clauses used as sentence modifiers. Is the sentence "The woman that was dusting the piano fainted" grammatical? ____

1999

The relative pronoun *that* is used only in relative clauses functioning as noun modifiers. Make a sentence with a relative clause from the insert sentence "The house was built in 1692" and the matrix "They bought a house." Use *that*. _____

356   ENGLISH SYNTAX

2000

One can tell whether a relative clause is a sentence modifier (and should be set off by commas) or a noun modifier (and should not be) by seeing whether *that* can be substituted for *who* or *which*. If *that* can be substituted, the clause is a noun modifier. If not, the clause is a sentence modifier.

MAIN POINTS OF LESSON FORTY

Sentence modifiers are set off from the matrix sentence by commas. Noun modifiers are not set off.

T-SM, which shifts a modifier to the beginning of the sentence, applies to sentence modifiers and not to noun modifiers. One can distinguish the two, therefore, by seeing whether **T-SM** can be grammatically applied.

That occurs in relative clauses used as noun modifiers but not in relative clauses used as sentence modifiers. One can therefore distinguish the two by trying whether *that* can be grammatically substituted for *who* or *which*.

Lesson Forty-One
PREDICATION

We have been using the terms *grammatical* and *ungrammatical* without any attempt to define the concept of grammaticality. This may be thought an illogical way to proceed, but it is not an oversight. Grammatical can only mean "corresponding to the grammar" and grammaticality can only be defined by specifying what the grammar is. In doing this, we must depend ultimately on our intuition, as native speakers of English, to tell us whether a sentence is or is not a good English sentence.

Notice particularly that we cannot take the easy way of calling grammatical that which speakers of English say or write. If we could, the task would be relatively simple. We would simply collect a body of English speech and writing and classify it in some way. However, such a collection would inevitably contain a great deal that we would simply not want to call grammatical. It would contain, for example, slips of the tongue. Someone intending to say, "He had a basket of bread" might come out instead with "He had a brasket of bed." We would not want to call this grammatical, even though it is uttered by a native speaker of English.

Indeed, if you listen closely to the conversation even of well-educated speakers of English, you will find that much of it is departure from the grammar rather than illustration of it. The eminent linguist Charles F. Hockett cites the following example, transcribed from a real conversation:

> It's uh . . . it's uh not . . . I mean he [throat cleared] actually well he he we we had just sort of . . . in many ways sort of given up . . . trying to do very much . . . until . . . bedtime. Unless it's something that he can be included in . . . whereupon he will . . . usually isn't interested for long enough to really . . . carry through with it.*

---

*From *A Course in Modern Linguistics* by Charles F. Hockett. Reprinted by permission of The Macmillan Company.

A good deal of actual conversation is like this. Obviously it is not grammatical, in any useful sense of the term. It contains within it many grammatical sequences, but as a whole it is a set of departures from the grammar, a going in and out of the grammar, rather than a succession of well-formed English sentences. Even when the speaker is being quite careful and formal, he will necessarily depart from the grammar very frequently, as the verbatim transcription of any presidential press conference will illustrate.

We are not saying that such ungrammaticality is a bad thing. It is, on the contrary, quite normal and suitable. Conversation in which all the sentences were perfectly grammatical would sound odd and unnatural. Sometimes in television programs speakers will pretend to be speaking spontaneously when in reality they are reading from a script hidden from the cameras. The very grammaticality of the sentences will usually mark such talk as contrived.

On the other hand, there are many sentences that we should certainly wish to call grammatical which we would never find in any collection of English speech or writing. Such sentences as "Pigs are pink" or "The principal exports of the planet Mars are sausages and paper clips" are undoubtedly grammatical, though they are not to be found used in English.

So in specifying the grammar, we necessarily fall back on our own feeling about whether a construction is grammatical or not. This seems vague, perhaps, and lacking in objectivity, but actually it presents very few problems. Generally we have no difficulty in distinguishing a grammatical construction like "Pigs are pink" from an ungrammatical one like *"Pinks was pig." When we are uncertain, we can generally agree that the construction is marginal.

One very common kind of ungrammaticality is an error in predication, in which the predicate is grammatically unsuited to the subject.

2001

Take the sentence "John terrified oatmeal." Is this sentence grammatical? _____

2002

*"John terrified oatmeal" is ungrammatical. People can terrify other people, but they can't terrify a dish of mush. Is the sentence "Oatmeal admired John" grammatical? _____

2003

Is "Oatmeal terrified John" grammatical? ____

2004

A dish of mush can terrify a person. Many children are terrified by oatmeal. Is "John saw the table" grammatical? ____

2005

Is "The table saw John" grammatical? ____

2006

Except in a story in which tables and chairs are personified—that is, made to act like people—*"The table saw John" would be ungrammatical. Is "The cat frightened the canned salmon" grammatical? ____

2007

Is "The cat frightened the salmon" grammatical? ____

2008

If the salmon is alive and not canned, the cat can frighten it. Is "The canned salmon frightened the cat" grammatical? ____

2009

Is "The mouse ate the cheese" grammatical? ____

2010

Is "The cheese ate the mouse" grammatical? ____

2011

In order to explain why some of these sentences are grammatical and some are not, we need to notice another general category of nouns: *animate* nouns. We can start by saying that animate nouns are nouns that can be subjects of verbs like *eat, see, feel*. In "The child ate the oatmeal," *child* is an _____ noun.

2012

Animate nouns of course refer to living things, or things thought of as being alive. If we say, "The canned salmon smiled at the cat," we are

360   ENGLISH SYNTAX

making some kind of joke that involves taking *canned salmon* as an animate noun. Ordinarily, the sentence would be ungrammatical. In "The mouse ate the cheese," *mouse* is an _____ noun.

2013

Nouns which are not animate are *inanimate*. Inanimate nouns are nouns that cannot be subjects of verbs like *see, eat, feel* or objects of verbs like *terrify, frighten, please*. Is "John's behavior pleased Sally" grammatical?

____

2014

Sally is an animate noun and can be the object of a verb like *please, frighten, terrify*. Is "John's behavior pleased the bananas" grammatical?

____

2015

*"John's behavior pleased the bananas" is ungrammatical because *bananas* is an _____ noun.

2016

Notice that *animate* and *inanimate*, as we are using the terms, refer to grammar and not to biology. A banana and a tree are living organisms, but *banana* and *tree* are inanimate nouns. The sentence *"John's behavior amused the tree" is ungrammatical because *amuse* is not the kind of verb that can have an _____ noun as its object.

2017

Many errors of what is called *predication* involve the wrong use of animate and inanimate nouns. An error of predication occurs when the predicate is grammatically unsuitable to the subject. Is the sentence "The desire hoped to get an *A*" grammatical? ____

2018

*"The desire hoped to get an *A*" is ungrammatical because *hoped* is the kind of verb that must have an _____ noun as subject, and the noun *desire* is _____ .

PREDICATION 361

2019

Except as a slip of the tongue, no speaker of English would say or write *"The desire hoped to get an *A*." But the following sentence might easily occur: "John's desire to excel in every subject he took actually hoped to get an *A* even in algebra." Is it grammatical? ____

2020

Such a sentence is an error in predication. The ungrammatical matrix sentence, which has been enlarged by transformation, is *"The _____ _____ an *A*."

2021

The matrix sentence is ungrammatical, and so the whole sentence is ungrammatical. What has happened is that in the building up of the sentence through transformation, the writer has forgotten what the matrix sentence was. Is this sentence grammatical: "John desired to excel in every subject he took and actually hoped to get an *A* even in algebra"? ____

2022

"John desired to excel in every subject he took and actually hoped to get an *A* even in algebra" contains the two principal base sentences "John desired to excel" and "John _____."

2023

Is this sentence grammatical: "The chairman's anxiety about not having enough money for expenses decided to poll the members about the possibility of raising the dues"? ____

2024

*"The chairman's anxiety about not having enough money for expenses decided to poll the members about the possibility of raising dues" is ungrammatical because it contains the ungrammatical matrix sentence *"The anxiety _____."

2025

"The chairman, being anxious about not having enough money for expenses, decided to poll the members about the possibility of raising the dues" is grammatical. It is built on the matrix sentence "_____ the members."

2026

The chairman can be subject of the verb *decide* because *chairman* is an _____ noun.

2027

*"Being anxious about the club's finances, a poll of the membership on the possibility of raising dues was taken" is ungrammatical because the participial phrase derives from the insert sentence *"A poll was _____."

2028

If any of the base sentences that make up a complicated sentence is ungrammatical, the whole sentence is ungrammatical. Is the sentence "His ideas of what he wanted to do when he grew older dreamed of piloting jet airplanes" grammatical? _____

2029

*"His ideas of what he wanted to do when he grew older dreamed of piloting jet airplanes" is ungrammatical because it is built on the ungrammatical three-word matrix sentence _____ .

2030

"His ideas of what he wanted to do when he grew older involved piloting jet airplanes" is grammatical. The matrix sentence is "_____ piloting jet airplanes."

2031

Is "The appointment was done by the chairman" grammatical? _____

2032

The passive sentence *"The appointment was done by the chairman" derives from the kernel sentence *_____ .

2033

We are always less likely to make a grammatical error in a kernal sentence than in a transformation of it. We would hardly say *"The chairman did the appointment" but instead "The chairman _____ the appointment."

2034

As we build up a complicated sentence through transformation, the possibility of error increases. The sentence *"The appointment which caused all the argument had actually been done by the chairman himself" is ungrammatical because it derives from the kernel sentence *_____ .

2035

Is the sentence "Each member was asked to name any possible speaker that he was acquainted" grammatical? _____

2036

*"Each member was asked to name any possible speaker that he was acquainted" is ungrammatical because it contains the ungrammatical relative clause _____ .

2037

The relative clause in *a speaker that he knew* derives from the insert sentence "He knew a speaker." Then the clause in *a speaker that he was acquainted* must derive from *_____ .

2038

We wouldn't intentionally say *"He was acquainted a speaker" but instead "He was _____ ."

2039

"He was acquainted with a speaker" transforms into the relative clause *a speaker that he was acquainted with* or *a speaker with* _____ _____ .

364 ENGLISH SYNTAX

2040

The sentence should have been "Each member was asked to name any possible speaker that he was acquainted with" (or "with whom he was acquainted"). Is the sentence "His long-awaited arrival in Portland for the meeting of the Beekeepers Association should have been by jet plane" grammatical? ____

2041

What is the matrix sentence at the base of *"His long-awaited arrival in Portland for the meeting of the Beekeepers Association should have been by jet plane"? _____

2042

However, we wouldn't ordinarily say *"The arrival was by plane" but instead "He arrived by plane." Is the sentence "His long-awaited arrival in Portland for the meeting of the Beekeepers Association must have been for some reason delayed" grammatical? ____

2043

"His long-awaited arrival in Portland for the meeting of the Beekeepers Association must have been for some reason delayed" derives from the passive matrix sentence "The arrival was delayed." This in turn derives from the kernel sentence "Something _____."

2044

Is this sentence grammatical: "The Mayor's bad temper offended many voters and was not reelected for a second term"? ____

2045

*"The Mayor's bad temper offended many voters and was not reelected for a second term" derives from two matrix sentences: the grammatical sentence "The temper offended many voters" and the ungrammatical sentence *"The temper _____."

2046

The passive sentence *"The temper was reelected" derives from the kernel sentence *"They _____."

2047

You can reelect a mayor but not a temper. Is this sentence grammatical: "The Mayor offended many people by his bad temper, and he was not reelected for a second term"? _____

2048

Is this sentence grammatical: "Mrs. Alva's pity for the hungry little boy gave him a hamburger"? _____

2049

Is this sentence grammatical: "Mrs. Alva, moved to pity for the hungry little boy, advised him to find a job and earn some money"? _____

2050

Any complicated sentence is derived from a number of kernel sentences. Each kernel sentence must be grammatical if the whole is to be grammatical.

MAIN POINTS OF LESSON FORTY-ONE

Errors in predication are those in which the subject is grammatically unsuitable to the predicate.

Many errors in predication result from the use of animate or inanimate nouns with verbs that cannot take the one type or the other as subjects or objects. An animate noun is one that can be subject of a verb like *eat, see, feel* or object of a verb like *frighten, amuse, terrify*. In general, animate nouns are those that refer to living beings, though the correspondence between biology and grammar is not exact. Nouns that are not animate are called inanimate.

Errors in predication seldom occur in simple sentences. They are not uncommon, however, in sentences that result from many transformations.

Lesson Forty-Two
SOME PROBLEMS IN MODIFICATION

It was explained in the introduction to Lesson Forty-One that not everything said by native speakers of English can be considered grammatical. It is equally obvious that not everything written by a native speaker of English will necessarily be grammatical. If it were not so, there would not be much motivation for courses in the improvement of writing.

Errors in writing are of two general kinds: mechanical errors and grammatical errors. Mechanical errors are those that result from inadequate control of the writing system—spelling, capitalization, conventions of punctuation. Some of these relate to the grammar of the language. We have seen relationships between grammar and punctuation, and there are many relationships between spelling and the phonological part of the grammar. However, mechanical errors are essentially different from such purely grammatical errors as predication, dangling modifiers, ambiguous construction, in which constructions that are not grammatical are written down as if they were.

One is not so likely to be ungrammatical in writing as in speech because of the nature of the two activities. In speech one ordinarily has to push right along, meeting the situation, filling the silences with sound, whereas in writing one can deliberate, select one construction or another, revise. On the other hand, in speech we enjoy various aids to communication—gesture, intonation, the actual presence of the person we are addressing—which we do not have when we write. For this reason, writing must be more grammatical than speech has to be. Departures from the grammar that would pass unnoticed in speech become serious errors in writing. They may impede understanding or stand out as ugly or foolish.

In writing, as in speech, we seldom depart from the grammar in kernel sentences. Errors come in transforms, particularly in sentences that are heavily transformed and complicated. Student writers, intuitively aware of this danger, sometimes try to avoid it by using only simple sentences. However, they then fall into the even more serious fault of childish writing, which is incapable of shades of emphasis and barren of variety. Complicated sentences are often needed and should not be avoided. The writer must take care that they are grammatical, however, and he can do this if he is aware of the relationship of the basic elements of which the sentences are composed and makes sure that these relationships remain intact through the transformations.

2051

In the sentence "The girl from Boston waved to us," what is the subject? _____

2052

In the subject of the sentence "The girl from Boston waved to us," the noun phrase *the girl* is modified by a _____ phrase.

2053

In "The girl who had come with Jim waved to us," the noun phrase *the girl* is modified by a _____ .

2054

In "The girl from Boston who had come with Jim waved to us," the noun phrase *the girl* is modified by a _____ , and then the expanded noun phrase is modified by a _____ .

2055

If the same noun phrase is modified by both a prepositional phrase and a relative clause, which of the modifiers comes first? _____

2056

What is the subject of the sentence "The girl by the bridge which spanned the creek waved to us"? _____

2057

The noun phrase *the girl by the bridge which spanned the creek* contains the relative clause _____ .

368   ENGLISH SYNTAX

2058

In the noun phrase *the girl by the bridge which spanned the creek*, is the subject of the insert sentence that produces the relative clause *the girl* or *the bridge?* _____

2059

The noun phrase *the girl by the bridge which spanned the creek* doesn't mean that the girl by the bridge spanned the creek. It means that the bridge did. In this noun phrase the object of the preposition *by* is the group of words _____ .

2060

In the sentence "The girl from Boston who came with Jim waved to us," the object of the preposition *from* is _____ .

2061

The two noun phrases (1) *the girl from Boston who came with Jim* and (2) *the girl by the bridge which spanned the creek* have almost the same structure: **NP + Prep + NP + relative clause**. The difference is that in (1) the relative clause modifies **NP + Prep + NP**. In (2) it modifies just _____ .

2062

Whenever the sequence **NP + Prep + NP + relative clause** occurs, the relative clause has two possible structures to modify: the whole sequence **NP + Prep + NP** or just the **NP** which is the object of the preposition. In the noun phrase *the girl from the city which I mentioned*, the relative clause modifies the words _____ .

2063

In *the girl from the city whom I mentioned*, the relative clause modifies the words _____ .

2064

The relative clause in *the girl from the city which I mentioned* derives from the insert sentence _____ .

SOME PROBLEMS IN MODIFICATION   369

2065

The relative clause in *the girl from the city whom I mentioned* derives from the insert sentence _____ .

2066

When a relative replaces an object in the insert sentence and the object refers to a person, the relative pronoun is *whom* or *that*, either of which can be deleted. When the object refers to anything other than a person, the relative pronoun is _____ or _____ .

2067

If the first **NP** in the sequence **NP + Prep + NP + relative clause** refers to a person and the second does not, and if the relative pronoun is *who* or *whom*, will the relative clause modify **NP + Prep + NP** or just the second **NP**? _____

2068

If the relative pronoun were *which*, the clause would modify the second **NP**. But if the relative pronoun were *that* or if it had been deleted, the clause could modify either construction. In the noun phrase *the girl from the city I mentioned*, the relative pronoun has been _____ .

2069

The noun phrase *the girl from the city I mentioned* is ambiguous—that is, it has two possible meanings. It has two possible meanings because it can be derived from two different insert sentences. One is "I mentioned the girl from the city" and the other is _____ .

2070

The noun phrase *the kitten in the basket that everyone liked* is also ambiguous. It can be derived from "Everyone liked the kitten in the basket" or from _____ .

2071

Whenever two noun phrases lie ahead of a relative clause, there must be some signal to tell what the clause modifies. The phrase *the man by the tree that was leaving* contains no signal. Men can leave (depart), and trees can leave (lose their leaves). The phrase *the man by the tree which was leaving* is not ambiguous. The signal lies in the word _____.

2072

In *the men by the tree that were leaving,* the signal lies in the word *were.* This relative clause can only derive from the insert sentence _____ _____ .

2073

When one noun phrase before the relative clause is singular and the other plural, the form of a *be, have,* or verb can be a signal. In the noun phrase *the men by the tree that was leaving,* the insert sentence for the relative clause has to be _____ .

2074

Various kinds of signals will work in structures like these. Anything in the clause that connects the clause to one noun and not the other is a sufficient signal. In "The girl in the car that was waving was Ann," the insert sentence is _____ .

2075

The verb *wave* usually has a human subject. Girls wave, but cars don't, so the sentence is not ambiguous. In "The girl in the car that was weaving was Ann," the insert sentence for the relative clause is probably _____ .

2076

Ann could have been weaving a basket, of course, but the other meaning is more likely. Whatever the signal is, there must be a signal when a relative clause has two noun phrases in front of it. Otherwise the sentence will be ambiguous. Adverbs may also provide ambiguity in sentences. In "Leslie worked frequently," *frequently* is an adverb of _____ .

2077

Adverbs of frequency can occur either after the verb or before it. We also say, "Leslie frequently worked." What is the adverb of frequency in "The girl sat with my cousins sometimes"? _____

SOME PROBLEMS IN MODIFICATION 371

2078

Is the sentence "The girl who sat with my cousins sometimes sang songs to them" ambiguous? ____

2079

"The girl who sat with my cousins sometimes sang songs to them" could derive from either of two sets of base sentences: "The girl sat with my cousins sometimes" and "The girl sang songs to them" or _____ _____ and _____ .

2080

Is the following sentence ambiguous: "The girl who sat with my cousins never sang songs to them"? ____

2081

The adverb *never* occurs only before the verb, not after it. *"The girl sat with my cousins never" is therefore not a possible insert sentence, and *never* must be part of the matrix. Is this sentence ambiguous: "The girl who sat with my cousins sometimes often sang songs to them"? ____

2082

"The girl who sat with my cousins sometimes often sang songs to them" comes from the insert sentence _____ and the matrix _____ .

2083

We see that the signals that indicate the base sentences that underlie transforms may be of many sorts, but there must be signals, or the transform will be ambiguous. In "Patrick went there quickly," *there* is an adverbial of _____ , and *quickly* is an adverbial of _____ .

2084

Adverbials can be adverbs, prepositional phrases, or noun phrases. In "Patrick went to the store on his bicycle," *to the store* is an adverbial of _____ , and *on his bicycle* is an adverbial of _____ .

2085

Now compare "Patrick went to the store on his bicycle" and "Patrick went to the store on the corner." In the first sentence *on his bicycle* modifies *went to the store.* In the second sentence, *on the corner* modifies _____ .

2086

Both these sentences have two prepositional phrases after the verb, but in the first the second prepositional phrase modifies all the rest of the predicate, whereas in the other it modifies just the object of the first prepositional phrase. Is either sentence ambiguous? _____

2087

In *went to the store on his bicycle,* the second prepositional phrase can't be an adverb of place, unless the store is on the bicycle, which is far-fetched. In *went to the store on the corner, on the corner* can't be an adverbial of manner, describing how he went there. Instead it is an adverbial of _____ .

2088

Is the construction *answered my mother in anger* like (1) *went to the store on the corner* or (2) *went to the store on his bicycle?* _____

2089

Is the construction "Vicki spoke to the woman in tears" ambiguous? _____

2090

"Vicki spoke to the woman in tears" is ambiguous because we don't know what *in tears* modifies and therefore don't know who is crying. Is the sentence "Robert found the money he had lost in the street" ambiguous? _____

2091

In "Robert found the money he had lost in the street," the prepositional phrase could come from the base sentence "He found it in the street" or from _____ .

SOME PROBLEMS IN MODIFICATION 373

2092

In "Robert left with a man he met last Monday," *last Monday* is an adverbial of _____ .

2093

"Robert left with a man he met last Monday" is ambiguous. The adverbial could derive either from "Robert left last Monday" or from _____ .

2094

Is "Stephen was telephoning a girl he met on the bus" ambiguous? _____

2095

The base sentence "He was telephoning on the bus" is hardly possible, so the adverbial must come from "He met a girl on the bus." Is "Stephen shared the candy he had bought reluctantly" ambiguous? _____

2096

In "Stephen shared the candy he had bought reluctantly," the adverbial could come either from the matrix "He shared it reluctantly" or the insert "He had bought it reluctantly." However, in "Stephen shared the candy he had reluctantly bought," the adverbial can come only from the insert sentence _____ .

2097

In "Alice answered the man with a smile," who is smiling? _____

2098

In "Alice answered the man with the smile," who is smiling? _____

2099

In "Alice answered the man with the smile that made her so pretty," who is smiling? _____

374 ENGLISH SYNTAX

A sentence derivable from more than one set of base sentences will always be ambiguous. There must always be signals, which may be of many different kinds, to show just what bases underlie the transforms.

MAIN POINTS OF LESSON FORTY-TWO

Any construction derivable from two or more underlying constructions will be ambiguous—that is, has more than one possible meaning. Ambiguities can occur in various parts of the sentence, but as perils for writers they are most common in certain modification structures.

A noun phrase of the general type **NP + Prep + NP + relative clause** permits a common kind of ambiguity. The relative clause may modify the sequence **NP + Prep + NP** or just the second **NP**. The construction must contain some signal to indicate which structure is modified. The signal may be the particular relative pronoun used or the number of the *be, have,* or verb or the normal use of the words (e.g., girls wave and cars don't).

Adverbials also permit ambiguity. Adverbials of frequency may apply to a preceding or a following verb phrase, as in "The girl who sat with the children sometimes sang songs to them." (This is traditionally called a "squinting" modifier.) After the verb, adverbials may be taken as applying to more than one of the preceding noun or verb phrases. This is possible only in transforms that complicate the matrix.

Lesson Forty-Three
REFERENCE OF PRONOUNS

We have so far been concerned with ungrammaticality mostly as something to be avoided, and indeed the ungrammatical sentences that we have exemplified are kinds that one would ordinarily wish to avoid in writing. But ungrammaticality is not necessarily bad in itself. We saw in the introduction to Lesson Forty-One that departure from the grammar is quite normal in speech, where for the most part it goes unnoticed. We should observe also that intentional ungrammaticality is an important device of writers, and particularly of poets. The poet gets many of his effects by departing from the grammar, by giving an unexpected syntactic twist to his sentence. Almost any poet will illustrate this. Here are a few examples from Gerard Manley Hopkins, with the poetic construction given first and the grammatical construction after in parentheses:

I caught this morning morning's minion. (I caught morning's minion this morning.)
The achieve of, the mastery of the thing! (The achievement of the thing and the mastery of it!)
And frightful a nightfall folded rueful a day. (And a frightful nightfall folded a rueful day. Or, folded a day ruefully, or both.)
Leaves, like the things of man, you with your fresh thoughts care for, can you? (Can you, with your fresh thoughts, care for leaves, which are like the things of man?)

It will be seen that the poet achieves not only variety and surprise by being ungrammatical but also a power and concentration of meaning that the rules of the grammar will not permit.

Some poets are more ungrammatical than Hopkins and some less, but all poets are ungrammatical in this good sense. For a perfectly grammatical line is completely predictable by the grammar so far as its syntax goes, and a wholly predictable line is wholly trite.

2101

In "I caught a cold," the subject is a _____ pronoun.

2102

The seven personal pronouns, in their subject forms, are ____ , ____ , ____ , ____ , ____ , ____ , ____ .

2103

In their object forms, the personal pronouns are ____ , ____ , ____ , ____ , ____ , ____ , ____ .

2104

The personal pronouns also have possessive forms, some one form and some two. *I* plus **Pos** is *my* or *mine*. *He* plus **Pos** is *his*. *She* plus **Pos** is ____ or ____ .

2105

The personal pronouns *he, she, it,* and *they,* in all their forms, generally refer to noun phrases. That is, they do not ordinarily occur unless some other noun phrase has previously occurred. In the sentence, "We all liked Jeff. He was always a lot of fun," the pronoun *he* refers to the noun phrase _____ .

2106

In the sentence "My father really wanted to help us, but he didn't have time," the pronoun *he* refers to the noun phrase _____ .

2107

In "Andrea had left her purse in the desk," the pronoun *her* refers to the noun phrase _____ .

2108

In "DeWitt glanced at the neckties, but he didn't find them very interesting," the pronoun *them* refers to the noun phrase _____ .

REFERENCE OF PRONOUNS

2109

In "DeWitt glanced at the display of neckties, but he didn't find it very interesting," the pronoun *it* refers to the noun phrase _____ .

2110

In "Anybody who wants his book autographed should step right up," the pronoun *his* refers to the noun phrase _____ .

2111

The noun phrase to which a pronoun refers is called the *antecedent* of the pronoun. The antecedent of *their* in "Those boys had better improve their behavior" is _____ .

2112

In "Richard felt that he was about to find the solution, but it still eluded him," the antecedent of *it* is _____ , and the antecedent of *him* is _____ .

2113

Pronouns agree with their antecedents in number. This means that if the antecedent is singular, the pronoun must be some form of *he, she,* or *it*. If the antecedent is plural, the pronoun must be some form of _____ .

2114

In "The birds sang beautifully, but they had no other virtues," the pronoun *they* occurs because the antecedent, *the birds,* is _____ .

2115

In "The bird sang beautifully, so I decided to buy it," the pronoun is *it* and not *they* because the antecedent, *the bird,* is _____ .

2116

The singular pronouns—*he, she,* and *it*—also agree with their antecedents in *gender*. English nouns have one of three genders—masculine, feminine, and neuter. By and large, nouns that refer to males are masculine, nouns that refer to females are feminine, and other nouns are neuter. In "John sold his car," the gender of *John* is _____ .

2117

In "Edith brought her lunch," the gender of *Edith* is _____ .

2118

What makes it absolutely clear that *John* is masculine in "John sold his car" is the *his*. The *her* in "Edith brought her lunch" makes it certain that *Edith* is feminine. The gender of nouns is not shown in the form of the noun but in the pronouns that refer to them. In "He bought the book, but he never read it," the gender of *the book* is _____ .

2119

The proper noun *Andy* may be a boy's name (short for *Andrew*) or a girl's name (short for *Andrea*). What is its gender in "Andy had been invited, but she wasn't able to come"? _____

2120

Gender is not the same thing as sex. Cats are either male or female, but the noun *cat* can be masculine, feminine, or neuter. Which is it in "The cat ate her salmon"? _____

2121

What is the gender of *cat* in "The cat ate its salmon"? _____

2122

We choose between *he, she, it,* on the one hand, and *they* on the other, according to whether the antecedent is _____ or _____ .

2123

We choose among *he, she,* and *it* according to whether the antecedent is _____ , _____ , or _____ .

2124

If we cannot tell which of two preceding noun phrases is the antecedent of a pronoun, the sentence will be ambiguous. In "John asked his

REFERENCE OF PRONOUNS 379

mother if he could help her," the antecedent of *he* is _____ , and the antecedent of *her* is _____ .

2125

In "John asked his parents if they could help him," the antecedent of *they* is _____ , and the antecedent of *him* is _____ .

2126

Now the sentence "John asked his father if he could help him" is ambiguous. The pronouns *he* and *him* could refer to either _____ or _____ .

2127

When there are two or more noun phrases ahead of the pronoun and when the noun phrases do not differ in number or gender, the sentence can be ambiguous. "Sally and her uncle discussed what she should do" is not ambiguous because the two noun phrases in the compound subject differ in _____ .

2128

Is "Sally and her aunt discussed what she should do" ambiguous? _____

2129

Is the sentence "Sally and her aunt discussed what they should do" ambiguous? _____

2130

In "Sally and her aunt discussed what they should do," the pronoun *they* refers unambiguously to the compound subject. "Sally and her aunts discussed what they should do" is ambiguous, however. *They* could refer to the compound "Sally and her aunts" or to the noun phrase _____ .

---

380   ENGLISH SYNTAX

2131

The sentence "He thought the card might be in the wallet, but he couldn't find it" is ambiguous because *it* could refer to either _____ or _____ .

2132

The sentence "He thought the cards might be in the wallet, but he couldn't find them" is not ambiguous. The pronoun *them* refers to _____ .

2133

Is "Mr. Smith told David to improve his manners" ambiguous? _____

2134

Mr. Smith could hardly tell David to improve Mr. Smith's manners, so the antecedent of *his* in "Mr. Smith told David to improve his manners" has to be _____ .

2135

What is the antecedent of *his* in "Anybody who wants to receive a copy should leave his name"? _____

2136

In "Anybody who wants to receive a copy should leave his name," *anybody* is an _____ pronoun.

2137

In "Anybody who wants to receive a copy should leave his name," is *anybody* singular or plural? _____

2138

The indefinite pronouns are generally treated as singular in writing, though not always in speech. If they are singular (and masculine), what pronoun will occur in the blank in "Everyone must decide what _____ wants to do"? _____

REFERENCE OF PRONOUNS

2139

If we take indefinite pronouns as singular in number, what personal pronoun will occur in the blank in "Under these circumstances, nobody can be sure of keeping ____ job"? ____

2140

In the sentence "Under these circumstances, nobody can be sure of keeping his job," what is the gender of *nobody?* ____

2141

What is the gender of *everyone* in "Everyone must be sure to bring her ticket"? ____

2142

If the people being talked about are all females, the indefinite pronouns are feminine. If the people are males or both males and females, the pronouns are masculine. In "All the boys and girls were puzzled, but no one was willing to raise ____ hand," the personal pronoun in the blank will be ____ .

2143

In the determiner, *demonstrative* is rewritten as a choice between **D₁** and **D₂**. Phonological rules give as the product of **Def + D₁** and **Def + D₂** the four words ____ , ____ , ____ , ____ .

2144

The demonstratives distinguish between singular and plural. The plural demonstratives are ____ and ____ .

2145

The demonstratives, like all determiners, occur before an **N**. The **N** may be deleted if the reference is clear: "This dress is Alice's" → "This is Alice's." "He left these letters" → ____ .

2146

Demonstratives do not have antecedents in quite the same way that personal pronouns do. Usually they refer to the following **N**, or to a deleted

382 ENGLISH SYNTAX

N. In "This is Alice's" from "This dress is Alice's," the demonstrative refers to the noun _____ .

2147

The reference of a demonstrative in conversation is thus usually to something pointed at or otherwise indicated. In writing it may be to a preceding noun phrase. In "Harold had a nice voice, but that wasn't what made him popular," *that* refers to the noun phrase _____ .

2148

Demonstratives, unlike personal pronouns, also may refer to whole clauses or sentences. What does *this* refer to in "Uncle Louie grew furiously angry, but this surprised no one"? _____

2149

What does *that* refer to in "He had a terrible temper, but none of us knew *that*"? _____

2150

There is no general rule about what a demonstrative should refer to. It can be a noun phrase, a sentence, or something pointed out. The only rule is that the reference be clear.

MAIN POINTS OF LESSON FORTY-THREE

Personal pronouns refer to noun phrases, except for the pronouns *I, we,* and *you,* which refer to the speaker or the person spoken to. Noun phrases to which pronouns refer are called the antecedents of the pronouns.

Pronouns agree with their antecedents in number and gender. If the antecedent is singular, the pronoun is *he, she,* or *it.* If the antecedent is plural, the pronoun is *they.* When the antecedent is singular, the pronoun is *he* for masculine antecedents, *she* for feminine, *it* for neuter. It is the choice of pronoun that establishes the gender of the noun phrase.

When a pronoun is preceded by two noun phrases which do not differ in number or gender, it may be impossible to tell which is the antecedent. The sentence will then be ambiguous.

REFERENCE OF PRONOUNS

The indefinite pronouns are as a rule treated as singular in writing and referred to with *he, she,* or *it.* This rule does not always obtain in speech.

The demonstratives *this, that, these, those,* when not followed by an **N**, may refer to a noun phrase, a sentence, or something pointed out or otherwise indicated.

Lesson Forty-Four
REVIEW

This is the end of this sketch of English syntax. It is proper to call it a sketch, for, though we have tried to characterize the principal features of the English kernel and of the transforms that derive from it, we have necessarily omitted a great deal. Any description of English syntax aiming at completeness would have to be many times the size of this one.

It is to be hoped, however, that enough has been given that the student who has persisted this far will have an understanding of the general nature of the English language in its syntactic component. He should perceive the essential simplicity and symmetry of the syntax. All of the meaning relationships among words are contained in the kernel and persist unchanged through transformations of the kernel. Thus, from a finite set of kernel rules and a finite set of transformational rules, we are able to generate a countless number of many correct English sentences, including many that have never previously occurred.

This goes a way toward explaining how human beings manage to learn and use languages. So also do the sets of symmetrical relationships we have observed, as, for example, in the transitive verb system, the question system, the modification system. Structures which superficially appear quite different are seen to be in fact very similar, to be simply variations of one another in highly systematic recurring patterns. We must suppose that the child learning the language somehow gets onto this system. From the random sentences that he hears from his parents, his brothers and sisters, his playmates, he somehow constructs for himself the grammar of his language. He does this quite unconsciously of course, but he does it and in the simplest possible way. To be able to do it is what it means to be a human being.

It is to be hoped also that the student who has worked through the text will have gained a clearer notion of the concept of grammaticality. We have seen that grammatical is not the same as meaningful. A grammatical sentence can be meaningless: "Oysters living on the moon don't whistle." It isn't the same as true. A grammatical sentence can be a lie: "My grandmother was President of the United States." Grammatical doesn't mean "capable of being said." Anything is capable of being said: "Fry don't stickle never Harold seeming." Grammatical means simply "corresponding to the grammar," to the system which we have all somehow managed to acquire but from which we all constantly depart, intentionally or unintentionally, in our use of language. To depart unintentionally from the grammar is to be a careless writer and probably a poor one. To depart intentionally is to be a poet.

Last and perhaps least, it is to be hoped that this syntactic sketch will be of practical use to the student in his writing and reading. It may help him to confront more successfully some of the problems of composition. He should perceive that most of the grammatical errors we make in writing occur not in kernel sentences but in transformations of the kernel, in which we lose sight of and confuse the kernel relationships. Understanding the nature of the system, he may be better able to keep relationships clear through complicated sentences. Knowing the various structures of the system, he may find it easier to manage the conventions of punctuation. He may become more acutely aware of the things going on in the language as he uses it and as others use it and may derive from this understanding satisfactions of many kinds.

We will conclude with a brief recapitulation of the chief features of the description of the syntax.

2151

There are two fundamental kinds of sentences: _____ sentences and transforms.

2152

Kernel sentences can be described by simple rewrite rules of the type $X \rightarrow Y + Z$. The first rule is $S \rightarrow NP + VP$. This means that every kernel sentence consists of a _____ and a _____ .

2153

The noun phrase of the kernel sentence functions as its _____ . The verb phrase functions as its _____ .

2154

The noun phrase can be one of three fundamental types. It can be a proper noun, an indefinite pronoun, or _____ + _____ .

2155

The rewrite of verb phrase is this:

$$VP \rightarrow Aux + \left\{ \begin{matrix} be + \left\{ \begin{matrix} substantive \\ Adv\text{-}p \end{matrix} \right\} \\ verbal \end{matrix} \right\}$$

In order to have a verb phrase, we must have an **Aux**. Then we must have either _____ or _____ .

2156

If we choose *be* in the kernel, we must then have either _____ or _____ .

2157

Verbal stands for all the different kinds of verbs, plus any objects, complements, etc., that accompany them. In addition to **VI** and **VT,** we identified the verb types **V**____ , **V**____ , **V**____ .

2158

Vs means a verb of the *seem* type; **Vb** a verb of the _____ type; **Vh** a verb of the _____ type.

2159

VI and **VT** are further subdivided according to whether the verb is followed by a particle or a complement or by neither. In "He walked away," the verb is a **Vi₂**. The word *away* is a _____ .

2160

In "We thought Edith attractive," the **VT** consists of the two words _____ .

2161

Aux → tense + (M) + (aspect). Aspect → (have + part) + (be + ing). For every verb phrase in the kernel, we may or may not have an **M** or a have + part or a be + ing. But we must have a _____ .

REVIEW   387

2162

The two tenses in English are _____ and _____ .

2163

The **Aux** of the sentence "John left" consists of _____ .

2164

The **Aux** of "John had left" consists of _____ and _____ + _____ .

2165

Part means whatever is done to the verb to make it a past participle. **Walk + part** is _____ ; **drive + part** is _____ .

2166

M stands for *modal*. The English modals are _____ , _____ , _____ , _____ , _____ .

2167

The symbol **past** means whatever is done to a verb, modal, *have,* or *be* to make it past. **Arrive + past** is _____ ; **have + past** is _____ ; **shall + past** is _____ .

2168

There are two kinds of transformations: obligatory and _____ .

2169

The kernel rules give us a K-terminal string containing the morphemes of a kernel sentence. But the morphemes are not all in their final order. To get a sentence from the K-terminal string **John + past + shall + have + part + be + ing + work**, the transformation **T-af** must be applied. Since it must be applied, it is an _____ transformation.

2170

T-af is **Af + v ⇒ v + Af**. Here **Af** stands for any **tense, part,** or **ing**. Small **v** stands for any _____ , _____ , _____ , or _____ .

388 ENGLISH SYNTAX

2171

If we apply **T-af** to **John + past + shall + have + part + be + ing + work**, we get _____ + _____ + _____ + _____ + _____ + _____ + _____ + _____ .

2172

John + shall + past + have + be + part + work + ing will give us finally the sentence _____ .

2173

However, before we apply **T-af**, we have the possibility of applying any of a number of optional transformations, to produce questions, negatives, modifiers, and the like. The transformation that produces questions like "Was John working?" is called **T-**_____ .

2174

This is **T-yes/no**:

    NP + tense-M   + X ⟹ tense-M   + NP + X
    NP + tense-have + X ⟹ tense-have + NP + X
    NP + tense-be   + X ⟹ tense-be   + NP + X
    NP + tense + verbal ⟹ tense   + NP + verbal

If we apply this to **John + past + shall + work**, we get **past + shall + John + work** and finally, after **T-af**, the sentence _____ .

2175

If we apply **T-yes/no** to **John + past + work**, we get **past + John + work**. **T-do** now becomes obligatory. This says that whenever we have a tense with nothing to be a tense for, that is with no **M** or *have* or *be* or verb after it, tense becomes **do + tense**. So we get **do + past + John + work** and finally the question _____ .

2176

This machinery works in the same way to produce not only *yes/no* questions but also many other structures. If you understand it here, you understand it everywhere. After the application of **T-yes/no**, but before

T-af or T-do, one of the varieties of T-wh may be applied. T-wh-NP applied to past + John + see + someone will substitute who + m for the word _____ .

2177

T-wh-NP applied to past + John + see + something gives what + past + John + see. Now T-do applies to give what + do + past + John + see and finally the sentence _____ .

2178

By very similar transformations we get "Whose brother did John see?," "Where did John go?," "What did John do?," etc. The closely related T-rel produces relative clauses modifying noun phrases. What is the expanded noun phrase in "The little boy who was crying went away"?

2179

Transformations which produce sentences like "The little boy who was crying went away" are called double-base transformations. They involve two base sentences: a matrix sentence and an insert sentence. Here the insert sentence is "The little boy was crying." What is the matrix sentence? _____

2180

In "Seeing Mary, John fainted," the matrix sentence is "John fainted." *Seeing Mary* comes from an insert sentence through T-rel, T-del-ing, and T-SM. What is the insert sentence? _____

2181

Most grammatical mistakes occur in transforms. If a transform derives from an ungrammatical base, the transform will be ungrammatical too. The sentence *"Seeing Mary, a frown appeared on John's face" is ungrammatical because it has the ungrammatical insert sentence _____ .

390 ENGLISH SYNTAX

2182

The sentence *"The decision about when to have the beach trip finally agreed to go on Wednesday" is ungrammatical because it has the ungrammatical matrix sentence _____.

2183

Sentences may also be expanded through the process of compounding. Sentences or parts of sentences may be compounded by conjunctions. The conjunctions *and, or,* and *but* join sentences or parts of sentences. What are the four conjunctions that compound sentences but not parts of sentences? ____ , ____ , ____ , ____

2184

The rule of compounding is that when conjunctions join parts of sentences, the structures joined must be the same. The sentence "We met Mary and the young ladies that were visiting her" is grammatical because the *and* joins two _____.

2185

The sentence "The young ladies whom we met and whose cousins were visiting Mary had an interesting tale to tell" is grammatical because the conjunction joins two _____.

2186

The sentence "People who live alone and have no one to talk to are often great readers" is grammatical because the conjunction joins two _____.

2187

However, *"John is a determined young fellow and who knows just what he wants" is ungrammatical. Here the *and* joins a _____ and a _____.

2188

Conjunctions are sometimes confused with sentence connectors. In "John was neither bold nor insolent; however, he knew exactly what he

REVIEW   391

wanted," the conjunctions are _____ and _____ . The sentence connector is _____ .

2189

When conjunctions connect two sentences, we usually have a comma, a semicolon, or a period before the conjunction. When a sentence connector connects two sentences, we usually have a _____ or a _____ before the sentence connector.

2190

Conjunctions and sentence connectors differ in that _____ _____ can occur at the end of or within the second sentence and _____ cannot.

2191

In "The lad helping Julia is my brother Ralph," *helping Julia* is a participial phrase. It is used here to modify a _____ .

2192

In "Helping Julia, Ralph cut his thumb," the participial phrase is not a noun modifier but a _____ modifier.

2193

In "Ralph, trying to help Julia, cut his thumb," the participial phrase is a _____ modifier.

2194

In "Anybody who tries to help Julia is asking for trouble" the relative clause is a _____ modifier.

2195

In "Stephen, a friend of Julia's, tried to help her," the sentence modifier is a construction called an _____ .

392   ENGLISH SYNTAX

2196

Noun modifiers identify or single out the noun phrase. Sentence modifiers do not. Sentence modifiers are set off by commas. Noun modifiers are not. In "Vidan's father who knew Yugoslavia very well laughed uproariously," there should be commas after the words _____ and _____ .

2197

A sentence is ungrammatical if part of it derives from an ungrammatical base sentence. It is ambiguous if part of it is derivable from more than one base sentence. The phrase *a smoking room* is ambiguous out of context. It can derive from either "The room is smoking" (i.e., *on fire*) or "The room _____ ."

2198

The sentence "She answered the people who had questioned her insolently" is ambiguous. The adverb *insolently* can either go with the matrix sentence "She answered the people" or with the insert sentence _____ .

2199

The sentence "David asked the watchman if he could open the door" is ambiguous. The antecedent of *he* could be either _____ or _____ .

2200

It has been said that this description of English syntax is not complete. It should also be said that it is not final. Like mathematics, chemistry, literature, the study of grammar goes on. Grammarians will continue to get new insights into the language, see new simplicities and relationships, find better ways of presentation, and our knowledge of the grammar of English will change and grow.

REVIEW 393

ABBREVIATIONS USED

This list gives the terms—mostly traditional ones—which suggested the symbols used in the text. It is to be remembered that giving the terms does not define the symbols, which are defined in the grammar. For example, v is suggested by the term *verb,* but v includes other structures in addition to those defined as verbs.

A	affirmation stress	NP	noun phrase
Adj	adjective	obj	object
Adv-m	adverbial of manner	part	participle
Adv-p	adverbial of place	Plur	plural
Adv-t	adverbial of time	Pos	possessive
Af	affix	Prep	preposition
affirm	affirmation	Prt	particle
Art	article	rel	relative
Aux	auxiliary	S	sentence
Comp	complement	SM	sentence modifier
Conj	conjunction	Sub	subordinator
Def	definite	v	verbal
del	deletion	VP	verb phrase
Demon	demonstrative	Vb	*become* class verb
Det	determiner	Vh	*have* class verb
M	modal	VI	intransitive verb
N	noun	Vs	*seem* class verb
Nondef	nondefinite	VT	transitive verb
NM	noun modifier	wh	*wh*o, *wh*at, *wh*ere, etc.

SOME SYNTACTIC RULES OF ENGLISH

Kernel Rules

S → NP + VP

NP → $\begin{Bmatrix} \text{proper noun} \\ \text{indefinite pronoun} \\ \text{Det + N} \end{Bmatrix}$

proper noun → John, Mr. Wheeler, France . . .

indefinite pronoun → some-, any-, no-, or every- + -one, -body, or -thing

Det → (pre-article) + Art + (Demon) + (number)

pre-article → several of, many of, both of . . .

Art → $\begin{Bmatrix} \text{Def} \\ \text{Nondef} \end{Bmatrix}$

Def → the

Nondef → $\begin{Bmatrix} a \\ \text{some} \\ \emptyset \end{Bmatrix}$

Demon → $\begin{Bmatrix} D_1 \\ D_2 \end{Bmatrix}$

number → $\begin{Bmatrix} \text{cardinal} \\ \text{ordinal} \end{Bmatrix}$

cardinal → one, two, three . . .

ordinal → first, second, third . . .

N → $\begin{Bmatrix} \text{personal pronoun} \\ \text{common noun} \end{Bmatrix}$

personal pronoun → I, you, he, she, it, we, they

common noun → $\begin{Bmatrix} \text{count} \\ \text{noncount} \end{Bmatrix}$

count noun → $\begin{Bmatrix} \text{animate} \\ \text{inanimate} \end{Bmatrix}$

animate → John, boy, cat ...

inanimate → table, tree, decision ...

noncount → mush, furniture, sarcasm ...

VP → Aux + $\begin{Bmatrix} \text{be} + \begin{Bmatrix} \text{substantive} \\ \text{Adv-p} \end{Bmatrix} \\ \text{verbal} \end{Bmatrix}$

Aux → tense + (M) + (aspect)

tense → $\begin{Bmatrix} \text{present} \\ \text{past} \end{Bmatrix}$

M → can, may, shall, will, must

aspect → (have + part) + (be + ing)

substantive → $\begin{Bmatrix} \text{NP} \\ \text{(Int) + Adj} \end{Bmatrix}$

intensifier → very, rather, pretty ...

Adj → good, sad, beautiful ...

Adv-m → happily, quickly, in a rage ...

Adv-p → there, downstairs, in the house ...

verbal → $\begin{Bmatrix} \begin{Bmatrix} \text{VI} \\ \text{VT + NP} \\ \text{Vb + substantive} \\ \text{Vs + Adj} \\ \text{Vh + NP} \end{Bmatrix} + \text{(Adv-m)} \end{Bmatrix}$

VI → $\begin{Bmatrix} \text{Vi}_1 \\ \text{Vi}_2 + \text{Prt} \\ \text{Vi}_3 + \text{Comp} \end{Bmatrix}$

Vi_1 → occur, laugh, wait ...

Vi_2 → glance, look, come ...

Prt → down, up, in, away ...

Vi_3 → stand, lie, stay ...

Comp → on the sofa, in the corner ...

$$VT \rightarrow \begin{Bmatrix} Vt_1 \\ \begin{Bmatrix} Vt_2 + Prt \\ Vt_3 \\ Vt_{to} \\ Vt_{ing} \end{Bmatrix} + Comp \end{Bmatrix}$$

$Vt_1 \rightarrow$ see, find, terrify . . .

$Vt_2 \rightarrow$ put, look, throw . . .

$Vt_3 \rightarrow$ consider, elect, give . . .

$Vt_{to} \rightarrow$ persuade, expect, try . . .

$Vt_{ing} \rightarrow$ enjoy, avoid, imagine . . .

Vb $\rightarrow$ become, remain . . .

Vs $\rightarrow$ seem, look, taste . . .

Vh $\rightarrow$ have, cost, weigh . . .

Transformational Rules—Single-Base Transformations

T-af: Af + v $\Rightarrow$ v + Af

Af means any tense, **part**, or **ing**; and v means any modal, *have*, *be*, or verb. This transformation is obligatory and applies after all other transformations. Its effect is, therefore, to produce a T-terminal string.

T-do: tense $\Rightarrow$ do + tense

This applies after all optional transformations and is obligatory for any tense not accompanied by a v.

T-yes/no: NP + tense-M + X $\Rightarrow$ tense-M   + NP + X
NP + tense-have + X $\Rightarrow$ tense-have + NP + X
NP + tense-be   + X $\Rightarrow$ tense-be   + NP + X
NP + tense + verbal $\Rightarrow$ tense   + NP + verbal

T-neg: NP + tense-M   + X $\Rightarrow$ NP + tense-M   + not + X
NP + tense-have + X $\Rightarrow$ NP + tense-have + not + X
NP + tense-be   + X $\Rightarrow$ NP + tense-be   + not + X
NP + tense + verbal $\Rightarrow$ NP + tense   + not + verbal

T-affirm: NP + tense-M   + X ⇒ NP + tense-M   + A + X
           NP + tense-have + X ⇒ NP + tense-have + A + X
           NP + tense-be   + X ⇒ NP + tense-be   + A + X
           NP + tense + verbal ⇒ NP + tense   + A + verbal

The symbol **A** means that the word preceding **A** will have the primary stress. For the sequence **NP + tense + verbal**, the *do* transformation will then apply automatically.

T-obj: $\begin{Bmatrix} VT \\ Vh \\ Prep \end{Bmatrix}$ + NP ⇒ $\begin{Bmatrix} VT \\ Vh \\ Prep \end{Bmatrix}$ + NP + m

This is obligatory whenever the **NP** is a personal pronoun or (for some speakers) *who*. Phonological rules then convert he + m to *him*, I + m to *me*, who + m to *whom*, etc.

T-wh-adv-p: X + Adv-p + Y ⇒ where + X + Y

This and all the *wh* transformations apply only to strings resulting from **T-yes/no**. X and Y mean whatever occurs in the positions indicated, or nothing, if nothing occurs there.

T-wh-adv-t: X + Adv-t + Y ⇒ when + X + Y

T-wh-NP: X + $\begin{Bmatrix} someone \\ something \end{Bmatrix}$ + Y ⇒ $\begin{Bmatrix} who \\ what \end{Bmatrix}$ + X + Y

When *someone* functions as object, **T-obj** will convert *who* to *whom*. This part of **T-obj**, however, does not exist in the grammar of some speakers and is optional for others.

As stated, **T-wh-NP** will produce "Who (or *whom*) did he give it to?" but not "To whom did he give it?" For the latter sentence a special rule is necessary.

T-wh-article: X + article + N + Y ⇒ $\begin{Bmatrix} which \\ what \end{Bmatrix}$ + N + X + Y

T-passive: NP_1 + Aux + VT + NP_2 ⇒ NP_2 + Aux + be + part + VT + (by + NP_1)

T-there: X + Nondef + Y + Aux + be + Adv-p ⇒ there + Aux + be + X + Nondef + Y + Adv-p

There are some restrictions on this transformation. It does not apply when the Y contains a proper noun or, usually, a personal pronoun. An alternative analysis would be to make Ø an alternative of *the* for **Def**. Then the subject of "John is here" would be **Def + John** and **T-there** could not apply to give *"There is John in the room."

Tranformational Rules—Double-Base Transformations

Most of the double-base transformations shown here are not fully formulated in the text, though the method is explained (p. 151). They are worked out here for the benefit of those interested in their formal statement.

T-Pos: insert: NP (1) — Aux + have + Det + N₁ (2)
matrix: X (3) — the (4) — N₁ + Y (5)
result: 3 + 1 + Pos + 5

The consecutive numbers refer to the segments separated by hyphens. The result line shows their arrangement in the transform. The subscript number 1 attached to the two N's indicates that these must be identical. *Example:*
insert: John (1) — has a car (2)
matrix: I bought (3) — the (4) — car (5)
result: I bought (3) + John (1) + Pos + car (5) (I bought John's car.)

Thus the effect is to substitute the subject of a *have* sentence plus the possessive morpheme for the definite article in the matrix sentence. The use of X and Y indicates that it doesn't matter what occurs in these positions, that the transformation works whatever occurs there. In the example given, Y is nothing.

Insert sentences with *have* account for most of the possessives, but there are a number of types for which they do not account: *Shakespeare's plays, a day's work,* etc. A complete grammar would give the full variety of insert sentences that account for these.

T-Vt₃: insert: NP₁ (1) — Aux + be (2) — substantive (3)
matrix: NP + Aux + Vt₃ (4) — Comp (5) — NP₁ (6)
result: 4 + 3 + 6

This is specifically the transformation that applies with Vt₃'s of the *consider* type. In variations, (3) must be an NP, an Adv-p, etc. *Example:*
insert: Mary (1) — was (2) — beautiful (3)
matrix: He thought (4) — Comp (5) — Mary (6)
result: He thought (4) + beautiful (3) + Mary (6)

T-Vt_to: insert: NP₁ (1) — Aux (2) — X (3)
matrix: NP + Aux + Vt_to (4) — Comp (5) — NP₁ (6)
result: 4 + to + 3 + 6

Example:
 insert: John (1) − past (2) − go (3)
 matrix: We persuaded (4) − Comp (5) − John (6)
 result: We persuaded (4) + to + go (3) + John (6)

T-Vt_{ing}: insert: NP₁ (1) − Aux (2) − X (3)
 matrix: NP + Aux + Vt_{ing} (4) − Comp (5) − NP₁ (6)
 result: 4 + ing + 3 + 6

Example:
 insert: John (1) − past (2) − study (3)
 matrix: We found (4) − Comp (5) − John (6)
 result: We found (4) + ing + study (3) + John (6)

A single-base transformation, **T-VT** applies to the results of the last three transformations and also, sometimes, to strings containing Vt₂.

T-VT: $Vt_x + \begin{Bmatrix} Prt \\ Comp \end{Bmatrix} + NP \Longrightarrow Vt_x + NP + \begin{Bmatrix} Prt \\ Comp \end{Bmatrix}$

This is obligatory for complement constructions unless the complement is long and complicated, in which case it is optional:

 John thought Edna foolish. (from **John thought + foolish + Edna**)
 John thought anyone who disagreed with him foolish.
 John thought foolish anyone who disagreed with him.

T-VT is optional for particle constructions unless the **NP** is a personal pronoun, in which case it is obligatory:

 John put the books away.
 John put away the books.
 John put them away.

The symbol Vt_x includes all transitive verb types that can be followed by a particle or a complement.

T-rel: insert: X (1) − NP₁ (2) − Y (3)
 matrix: Z (4) − NP₁ (5) − W (6)
 result: $4 + 5 + \begin{Bmatrix} who \\ which \\ that \end{Bmatrix} + 1 + 3 + 6$

There are some variations according to whether the resulting relative clause is a restrictive or nonrestrictive modifier and according to whether it functions as modifier of an **NP** or as a substitute for an **NP**. In the latter case, for example, the relative pronoun can be *what* but not *that*. The formula above is for relative clauses functioning as modifiers of **NP**'s. The symbols **X, Y, Z,** and **W** mark the positions and can stand for anything or nothing. *Example:*

insert: the police arrested (1) — the boy (2) — last night (3)
matrix: Mary sent (4) — the boy (5) — some flowers (6)
result: Mary sent (4) + the boy (5) + that + the police arrested (1) + last night (3) + some flowers (6)

An example in which some of the positions are empty:
insert: the police arrested (1) — the boy (2) — Y (3)
matrix: W (4) — the boy (5) — is Mary's friend (6)
result: Ø (4) + the boy (5) + that + the police arrested (1) + Ø (3) + is Mary's friend (6)

When the result of **T-rel** contains the sequence **NP + relative pronoun + tense + be + X**, the deletion transformation may be applied. Deletion is possible in many parts of the grammar, and by *deletion transformation* we mean any of these possibilities. The following is one:

T-del: NP + relative pronoun + tense + be + X ⟹ NP + X

This converts the relative clause into a participial phrase, adjective phrase, appositive, etc. Some relative clauses cannot contain *be*. For these, a related transformation, **T-del-ing**, may apply.

T-del-ing: NP + relative pronoun + Aux + X ⟹ NP + ing + X

Thus *people who own property* becomes *people owning property*.

When the result of **T-del** is a single-word modifier, **T-NM** is usually obligatory:

T-NM: Det + N + modifier ⟹ Det + modifier + N

This is obligatory when "modifier" is an adjective, a noun, or a participle, often optional when "modifier" is an adverb.

In certain conditions—i.e., when the **NP₁** of **T-rel** is a proper noun—**T-SM** will apply to the result of **T-del**, putting the modifier at the beginning of the sentence:

T-SM: NP + modifier + VP ⟹ modifier + NP + VP

Another single-base transformation produces the somewhat similar structure called a nominative absolute:

T-nom-abs:
$$NP + tense + \begin{Bmatrix} be \\ verbal \end{Bmatrix} + X \Rightarrow NP + ing + \begin{Bmatrix} be \\ verbal \end{Bmatrix} + X$$

T-for-to: insert: NP (1) — Aux (2) — X (3)
matrix: it + Aux + be + Adj (4) — Comp (5)
result: 4 + for + 1 + to + 3

Example:
   insert: John (1) — past (2) — milk the goats (3)
   matrix: it was easy (4) — Comp (5)
   result: it was easy (4) + for + John (1) + to + milk the goats (5)

Deletion and transposition transformations will then produce:
   It was easy to milk the goats.
   For John to milk the goats was easy.
   To milk the goats was easy for John.
   To milk the goats was easy.

T-Pos-ing: insert: NP (1) — Aux (2) — X (3)
   matrix: X (4) — NP (5) — Y (6)
   result: 4 + 1 + Pos + ing + 3 + 6
Example:
   insert: John (1) — past (2) — insist on milking the goats (3)
   matrix: we were surprised by (4) — NP (5) — Y (6)
   result: we were surprised by (4) + John (1) + Pos + ing + insist on milking the goats (3) + ∅ (6)

T-sub: insert: S (1)
   matrix: X (2) — NP (3) — Y (4)
   result: 2 + Sub + 1 + 4
Example:
   insert: John could come (1)
   matrix: I knew (2) — NP (3) — Y (4)
   result: I knew (2) + that + John could come (3) + ∅ (4)

T-conj: insert: X (1) + A (2) + Y (3)
   matrix: X (4) + B (5) + Y (6)
   result: 4 + 2 + Conj + 5 + 6
Example:
   insert: Mary liked (1) + John (2) + very much (3)
   matrix: Mary liked (4) + Bill (5) + very much (6)
   result: Mary liked (4) + John (2) + and + Bill (5) + very much (6)

Here there is no particular reason to call one of the base sentences the insert and the other the matrix, but we do so to avoid adding terminology. The general condition on the transformation is that **A** and **B**—(2) and (5)—have the same grammatical structure—i.e., be both **NP**'s, both **VP**'s, both relative clauses, etc. The transformation can be easily expanded to account for series of three or more.